F.P.A.

F.P.A.

THE LIFE AND TIMES OF
FRANKLIN PIERCE ADAMS

Sally Ashley

BEAUFORT BOOKS
Publishers
NEW YORK

The copyright page continues on page 253.

Library of Congress Cataloging-in-Publication Data

Ashley, Sally.
F.P.A.: the life and times of Franklin Pierce Adams.
Bibliography: p.
Includes index.
1. Adams, Franklin P. (Franklin Pierce), 1881-1960—
Biography. 2. Authors, American—20th century—
Biography. 3. Journalists—United States—Biography.
I. Title. II. Title: F.P.A., the life and times of
Franklin Pierce Adams.
PS3501.D24Z54 1986 070'.92'4 [B] 85-26723
ISBN 0-8253-0256-0

*Published in the United States by
Beaufort Books Publishers, New York.*

Designed by: Christine Swirnoff / Libra Graphics, Inc.

Printed in the U.S.A. First Edition

10 9 8 7 6 5 4 3 2 1

DEDICATION

When you have the love of your parents at your back, the world opens, shining, in front of you. So this book is dedicated with love and gratitude to my parents, Ruth Stewart Sloan Ashley and James Mansfield Ashley III.

ACKNOWLEDGMENTS

Without the support and encouragement of my agent, Elise Goodman, this book would not have been written.

And the contribution of Peter Dolgenos —researcher, fact-checker and historical detective *extraordinaire*—is incalculable.

C O N T E N T S

INTRODUCTION

THE IDEA held firmly by its residents is that New York City is the center of all things glamorous, intellectual, sportive, and generally worthwhile. The Saul Steinberg poster (originally a cover of *The New Yorker*) isn't wrong when it portrays everywhere west of Manhattan's Tenth Avenue as vague and beyond even the imposition of perspective: That's how the world looks to New Yorkers who gripe endlessly but wouldn't live anywhere else.

Seeds of this strange conceit can be traced to the turn of the century when adventurous Americans changed direction and began going East to seek their fortunes. They were youngsters with the familiar pioneering spirit who wanted, instead of ranching and homesteading, to write plays, books and songs, to star on Broadway, to report on sports or events of the day in the scrappy New York newspapers.

Among other midwesterners inexorably drawn to New York City was, in 1904, Franklin Pierce Adams. He left Chicago at 22 in lovesick pursuit of a chorus girl, whom he married and lived with for 20 years. Adams never returned to Chicago except on infrequent visits and in fact became integral in the genesis of the New York City myth. It's ironic that nowadays few people have heard of him. Once he was a towering figure and it's because of him and the legendary literary and theatrical friends he helped that the notion of New York's School of Wit and Glamour came about. He and his group predated the combative Mayor Koch and the "I Love New York" public relations campaign by decades. And if it weren't for Adams and the others, what we ♥ about New York would be quite different. And not nearly so much fun.

Everybody is familiar with the myths of the madcap '20s. Anecdotes circulate endlessly about Scott and Zelda cavorting in the Plaza fountain and the group that ate lunch at the Algonquin Hotel—Robert Benchley, Dorothy Parker, Alexander Woollcott, and F.P.A., among others. What isn't so well appreciated is the importance of these people in the evolution of American humor. Mel Brooks, Woody Allen, Neil Simon, Fran Lebowitz, Joseph Heller, Nichols and May, Philip Roth, and Johnny Carson owe tips of their expensive hats to F.P.A. and his friends.

For if it's possible (as Margaret Mead pointed out) to describe the American system without mentioning class, it's impossible to do so without mentioning the national sense of humor. The Bronx cheer is as much a part of the American fabric as is Federalism. If Karl Marx, with his stolid intelligence, was archetypically German, then the Marx Brothers were indubitably American.

After World War I, Americans returned from overseas, hardly scratched and with a college senior cockiness. All of Europe had lost the war—not just Germany—and the brash American youngsters who hadn't been in it long enough to get tired walked off with the future. Eyes were focused on New York, where the new American persona first appeared. This fresh personality fused the seemingly contradictory combinations of straightforwardness and whimsy, irreverence and earnestness, individualism and team spirit, lunacy and practicality. Most important, its humor depended on wit instead of storytelling. The fable and the tall tale were tools used by the American humorist before the war. Afterward it was wit Americans displayed, and wit is quicker than storytelling, leaner and more cerebral. The smart alecks at the Algonquin Round Table changed America's image from the frontiersman in his homespun to a different prototype, at once sophisticated and innocent, a direct descendant of the man from Roaring Camp, closer to Ben Franklin than to Paul Bunyan, but wearing earrings or a dinner jacket and sporting a big city manicure and often a college diploma.

In those days of wildly competing newspapers and hired girls, no New York City name was better known than Franklin Pierce Adams, no printed space more coveted than the top of his column, "The Conning Tower" in Herbert Bayard (everybody had middle names then) Swope's celebrated *New York World*, and before that in the *Mail* and the *Tribune*, and after it in the *New York Herald Tribune* and the *Evening Post*. The column appeared consecutively from 1904 to 1937—except for a twenty-four-hour long hiatus in 1934, when Ogden Mills Reid, who ran the *New York Herald Tribune* much like George Steinbrenner runs the Yankees, was a day late renewing F.P.A.'s contract. No other by-line before or since has matched that record of thirty-three straight years; F.P.A. was the Lou Gehrig of newspaper columnists, and while his column at its height was syndicated in only six papers, everybody read it.

Ring Lardner, Eugene O'Neill, Edna Ferber, Ira Gershwin, Dorothy Parker, E. B. White, Robert Sherwood, and Edna St. Vincent Millay contributed original material to the Tower. Robert Benchley, John O'Hara, James Thurber, and George S. Kaufman appeared there before they appeared anywhere else. Much of the Tower's format and F.P.A.'s impatience with superciliousness found its way later into the pages of *The New Yorker*, and remained.

F.P.A. recognized talent and spotlighted it, cared for and nurtured it through unfailing encouragement, meticulous editing. He prowled typesetting rooms and was known among proofreaders, not kindly, as "the comma-hunter of Park Row." That he didn't pay for material when he published it was of no concern to his contributors because appearance in the column was often enough to begin a fine career. Besides, people could send messages to each other in the Tower, as if it were a bulletin board or a school newspaper. Young swains submitted anguished or ironic or belligerent—mostly funny—work, and if it met his standards, F.P.A. printed it and everybody read it. Such attention was thrilling. E. B. White remembered that he was "perennially in love in those days . . . a fine time for a young fellow like me to be alive in. . . . The Tower [meant] you had something to wake up to in the morning, you had a place to mail your deathless prose and verse, and you felt yourself to be part of a group."

When Adams died in 1960, he'd lived past the time when people were interested in what he thought or did. Sadder, the world had passed beyond his interest in it. The obscurity of his once famous name demonstrated the fleeting nature of reputation, the inexorability of time and loss. Yet much of the work by people F.P.A. discovered and nurtured remains. His role as talent scout and mentor to American writers in the first half of the twentieth century stands today, one of a kind, important, worthy of attention. He was a tastemaker, a rigorous editor, and a generous friend; much of the stature of our literature in that long period owes something to him and to the standards he set.

Many young newcomers to New York City still call at the Algonquin first, before they visit the art museums or the opera houses. They want to say hello to those special ghosts from the Round Table. There are few other places where they can touch unmistakably the hopeful youngsters who preceded them, where they can become inspired momentarily with the notion of endless possibility. Knowledge of this unique group fleshes out the picture of the national past and is, in part, what continues to bring Americans to New York City and gives them pride in it.

Born the same year that President James A. Garfield was assassinated, Frank Adams died a few months before John F. Kennedy was elected. The story of his rich American life touches us still, and rates telling.

PART ONE

PART
ONE

CHAPTER ONE

Chicago

The past is a bucket of ashes.

—CARL SANDBURG

I Franklin Pierce Adams was born before there was any such things as world war or Sigmund Freud, when a belief in America's Manifest Destiny was as generally accepted as the certainty that God favored the Protestants. Yet Adams, a Jew, lived a classic American life. Like his immigrant grandparents, he was restless and ambitious, fleeing his hometown as soon as he could. He left Chicago at twenty-two and tackled the golden streets of New York City, where he lived the rest of his life. Easily transplanted, he scarcely saw his family after 1904 and claimed no midwestern ties except during football seasons. Other than a lifelong love affair with the Wolverines of the University of Michigan, no one would have guessed he came from anywhere but West Tenth Street, Manhattan.

In Chicago his parents sent him to private school, where he learned Latin, a knowledge he treasured and used. But if he knew the names of his German grandparents, they weren't important enough to save by telling his children. It was as if he was himself new, self-invented, forward-looking and optimistic, unburdened by the past and its story of finished possibilities. His ancestors were of no more importance to him than his descendants.

In this way he was remarkably akin to the city of his birth.

From its beginnings as a station on the way West, Chicago was a booster town. There, "big" meant "terrific," and this afternoon was a thousand times better than yesterday. Like Adams, Chicagoans were resourceful, practical, and energetic. They encouraged the purveyors of local and national hoopla and welcomed visitors with their own brand of boisterous hospitality. (An early innkeeper boasted, "Every night I play the fiddle like the devil and keep the hotel like hell!")

Yet shoulder to shoulder with the blowhards and drummers stood a group of Chicago writers who shaped and muscled American literature: Theodore Dreiser, Sherwood Anderson, Carl Sandburg, Edgar Lee Masters, George Ade, Eugene Field, Ben Hecht, Richard Wright, Finley Peter Dunne, Nelson Algren, Ring Lardner, Edna Ferber, Frank Norris, James T. Farrell, Willa Cather, Booth Tarkington—all of whom sprang in one way or another from the Chicago incubator. There were others. Some were idealists, many were irreverent and cynical, but all shared a searching, impatient vision and a powerful way of expressing it.

Like them, Adams was determined to participate in the creation of literature for the new century. He did, but not by writing it. His role, that of editor of a literary newspaper column, was invented by him and has yet to be duplicated. And because he grew up where the creative force was well-nigh palpable, it's important to look at the story of Chicago to see how it came to be the place it is, to set the stage for the razzle-dazzle of the New York literati and the story of F.P.A.

II

In 1818, when Illinois became a state, the village of Chicago numbered a hardy 150 souls. It grew fast.

Its frontier arrogance was captured and hurled at the world in the town motto, "I Will." Many of its residents were fugitives from who-knew-what-kind-of-disreputable past, and they were eager to Make It Big. By the time New Yorker John Jacob Astor retired from the fur-trading business in 1834, the Illinois and Michigan Canal had been dug to link the Great Lakes with the Mississippi. The first railroads were in action. Shrewd Chicagoans bet on the railroads despite the obvious and historic advantages of the canal and river system radiating from the shores of oceanlike Lake Michigan. They were right. The waterways made the city rich, but the railroads made her great.

The town was built on prairie as flat as a dollar bill, but its proximity to Lake Michigan was disastrous for the brave homesteaders who tried to erect dwellings. The land was a swamp in the spring and a dust bowl in the summer, when dust was inches thick, choking the yellow air, muffling the sound of horses' hooves.

On rainy days the roads and walkways turned to quicksand. The story circulated about the farmer buried to his neck in mud, who re-assured worried onlookers by commenting, "It's all right. I'm standing on a mule."

The indefatigable settlers laid planks across the mud and raised some of them on pilings. In a single block there could be three sets of stairs from the sidewalk to six or twelve feet higher platforms and other sets down again. A journey through the bustling business district was at once tedious and perilous, especially on snowy days when everything was covered with ice. Occasionally somebody attempted to pave the streets, once with stove lids—a failure. In 1855 an enterprising engineer from New York, George Pullman, supervised the six feet lifting of the entire five-story Tremont Hotel. The feat was accomplished without causing a crack in the brick edifice or alarming any of the guests, most of whom never guessed what had happened.

While prominent Chicago families had names like McCormick, Ogden, Wright, Hubbard, and Clark, and were descendants of Eastern families who'd sent their children westward with an eye to the Main Chance, the popular definition of Chicago as a Yankee stronghold was curiously blind to an 1855 fact of life: Nearly a third of the population of 100,000 was made up of German immigrants.

They formed an industrious colony boasting its own newspapers, civic and religious associations, grocery stores, butcher shops, and beer gardens. Among them were several thousand Jews who attended one of the city's five synagogues.

The Germans tended to keep to themselves and didn't do much fraternizing with other groups. The Melting Pot was a post-World War I notion. In 1855 Chicago's Know-Nothing party, whose members hated foreigners and blathered about the superiority of native-born Americans (although their definition of native-born didn't stretch to include local denizens of the Ottawa, Potawatomi, and Chippewa nations), elected the mayor and a majority of the members of the city council. Immediately they enacted a law raising the saloon tax from $50 to $300. The politicians justified their action as one intended to wipe out Chicago's lowlife saloons. But the Germans knew that the 600 percent increase was enacted to harass the city's immigrants, most of whom weren't yet voters. Shortsighted insiders have always believed that insulting newcomers will make them go away. As might have been expected, the ruse didn't work.

The Germans, stung, reacted with fierce nationalistic pride, and they rioted. A thousand of them battled the two-hundred-man police force in what became known as Chicago's Beer War. When the tax increases were tabled indefinitely, it signaled emergence of the powerful German community in Chicago. No politician ignored it again.

With the onset of the Civil War, Chicago families with the rest of America patriotically sent their sons off to win it. The times were turbulent and emotional, and the voices of preachers, newspaper editors, and politicians harangued the multitudes. Volunteers rushed to fill the ranks of the Illinois regiments.

Ever watchful entrepreneurs conceived and ran several wartime "sanitary fairs." The most successful of these, sporting a midway *and* cultural exhibits, raised $100,000 for the war effort, which the sponsors, with characteristic fanfare, turned over to the U.S. Treasury. Crafty Chicago merchants took note.

When the tragic war ended, Abraham Lincoln and Stephen Douglas were both dead, and the country staggered to bind its wounds.

Life ripped open in boomtown Chicago, and the "sporting life" thrived, despite the efforts of responsible citizens, zealous in their endless battle with the wages of sin and debauchery. An editorial clucked that "the shooting of people upon the most trifling provocation is becoming altogether too prevalent in this city." Evidence of the shoot-'em-up mentality abounded in the squalid collection of saloons, fleabag hotels, and brothels lying between State Street and Dearborn, known to all as "Hairtrigger Block."

Visitors and speculators continued to pour into town, and in consequence lavish new hotels were built. With the inns and restaurants came another Chicago institution: the business of entertainment. It grew from the need of practical citizens to take as much money as possible—legally, if necessary—from the swarms of newcomers and visitors.

In addition to their desire to capitalize on the boom, Chicagoans yearned for culture and respectability. So when one theater opened, it wisely proclaimed itself a "museum" to deflect certain disapproval from the scions (and their wives) of the South side, who approved of culture but sneered at people who put on shows. Not only did the Woods "Museum" contain "150,000 curiosities of every kind," including a ninety-six-foot-long fossil, a sea lion, a lighted panorama of London, and a hall displaying original oil paintings, it also boasted a lecture hall seating fifteen hundred people. Not accidentally, during the spring to September season, a theatrical stock company performed on its stage.

There were other well-known theaters, as well as two opera houses and a symphony music hall at the Tremont House—where the fabulous Adelina Patti sang. Her first of several concerts there was greeted by an orgy of self-conscious sophistication: Uniformed ticket takers and ushers patrolled the aisles, girls put up their hair for the first time, and their mothers threw elaborate pre- and post-concert parties, where the ladies wore above-the-elbow evening gloves and their escorts sported tails. Chicago society was born.

At Rice's and McVicker's theaters, actors of national reputation appeared. And when booze tycoon Uranus H. Crosby built an opera house at the stupendous cost of $600,000, it was the plushest opera house anywhere. Knowing he'd hopelessly extended himself, Crosby devised an ingenious plan to recoup. He raffled off the opera house at $5 a chance. Scuttlebutt circulated that he succeeded in selling $850,000 worth of raffle tickets. When the winner's name was drawn, Crosby acted quickly by buying back the building for $200,000—a huge profit, even allowing for probable exaggeration. The press grumbled that no matter what name had appeared on the winning ticket, it had turned out to be Uranus H. Crosby, as everybody should have known. But the deal was done. Soon everybody good-naturedly shrugged it off. So many of them had wanted to own their own opera house! It was all part of the young city's boast that any mother's son was good enough to own an opera house or an art museum or a store that sold pianos. It was democratic. Long afterward people recounted the episode with relish. Even Chicago bamboozles were bigger and more fun than anywhere else.

In 1870 Chicago was the fifth largest city in the United States—behind New York, Philadelphia, Brooklyn, and St. Louis.

Then, on October 8, it went up in smoke. Marshall Field's department store and the Palmer House hotel along with Conley's Patch—"The Abodes of Squalor and Vice." Stores, hotels, opera houses, churches and synagogues, lumberyards and livery stables, factories, Booksellers Row ("Where More Books Are Sold Than In Any City Twice The Size!"), twenty-two wooden schoolhouses, five railroad depots, theaters, banks, seventeen grain elevators containing 6.5 tons of grain, even red-light districts. All burned democratically.

More than 2,100 acres was destroyed, 300 people died, and 100,000 were homeless overnight. Some $200 million worth of property vanished, and the effect on the markets of the world ricocheted for months afterward. It was as if the city had been designed to carry fire from one end of itself to the other. Space beneath the wooden sidewalks served as a chimney as the fire raced up and down streets, cut across vacant lots, roared over the walkways, along picket fences, and through alleys. Downtown, warehouses and stores were jammed with flammable goods on floor-to-ceiling wooden shelves. In the railroad yards, wooden freight cars stood in long lines on wooden tracks. Winter fuel and oil for lamps awaited the inferno in barns and sheds behind every house. The galelike winds sweeping up from the south helped too, as did the long drought.

Stories of bravery, greed, stupidity, and general feistiness in the face of disaster blazed into the myth of the Great Conflagration. The wife of evangelical preacher Dwight Moody begged her husband to save his portrait as they frantically evacuated their home. "I can't do that, my dear," he's supposed to have said. "What if I'm met on the street by friends in the same plight and they say, 'Hello, Moody, glad you've escaped. What's that you've saved and cling to so affectionately?'—It wouldn't do to reply 'I've got my own portrait!' "

The fire lasted two days. When it ended, the city was destroyed. There were few landmarks or clues as to what had stood before. Even the distances were erased, as were the boundaries that might have told where properties began and ended. All was smoking rubble and ashes.

Merchants doubted the city could be rebuilt or made workable again. One businessman declared, "Our capital is wiped out of existence. . . . All loss is total. The trade of the town has gone up, and we might as well get out of it at once."

He was wrong. Within twenty-four hours enterprising men and women had returned to the smoldering remains of their city and set up businesses. One resourceful young man somehow found some oranges and tomatoes and constructed a fruit stand by nailing together a few charred planks and covering them with tar paper. An enterprising photographer posed him standing in front of the improvised structure, grinning and looking pleased with himself.

People poked and bustled among the ashes with wheelbarrows and set about homesteading all over again.

After a great rain fell on October 16, they started looking to the future once again. When the waterworks reopened the next day, Chicagoans knew that although they were down, they were characteristically scrambling and preparing to rise again.

One of the less obvious problems resulting from the fire was that practically all the city records and statistics were destroyed. Anybody born or dead before 1871 had no birth or death certificate. School and tax records were lost, as were city directories, deeds, bank records, newspapers, and censuses. Whole pages of history had been incinerated.

Nevertheless, the loss fit in with the forward-looking attitude of the entrepreneurial Chicagoans who didn't give a hoot about yesterday. They focused instead on today's excitement, tomorrow's promise. Family trees were of no use to them.

III In 1876 Rutherford B. Hayes was elected president, and General George Custer was clobbered by the Sioux at Little Big Horn. In Boston young Moses Adams decided to leave the city of his birth and journey westward. It was an auspicious time for unmoneyed but daring young men to forge ahead, and Horace Greeley had told them in which direction to go.

Moses' father Isaac owned a grocery store in Boston, which he'd opened soon after immigrating from Germany with his wife Rachel. Although the family name was originally Adam, circumstances had changed it. A wooden sign hanging above the shop entrance ("I. Adam, Prop.") blew down in a heavy storm and shattered. When Isaac hired a local painter to make a new sign, an *s* was added. Since Boston was a place where the name was revered, Isaac believed keeping it could only help business. So the *s* stayed. And when his son Moses was born on January 12, 1851, the newcomer's name became Adams, as did his father's—with a stroke of the registrar's pen.

Once grown, Moses ached to try his chances elsewhere. He didn't intend to remain in Boston and help run the grocery store. He had the same restless nature that had brought his parents to America in the great German migration of the 1840s, and so he left Boston as soon as there was money for the trip. He'd read about the tremendous fire and the way Chicago was rebuilding itself. It sounded like a hustling place where a bright man could succeed. Like his father, he never looked back.

Moses was dark-haired and good-looking, a gifted man who sang and told stories with an Irish flair for blarney, a German's love of friendship, an Englishman's talent for language, a newcomer's curiosity, topped with a sprinkle of his own quickness and audacity. He was a typical American.

After the night-and-day-long journey, he got off the train and trudged the dusty streets of Chicago lugging his valise. He was amazed at the vitality he saw and was immediately infected by it. Although he was new in town and awed, he was no hick. City born and bred, his was the drummer's easy confidence. And he was old enough (twenty-six), experienced in meeting the demands of life's hurlyburly and equal to its challenge. He found a room in a boardinghouse on Michigan Avenue not far from the lake. Somebody told him about a job as clerk in a dry goods establishment downtown on Wabash Avenue. He applied, describing for the boss his extensive Boston retail experience, and was hired. Because the hours were long and the chores excruciatingly tedious, he wanted to step out, so he found time to join a synagogue. His choice, *Kehilath Anshe Maarev* (The Congregation of the Men of the West), had a membership of prosperous second and third generation German families. Many of them owned stores and offices located along Market Street and Fifth Avenue, near his workplace.

Hard-working and well-spoken, he was soon welcomed into the homes of several of the most respectable families. Within a few months he opened a business with a new friend, Oscar Stern, who'd moved into his boardinghouse. They named their enterprise "Stern and Adams, Dry Goods," and launched themselves as commission merchants at 202 Monroe Street, in the midst of the thriving textile and garment district. Mothers in the congregation smiled and encouraged their daughters when Moses called.

The Schlossmans were a well-connected family. They'd been Americans for three generations, and their relatives included outstanding Chicago families like the Leopolds and the Strausses. Schlossman had a prosperous men's furnishings business on Clark Street, and there were brothers and sisters and aunts and uncles all over town. It was an attractive, energetic family, and Moses spent many afternoons and evenings visiting with Leon, one of the sons he'd met at temple. Soon it became evident, however, that the main attraction at the big house wasn't Leon but instead his younger sister Clara. She was tall and intelligent, with a special earnestness that appealed to Moses, who liked a good listener. And she laughed at his stories.

There was a piano in the parlor, and when Moses called, he brought sheet music from the latest shows. He and Clara shared the piano bench as he played and she sang. Sometimes she played, and he stood behind her and sang along with the rest of the family.

Nobody was surprised when Moses proposed and Clara accepted. Her family liked him and believed he was going places, as he did. When they were married on January 12, 1881, it was Moses' thirtieth birthday, and Clara was just twenty. He wore a traditional white yarmulke and a shawl over his suit. After he'd stamped on the goblet, he caught his bride in his arms, kissed her, and they came away laughing. Everybody cheered.

That winter was the second coldest in Chicago's history (or since 1871, when the first records were available). Temperatures ranged from ten to twenty degrees below zero, day after day, but the young couple ignored the icicles forming on the insides of their windows. They set up housekeeping on the second floor of a clapboard house with a large sun porch at 84 Twenty-sixth Street. It was a shady street of big houses and big families. Clara watched from her living room windows as neighborhood women bundled their fat babies in carriages to take the morning sun while older children in mittens and leggings made snowmen and went sledding. Here she saw an avenue of three-story frame houses with gateposts, picket fences, and great sheltering trees. An alley ran along the backyards, where shivering housemaids hurried out to speak to men in wagons who sold them milk and eggs and sometimes secondhand clothes. The Erring Woman's Refuge was a brick house standing on the corner of Indiana Avenue. Not much was known of the unfortunates there, since the shades were invariably drawn and Clara rarely saw people coming in or going out. Curious little boys were shooed away by a stern matron in a long black dress, who stood dauntlessly on the porch with her arms folded across her chest.

Soon Moses and Clara told the Schlossmans that they expected their first child. The baby's birth was scheduled for ten months after the wedding, indicating that fortune smiled on the new family.

That fall President James A. Garfield was assassinated, and his murderer was tried amid public clamor and outrage. The newspapers were obsessed with the tragedy, comparing Garfield to Lincoln, the deranged Charles Guiteau to Judas Iscariot (though curiously not to John Wilkes Booth).

But the world outside, with its hysteria and momentous events, seemed remote to the Adamses. At home on November 15 Clara gave birth to a baby boy. They hadn't decided on a name—being superstitious like many of their friends, they hadn't even borrowed a cradle before-hand. But after considerable family discussion, the name Franklin was selected, and a middle name of Leopold, after that prosperous branch of Clara's family.

Thirteen years later, when Franklin was confirmed at the Sinai Temple, he chose another middle name, Pierce, presumably after one of the dimmer lights of the U.S. presidency, and Leopold was laid aside. Until he was thirteen he was Franklin Leopold Adams.

IV   Frank was almost three when his sister Amy was born. Baby Evelyn came along three years later on a snowy morning in February. The family moved to a yellow frame house a few houses down Twenty-sixth Street.

In the manner of little boys in love with their nursemaids, Frank thought Civil War cavalry officer Philip Sheridan the greatest of generals because black-haired Maggie Sheridan was his sisters' nanny—even though she and the dashing general weren't related. It was Maggie who taught Frank to read. The first book he tackled, with her patient help, was called *Davy and the Goblin*.

Primary school for Frank was the Douglas School, on the southeast corner of Forest Avenue and Thirty-second Street. He learned to walk there by himself from the Adamses' new house on Calumet Avenue, and later from their big house on Grand Boulevard. The family moved four times in Frank's first seven years.

In those days educators had a firm grip on what they wanted to teach and how it was to be learned. Classes for even the youngest children were heavy with rote and recitation. Elocution was taught in all grades, poetry memorized about boys on burning decks and babies touched by angels while sleeping in their mothers' arms.

Requisite gestures during recitation included an arm across the forehead for despair, hands clasped breast high "to implore." A hand placed delicately upon one's heart and lowered eyes was "a maiden's answer."

The parsing of sentences was a daily at-the-blackboard ritual for the children, with arrows and predicates in boxes, and modifiers dangling at angles. The boys and girls dreaded drills on grammar and parts of speech and multiplication tables, but they were resigned. Years later Clarence Darrow remarked about his school days, "Grammar was a hideous nightmare. I tried and tried but even now I can hardly tell an adverb from an adjective, and I don't know that I care." Even President Garfield had said, "It is a perpetual wonder that any child's love of knowledge survives the outrages of the classroom."

But in the 1880s and 1890s, criticism of accepted methods of educating children was rare. Dedicated teachers like Miss Graham, in room 24, and Miss Store downstairs in room 12 held sway at the Douglas School. They were empowered to use corporal punishment whenever they decided it was appropriate. Children's well-being utterly depended on the teacher's mood because her rule was absolute, her decisions invariably upheld by the principal. Daydreamers or unruly types didn't benefit from this brand of authoritarianism, but nobody had yet come along to question it, so what Frank learned, he learned tensely and with an eye to pleasing the teacher. Luckily, quickness and agile memory counted at Douglas, so Frank thrived. He excelled at spelling, word usage, arithmetic, vocabulary, and penmanship, called "vertical handwriting." "Coal and peat are of vegetable origin," announced the opening sentence in elaborate curls across the first page of his first copybook. He remembered that fact unwillingly for the rest of his life.

Geography and history were solemn subjects, painstakingly taught. Colton's *Geography*, a widely read text of those days, announced that "Islamism is the religion taught by Mohammed, an imposter who recorded his doctrines in a book called the Koran. It consists of a confused mixture of grossly false ideas. . . . Christianity is the only system which elevates men to a true sense of his moral relations, and adds to his happiness." Further on, Colton described the Chinese as "ingenious, industrious and peaceful, but miserably conceited. They cling to the customs of their ancestors."

Cruikshank's *Geography* clumped together and dismissed the disparate cultures of millions of the world's inhabitants. "Half civilized peoples like the Chinese and Mexicans have towns and cities, cultivate the soil and exchange products; but have few arts and little intelligence."

The physical world of rivers and cities was attended to carefully. Frank and the other children at Douglas learned to sing about the rivers of Europe and they memorized state capitals in an interminable series of unrhymed phrases. ("New Jersey, Trenton, on the Delaware River, New Jersey, Trenton, on the Delaware River. Delaware, Dover, on the Jones Creek, Delaware, Dover, on the Jones Creek. Pennsylvania, Harrisburg, on the Susquehanna River, Pennsylvania, Harrisburg, on the Susquehanna River," and so on.)

Frank learned to memorize facts as if he were a vessel to fill with information. It was their elaborate collection and display that American education stressed. Curiosity was rewarded when it led to conventional conclusions and more facts.

Frank's interest in popular songs was kindled early when he and his classmates gathered in the music room and sang "The Landing of the Pilgrim Fathers," "Where Do All the Daisies Go?" and "Old Jack Frost Has Come to Town, Boys." He pooh-poohed the ability but remembered odd details from his school days anyhow. Years later he recalled from Barnes' *History of the United States*: "I remember best that Ethan Allen asked somebody at Ticonderoga to surrender 'In the name of the Great God Jehovah and the Continental Congress!' and that Charles C. Pinckney said, 'Millions for defense but not one cent for tribute,' and that the quotation was at the bottom of a left-hand page, in small type, as a footnote; and that somewhere in the book, though in connection with what, I don't know, it said, 'The effect of this brilliant event was electrical.' And I remember particularly a picture, 'John Smith Showing His Compass to the Indians.' "

A favorite book was Horatio Alger's inspirational biography of the much admired President Garfield, *From Canal Boy to President*. He read it many times. (Less than common knowledge was that Alger, trained as a Unitarian minister, had been banned from his pulpit in Brewster, Massachusetts, for "unnatural familiarity with boys.")

Frank was an outstanding student, with a genial classroom bravado and enviable status, year after year, as the teacher's pet. He and his friends played Pom-Pom-Pete-Away after school and raced their bicycles—called "wheels"—daring each other to frenzied displays of expertise and inviting the dismay of their mothers. He rode his Barnes White Flyer bicycle wearing a cap, short trousers caught at the knees with buckles, long plaid socks, and a white shirt with a high collar.

> These are the things I used to know:
> A book called "Remember the Alamo,"
> Written, I think, by Amelia Barr;
> And the Cottage Grove cable car—
> It was purple, but the State Street car was red
> That passed by the bakery of Livingston's bread.
> In our yard, near the drying shirts and socks,
> I planted nasturtiums and four-o'clocks,
> And in winter I often used to glide
> On Johny Cudahy's toboggan slide—
> (He had a pair of pants with stripes,
> And lived just across from the Conrad Seipps).
> And Toots McCormick and Alma Meyer
> Yelled when I passed on my Barnes White Flyer;
> And a thousand other things I knew
> In that sweet Chicago of '92.
>
> F.P.A., 1943

Bold as he was with his buddies, he was shy with girls. He timed his departure from home in order to follow the adored Corinne Zimmerman to school. But although he walked behind her every day for three years, he never summoned the courage to speak to her.

During the seventh and eighth grades, Frank's life was enriched by the opening, in 1893, of the World's Columbian Exposition, held in Chicago to celebrate the four hundredth anniversary of Columbus' discovery of the new world. It became a world's fair to challenge world's fairs. True to flamboyant Chicago tradition, civic leaders announced that the exposition was a miracle of the age. Their fair offered a new, perfect city set upon the shores of the world's most beautiful lake. The federal government put up $10 million for the fair, and the city fathers provided double that by selling subscriptions (Marshall Field bought the largest one) and issuing stocks and bonds. Frederick Olmsted, famous for creating New York's Central Park, was hired to landscape the fairgrounds. He arranged to dump railroad carloads of fill on the miles of sandy marsh, set special trees and shrubs and flowering plants in ordered displays on the man-made wooded island in the middle of the man-made blue lagoon; he manicured and tended the walks and canals and flower gardens until the scene was breathtaking.

Architects from all over the country were invited to design the various buildings. Stanford White's New York firm of McKim, Mead and White was responsible for the Agriculture Building and Boston's Peabody and Stearns for the Machinery Building. Van Brunt and Howe from Kansas City, and Richard Morris Hunt and George Browne Post from New York, were other out-of-towners who participated in the design and erection of the White City, a collection of glistening neoclassical structures of Indiana limestone.

Sociologist Charles Zeublin called the exposition "a symbol of regeneration." Famous Victorian-era sculptor Augustus Saint-Gaudens claimed the fair provided the opportunity for "the greatest meeting of artists since the fifteenth century" and went on to extol the Palace of Fine Arts (designed by Chicago's own Charles B. Atwood) as "the greatest achievement since the Parthenon."

Visionary architect Louis ("form must ever follow function") Sullivan, who designed the Transportation Building, felt otherwise. He said the exposition was "an appalling calamity, architecturally," and that "the damage wrought by the fair will last for half a century."

The exposition opened a year late, after two winters of frantic excavating and building, in May 1893. There were endlessly diverting carryings-on: parties, parades, opportunities for speechmaking and the hawking of souvenirs. President Grover Cleveland came from Washington, D.C., to lead the opening day parade of twenty-three carriages (many of them occupied by foreign dignitaries, mostly Spanish royalty). The procession passed through the midway, where the crowds yelled and threw their hats in the air, tom-toms sounded, lions from the Hagenbeck traveling animal show roared and caused pandemonium in the still muddy stretch facing the speakers' platform called the Court of Honor. President Cleveland touched a key to an electric circuit and suddenly lights blazed, flags unfurled, and water gushed from the MacMonnies fountain, which Saint-Gaudens with his customary understatement called "the masterpiece of masterpieces." A drape fell to reveal the Statue of Liberty. Guns boomed from warships standing offshore. Later in the afternoon, glass tycoon Edward Drummond Libbey presented the Infanta of Spain with a gown made entirely of fiberglass. The dress weighed eighty pounds, but the razor-edged threads made it unwearable anyway.

The members of the American Historical Association, meeting in convention at the fair, heard Frederick Jackson Turner's depressing news that the days of the American frontier had ended. But even this information made little impact on the giddy Chicagoans and their guests. Strolling the paths of their fair invited comparisons with fairyland; reality was as unremarked as December is in June. Yet within three years the most severe economic depression in its history hit America, closing 500 banks and 70 railroads, bankrupting more than 15,000 small businesses—including, ultimately, Moses'. But at the summer of the fair, the first chords of dissonance were out of earshot, far offstage.

Moses and Clara were impressed with the stories about the exposition appearing daily in the papers. They decided its presence in their city afforded an excellent educational opportunity for their son. He was twelve, and they wanted him to develop self-sufficiency and confidence, as well as to be exposed to the finest sights and lessons of the day. Moses took Frank downtown to have his photograph taken for a season's pass. Frank used it all summer. There was nothing he didn't want to taste or see, and he and his friends rode the horsecars to the fairgrounds almost every day, just as Moses and Clara wanted. Every night at supper he described what he'd seen, and his little sisters were amazed. Not only were the large buildings and their contents fascinating and edifying, but the midway offered delights beyond imagining. And it wasn't only the newly invented Ferris wheel, which towered 250 feet above the midway and carried hundreds of terrified passengers at once, or the Wild West Show starring Annie Oakley, or even the games of chance and daring stretching in all directions. It was the vistas of free exhibits and shows that thrilled him and brought him back again and again. There stood an entire Irish village with thatched roofs and a cow, a panorama of the Burmese Alps, Persian and Moorish palaces, a replica of St. Peter's in Rome, Parisian and American glass spinners, a noisy Asian Indian bazaar with hanging pots and rugs and mysterious women in long silken dresses with red spots on their foreheads. A realistic model of the volcano of Kilauea steamed and gurgled next to an authentic Chinese theater and a model of the Eiffel Tower. Frank saw the wild animals at the animal show do tricks, and he stood inside a log cabin circa 1776, near a street exactly like one in Cairo, Egypt. And, of course, there was Little Egypt herself, the belly dancer, celebrated and excoriated throughout the country, who wiggled and bumped to toodly music during four shows a day.

It was a fine time and place to be alive.

At home Clara and Moses talked about their plans for Frank, and worried about where they should send him to high school.

They were perplexed. They wanted the best possible education for their precocious son, so a private school seemed best. But most private schools in Chicago were Christian church affiliated. Still, they wanted him to learn and value English culture because that was the way of prosperous, well-educated Americans. It was a dilemma. How much inculcation into English mores did they want, and how much of themselves would such an education force him to abandon? What did it mean to become *Americanized*? Did you have to give up your religion for it? Was that desirable? Family discussions were heated. Clara and her family went regularly to services at the Sinai Temple and celebrated the Jewish holidays. Their rabbi had approved religious services on Sunday instead of on Saturday to fit in more conveniently with the ways of the majority of their neighbors, but even so it wasn't easy being an American Jew. Practically everybody of power and importance was Christian. It was hard to keep the Jewish traditions, but Clara made the effort.

When she and Moses learned about the newly established Armour Institute, founded in 1893 by Philip D. Armour of the meat-packing family, they were overjoyed. The school was heralded as forward-looking. Armour and his handpicked school administration (including Dr. Francis Wakely Gunsaulus, nationally known pastor and a neighbor of the Adamses on Grand Boulevard) wanted the benefits of their "broadly philanthropic" educational philosophy to reach everyone. And while its prospectus described the school's values as "avowedly Christian," and even though it stressed that Christian standards of culture would be emphasized in the curriculum, there was to be no "intrusion of denominational or sectarian bias."

It was to be a modern school and promised to use every up-to-date method. It would accept only those students who had demonstrated a desire to learn and would advocate education of "head, hand and heart, with whatever teaching and material most appropriately contributes to the elevation of sentiment, purity of tastes and refinement of manners." There was to be little regimentation because the students would be too busy with their studies and too well motivated to need intrusive supervision.

Clara and Moses visited the school, located at the corner of Armour (later Federal) Avenue and Thirty-third Street. They found a six-story fireproof building constructed of huge blocks of red granite providing "every convenience": a gymnasium, a technical museum, and a library consisting of five thousand volumes. Even though it was barely two years old, the library—with a special collection of early printed books—was described as "a rallying place for the forces of intelligence in the community, and *entirely free.*" Andrew Carnegie had yet to dot the national landscape with free libraries, so Armour's pride in its own freely circulating books was understandable. Later the Armour Institute library merged with the Crerar library, endowed by Chicago philanthropist John Crerar in 1889. Crerar had directed that the library named for him hold books and periodicals selected with a view to creating and sustaining a "healthy moral and Christian sentiment in the community, all nastiness and immorality to be excluded." He didn't mean to preclude everything except hymn books and sermons but intended to keep out "dirty French novels, all skeptical trash and works of questionable moral tone."

It was a self-conscious time. Civic improvement and indeed the perfectability of humans themselves seemed within their grasp as long as they followed the right path. And wealthy men like Crerar and Armour genuinely believed they knew the right path. Their philanthropy won dominance for their views.

Etchings and works of art hung in the Armour Institute hallways, including Moschelle's oil portrait of Robert Browning, Whistler's King Lear, and a copy made in 1520 of a genuine Raphael.

In fact, the Armour Institute ("of Technology" was added in 1895, the change occurring "to harmonize with the advanced ideas of The Founder") rapidly became a much respected institution in Chicago. It was divided into two parts: the Academy, a four-year high school course designed to prepare students for college, and the Institute, which was itself a college offering scientific and technical courses such as civil, mechanical, and electrical engineering, awarding the B.S. degree. Tuition at the Academy was $60 a year.

After passing the English, arithmetic, and history entrance exams given in June, Frank entered as a freshman in September 1895. His was the class of 1899.

The program was rigorous. Not only was the five hour per week study of Latin required, but so were regular recitations in rhetoric and assignments in algebra, history, and civil government—including the ancient, medieval and modern eras. Instruction was supplemented by stereopticon illustrations, map drawing, notebook work, reading, and frequent exams. As a fourteen-year-old freshman, Frank was expected to read and discuss Pope's translation of *The Iliad*, the de Coverley Papers in *The Spectator*, Coleridge's *The Rime of the Ancient Mariner*, De Quincey's *Flight of a Tartar Tribe*, Cooper's *The Last of the Mohicans*, Hawthorne's *The House of the Seven Gables*, Dryden's *Palamon and Arcite*, and Goldsmith's *The Vicar of Wakefield*. By the time of his senior year, he was to have also studied Shakespeare's *Macbeth* and *The Merchant of Venice*; Milton's *L'Allegro, Il Penseroso, Comus, Lycidas*, and *Paradise Lost*; Sir Walter Scott's *Ivanhoe*; Eliot's *Silas Marner*; works by Edmund Burke, Thomas Carlyle, Jonathan Swift, Macaulay, and other English poets and essayists. In addition, he was to have completed four years of Latin, from Caesar to Cicero and Virgil, and at least two years of a modern foreign language, as well as chemistry, geometry—both plane and solid—botany, physics, and trigonometry.

It was a stiff curriculum, but exclusionary. No translations of German poets were read, no Russians or eastern Europeans, no Spaniards, South Americans, Chinese or other Asians. The development of Western civilization was called "World History," and there was no mention of the eastern hemisphere or Africa except as they related to the West. England and its empire were the norm against which everything else was measured.

V High school opened windows to Frank's imagination that his mother and the purveyors of English culture at the Academy never dreamed of. His youth unfolded simultaneously with the golden years of vaudeville, and Chicago was the gemstone of the circuit. By the time he was fifteen, he spent at least one afternoon a week in the audience of the Olympic Theater, Chicago's first-class vaudeville house. Earlier he and his father had attended shows at Trocadero Hall, overlooking the lake. Frank felt special when he and his father indulged in these manly pleasures without the intrusion of the females in the family.

He and his friends were familiar with the exhibits at Chicago's London and Globe dime museums, homes to freaks and harmless exhibitionists. Frank's Monday eighth-grade class in manual training regularly convened downtown in the basement of the Jones School, located in the tough first ward, where aldermen had names like Bathhouse John and Hinkydink Kenna. "To us somewhat effete boys from Grand Boulevard,'' said Frank, "the Jones School and its vicinage were romantic heaven.'' They journeyed there by way of an unchaperoned trip downtown on the horsecar as soon as they'd finished lunch. Although class instruction didn't begin until 1:30 P.M., their group invariably arrived early. Not only did they enjoy impersonating men by working with the fearsome machinery, but with their early arrival they avoided the roughnecks from Jones, whose turf they invaded under the auspices but not necessarily the protection of the local school board. Surprisingly, several encounters with the Jones boys ended without significant damage or loss of face on either side. Scuffles on the cement floor of the school basement left Frank with "nothing but contempt for the modern effeminate game of football.''

A major enticement for these Monday afternoon forays was the dismissal time—3:30 P.M.—which left the dozen prepubescent boys downtown only a couple of blocks from the dime museums. Frank couldn't pay the admission price consecutively, but by walking the five miles home on alternate Mondays, he could afford entry every other week. He thrilled at the opportunity.

Freaks were the main attraction at Kohl and Middleton's Globe, and they included the armless woman (for an additional nickel she wrote your name with a pencil grasped by her toes), the rubber-skinned man who snapped his skin as if it were made of elastic, Mexican Frank who jumped barefoot on broken glass, Miss Emma Shaler, the Ossified Girl who was gradually turning to a Solid Mass of Bone, a mind reader, and the fat man who guessed your weight at no additional charge.

Years later escape artist Harry Houdini told Frank about his early trouping days among the sword swallowers, bearded ladies, and human stepladders at the dime museums. Houdini remembered Jonathan Bass, the Living Headstone (one can only guess what that meant), and Blue Eagle, an ''Indian'' who broke boards over his head in a curious demonstration of the strength of his skull. Houdini also remembered the pathetic final days of Billy Diamond, who'd permanently injured himself as the frequent subject of a team of hypnotists who put him into a ''trance'' and then made him dive onto cement floors. Cross-eyed Ben Turpin and other stars of the silent movies got started in the tawdry dime museums. Houdini described how he and the other entrepreneurially minded performers and freaks had tipped the barkers, ensuring rhapsodies of hyperbole about their acts (or deformities). Only the deaf or unfeeling could keep their dimes and walk away.

As he grew older, his taste changed, and the freaks lost their fascination. Gruesomeness was good for a gasp and a shudder, but once

Frank had spent the summer at the world's fair, he began to search for other kinds of enlightenment: songs that told stories, beautiful women in daring costumes, dancers, comedy acts, skits and routines to make him laugh or thrill. Gradually he and his friends began attending the Olympic, where vaudeville reigned and the best acts in America played regularly.

At the Academy he was given the choice of taking German or French for his foreign language requirement. He chose German because the class ended at noon, and once a week this gave him the rest of the afternoon off. He and his cousin, Charley Strauss, and his friend, Arthur Loeb, were able to get downtown in time for the first show, which started at 12:30 P.M. Frank's weekly allowance covered carfare as well as 30 cents for the best seat. A spot in the gallery was a dime, and 20 cents bought a hard chair in the balcony, but the boys, children of prosperous fathers, sat in the center seats on the first floor. Seats weren't reserved, so the first arrivals grabbed the best ones. The boys raced downtown to arrive as early as possible, although they learned quickly that the first acts on the program were rarely of any consequence. They were performed while members of the audience tramped in, took off their coats, talked to one another, sneezed, spat, blew their noses, and generally ignored the performers. It was a four-hour show, and the audience liked to get comfortable, noisily.

As they settled into their seats, Frank and his friends outdid each other showing off. Often they interspersed their remarks with rude noises. They groaned and stretched in exhibitionistic boredom, scrunching in the hemp-filled chairs and dangling their legs over the seats in front until the ushers ordered them to desist.

But they sat up attentively when the headliners appeared.

To the uninitiated the Olympic didn't appear a conventional place of worship. The damp air was heavy with stale, unexotic smells. For the convenience of the men in the audience, spittoons stood at the end of every other aisle. The carpet nearby was odoriferous and rancid. Nor was the place thoroughly swept or cleaned. Along the walls the gas lights flickered unsafely, failing to illuminate beyond an arc of two or three feet.

Cold in the winter, stifling in the summer, the theater was undeniably uncomfortable. Yet it was always packed. It was "the Big O, it was the Honey Dew. It was Grade A Milk of Paradise," said Frank years later. His adolescent taste ran to humor and innuendo, and he keenly appreciated, among other headliners, Lady Sholto Douglas who wore a diamond garter and sang with gusto and ineffable sex appeal.

When she grinned at the boys in the front rows, they whistled and stamped. The Lady winked and sang again.

Classic comedy teams of Weber and Fields, Williams and Walker (the only Black men featured regularly), and Johnny and Emma Ray played often. Dixon, Bowers and Dixon, "The Three Rubes," pantomimed a pitcher, a near-sighted catcher, and a terrified batter. Frank saw Barney Fagan and Henrietta Byron sing and dance to "My Gal's a High Born Lady." Caron, a clown, and Herbert, a sensational acrobat, climaxed their routine when Herbert dove from a tower of stacked chairs into the waves painted on the backdrop. And the four Cohans regularly appeared on the bill with the frenetic George M. beginning their turn with his announcement "If I can't say RAH RAH RAH before breakfast every morning I get nervous!"

Years later Frank explained his legendary total recall of songs written and forgotten before 1900: "There were ballads then that told stories, and no silly 'Hutsut' something or other. Who can help remembering 'Just Tell Them That You Saw Me' when it has lines like 'Is that you, Madge? I said to her, and she quickly turned away'?"

Despite these weekly forays, Frank did first-rate work at the Academy. He was diligent, well organized, and responsible, first in his class every year. His outstanding grades weren't equaled for many years after his graduation.

One Field Day, Armour Institute competed with its rival, the Lewis Institute, and won five events; although Frank was too small to participate, his enthusiasm was total. That week dinner-table talk took a vacation from vaudeville and ran to tales of their mighty shot-putter and the other track and field stars. He was fascinated with sports and the gifted men and women who excelled in them. His lifelong zealous attention to his own tennis was a reflection of this fascination, and there was more than a little envy involved.

Often he and Clara sat in the parlor before supper while he read aloud from the paper. One of their favorite columnists was Finley Peter Dunne. As Mr. Dooley, the Chicago bartender, Dunne wrote with hilarious irreverence in the *Chicago Evening Post*. (James Joyce was another fan who later tipped his hat to Dooley in *Finnegan's Wake* in his poem, "Dooleysprudence.") " 'Ye cud niver be a rale pathrite,' " read Frank as Mr. Dooley, " 'ye have no stock tikker in y'er house.' "

Frank enjoyed companionship with his mother, and he admired her for being both intellectual and cultured. She was quieter than his father, read more than he did, and discussed issues without his impassioned advocacy. While Frank was attracted to the backslapping, stand-you-to-a-drink side of his father, it sometimes made him uneasy. Clara was impatient with imprecise or sloppy speech and, as far as she was concerned, exaggeration robbed the truth of its value. She was careful and literal, appreciated humor in others but wasn't a storyteller herself, and less charmed by the ebullient aspect of Moses' personality as the years passed. Yet Frank admired his father's ability to make friends and tell stories. He saw that Moses was charming and well liked despite his lack of formal schooling. And it was Moses who'd taken Frank to his first vaudeville, Moses who understood about the magic there. Clara was suspicious of it. There was a clean distinction in their household between substance and bravado, between the authority of scholarship and the insecurity of charm. And it was clear which parent represented which characteristics.

Yet it was a solid marriage. If there wasn't often softness between Moses and Clara, neither were there ugly disputes. Their roles were clearly delineated and accepted. It was a fact of life that people were different from one another. While he may have been pulled in different directions because of conflicting loyalties, Frank learned to conceal his anxiety with a shrug or a wisecrack. He didn't often reveal or examine his feelings, preferring instead to maintain a detached, ironic manner. Orgies of emotion—in himself or in others—embarrassed him.

He credited his mother with the intellectual side of his personality, with his good taste and his ability to determine the way things should be. His standards were hers. He knew his father's gifts to him had to do with style—his quickness, geniality, flair. And, of course, it was Moses who was responsible for his love affair with show business. Further exploration into the mysteries of the psyche didn't interest him.

Suddenly, it seemed, his high school years were over. He was seventeen and possessed only a suggestion of whiskers when it was time to graduate. There were celebrations and ceremonies of all kinds for the graduating seniors, including a seven-course banquet, a Senior Hop, several receptions, and tea parties. Faces were scrubbed and adolescent rowdiness curtailed momentarily for inspirational readings and speeches. President of the class was Beatrice Gunsaulus (her important post resulting perhaps from a connection with the director of the Institute, who was her father), a serious young woman who gave the commencement address. The class numbered twenty-eight boys and nine girls. Frank, in his rimless spectacles, wore a stiff, high-standing collar (called a Waubunk) and a two-piece suit with a jacket of five buttons, all buttoned, and narrow pegged pants. His abundant dark hair was parted in the middle and plastered down much like Billy Clifford's, an idol who danced the cakewalk with Maud Huth at the Olympic Theater.

The future looked promising. Despite increasingly portentous economic signals, Moses continued to expect prosperity and, of course, Frank would be sent away to college. Clara's relative, Lewis Strauss, was an instructor in the English department of the University of Michigan in Ann Arbor, so Frank and cousin Charley decided to go there.

The young men jumped into college life with enthusiasm. They wore freshman beanies, talked the lingo, horsed around with new friends, and even enjoyed hazing. They were comrades in a large, tightly knit group that felt like a family except that participation came from choice instead of accident. This feeling of community served as a substitute for the life of belonging they'd missed as grandchildren of immigrants. Frank and Charley had spent most of their lives trying to behave like Americans, eschewing the traditions connecting them with their foreign roots. But abandonment of their families' cultural conventions hadn't provided a satisfactory substitute. At Armour Institute most of the other students had gone to church on Sundays and participated in various mysterious cultural rituals (like coming-out parties or Sunday dinners, Christmas and Easter celebrations, and giving up things for Lent). Such activity clearly differentiated the ones who belonged.

And despite their parents' best efforts, "Americanization" hadn't been possible for other inescapable but more subtle reasons. Urban life—even urban life in houses with front yards and hired girls—wasn't recognized by popular culture as legitimate Americana. Tastemakers were still harking back to the farm and rugged individualism when they described the national ideal. A city upbringing didn't represent that. In 1899, rural America was celebrated as authentic America. The sprawling new cities with their blocks of foreigners crammed into squalid tenements weren't that. Even the lives of prosperous men with English names who worked in offices and raised their families within the city limits were thought untypical. So Jewish boys from a city felt like outsiders at home, and away—because of their Jewishness *and* their urban background.

At the University of Michigan, Frank joined a respectable American community complete with football games, academic departments, favorite and unfavorite professors, undergraduates, and alumni weekends. Life there was unlike any he'd been part of. And roots didn't seem to matter. The college sense of community manifested itself in something called "school spirit." In it this year's achievements mattered greatly, and improvement, progress, and expectations were important. The past didn't matter much except in exams.

This valuable experience of belonging greatly influenced Frank.

Like other students in those predormitory days, Frank and Charley lived in a boardinghouse. A huge framed sampler hung in the dining room: "GOD HATES A GLUTTON." Despite the warning the boys gained weight on the cheap, abundant meals.

The university courses were interesting and demanding, and Frank made friends easily. Students came to Ann Arbor from all over the country, even New York, and talk of that great city excited him. He began to consider moving there some day. But he didn't mention the notion in letters to his mother. She was sick.

The illness had started imperceptibly. First her moods swung from optimism to despair and back again, sometimes in the same afternoon. Little things threw her into tizzies of exasperation. She wept easily, complained of a galloping heartbeat. She was always too warm and couldn't seem to relax. Despite constant hunger she began to lose weight. In a few months her clothes hung on her emaciated frame as if they belonged to somebody else.

His mother's age of thirty-nine seemed antediluvian to eighteen-year-old Frank, but he suspected that the unpleasant swoops and dips in her personality had to do with something other than the change of life. He wasn't sure. There wasn't anybody he felt comfortable asking about it. He and Moses didn't discuss such matters. There'd been no fatherly explanation of the birds and bees for Frank, who'd been left to discover the romance of biology by himself. But Clara's shortness of temper, her impatience and out-of-character anxiety were hard to ignore. Evelyn and Amy kept to their rooms, and when Frank came home on vacation, he arranged a busy social life that prevented him from spending much time with her. In the few months since he'd left, her eyes had begun to protrude eerily, and stared without blinking. Her moist hands trembled so that she had to grasp them in her lap. When she played the piano, it was an ordeal for everyone. The illness embarrassed and frightened her, but she hoped to conquer it with a stern dose of willpower.

Certainly Moses didn't need extra worries. Oscar Stern had died, and their business was suddenly facing great difficulty. Moses pored over its ledgers as he struggled to cover the leaks and ruptures of the once thriving little firm. Repercussions from the nationwide economic panic had been slowly affecting their business since it ran a season ahead of the current year, but orders had been on a slide for three years, and suddenly they'd dried up entirely. Moses was hardly a business manager. After Oscar died, he had to relearn administrative areas like cash flow management and credit maintenance even while receivables vanished and new business didn't materialize. He was rarely home and preoccupied when he was. Failure was a humbling, shameful experience, and there didn't seem to be an end to it. He gave up his office and showrooms and moved his desk to a third-floor room at 254 Market Street, but there still weren't any customers. Finally in May he decided to send for Frank, who hadn't quite completed his freshman year. Although Clara had some inheritance, there wasn't enough money to spare. They needed what was on hand to take care of the family and the medical bills until business improved. Frank would have to go to work. The news was heartbreaking, but he hid his bitter disappointment and came home without taking his final exams.

Frank tried not to blame anybody and obtained a position as an insurance supply clerk at the Transatlantic Insurance Company. Adolph Loeb, Arthur's father, was his boss. Frank collated and wrapped insurance policies and distributed them to out-of-town salesmen. Sometimes he served as bill collector. Except for a little pocket money, he gave everything he earned to his father.

Clara's condition continued to deteriorate. The doctor visited regularly and prescribed various balms and medicines that she took faithfully, announcing with every dose that she felt stronger. But she had difficulty negotiating the stairs and spent most afternoons in bed. The house took on a peculiar anticipatory stillness.

Her illness was finally identified as an obscure glandular malady called Basedow's disease, with complications affecting the kidneys and lungs. There was no known cure.

Ten days short of Frank's twentieth birthday, Clara died. She'd just turned forty.

A silent, red-eyed Moses followed her wooden coffin out of their home and down the steps to the buggy at the curb. Frank and his sisters followed with the rest of her family. A long line of horses drawing carriages draped in black bunting marched at half-gait through the South Side to the Rosehill Cemetery. Clara was buried there on a white-skied November afternoon, Moses lifting the first shovelful of earth into her grave.

His business never recovered, and he was buried next to her nine years later.

The children continued living with him in the house on Grand Boulevard. Her small inheritance dwindled, and the nearly helpless father depended on the earnings of his son.

Frank's comfortable world collapsed with stunning swiftness.

VI

Like the stereotypical Chicagoan, Frank was incapable of grieving long. If his mother had died when she was still the most important woman in his life, that was too bad, but other people had lost their mothers. If he had been forced to abandon the class of 1903, well, going to college at all had been a remarkable opportunity. The important thing was to avoid looking back. It was crucial to get on with life. Soon he left Loeb and, together with his ever-present cousin Charley, went into business as a full-fledged agent with the Equitable Life Assurance Society. The young men rented space in the splendid new Marquette Building.

Life as an entrepreneur wasn't exactly what Frank yearned for, though he enjoyed getting together with friends to shoot the breeze, selling enough insurance in the process to justify his sociability. Conversation was a gift he had. Yet, except for this component of meeting people and spending time with them, his work bored him. As often as he could afford, he spent evenings at shows, musical reviews, and plays on tour from New York. He wished there were some way he could integrate these after-hours pleasures into his workaday world. Gloomily, he thought it improbable. He pictured himself ending up like his father, who loved the glittering life of imagination but spent most of his days scrambling to keep himself in polished shoes. For Moses there was a distinction between work, which you performed because you had to, and play, which occupied you as a vacation from work, without value except as escape. Frank saw the way it was for his father was the way it was with most people. Growing up meant you had to stop expecting to have a good time. That somber philosophy had been hammered into him in school. There he'd learned that life was real and earnest, a difficult journey of troublesome responsibilities, culminating finally in the release of death. Yet it was hard for Frank to accept that the days ahead stretched endlessly and alike, that he'd have to get up early every morning and go to work till he dropped in his tracks.

Then, on February 22, 1901, he rashly called on George Ade at his club for the purpose of selling him insurance. With the visit Frank's perception of possibility changed, happily and for all time.

Ade was an irreverent bachelor who wrote a column for the *Chicago Record* and at thirty-five was one of America's established humorists. He invented characters who remarked with gentle irony on the passing parade, like Pink Marsh, the black heard observing, "We got mo' rights 'n anybody, but it sutny ain't safe to use 'em." Frank admired Ade extravagantly, and one of the first books he purchased after his homecoming was Ade's *Fables in Slang*. The volume contained a collection of Ade's newspaper columns. One of them, "The Fable of Sister Mae, Who Did as Well as Could be Expected," described

> hard working Luella, Short on Looks but long on Virtue, [who] Slaved in a Factory for three Dollars a Week, while her lazy, empty-headed but Shapely Sister Mae became Cashier of a Lunchroom, had practically to Fight Off her Masculine Admirers, and Landed a Wealthy Husband and Crashed Society. Did Mae then Forget Luella? Certainly Not. She gave Luella a Job in her Home as Assistant Cook at five Dollars a week. The Moral of this Tale: *Industry and Perseverance Bring a Sure Reward.*

Among other stern truths laid bare by the Fables were: Never Believe a Relative; Avoid Crowds; Genius Must Ever Walk Alone; In All the Learned Professions, Many are Called but Few are Chosen. Ade's comic plays, *The Sultan of Sulu* and *The College Widow* among them, made him a millionaire before he turned forty.

One of the most significant characteristics of Ade's writing, as far as Frank was concerned, was that he used slang.

Frank knew of the centuries-old battle among English language purists who insisted the tongue be written and spoken without the ugly intrusion of Americanisms—slang. Frank loved the language, he enjoyed playing with words and making puns and intricate patter jokes, and he especially liked the American version of English because of its punch and vitality. He approved of slang because of, not despite, its originality. At the University of Michigan, a course in the American language had excited him because it gave credibility to the New World version of English—not as a grotesque caricature of a remote and unchanging ideal, but as a respectable, even equal partner to it. This refreshing outlook viewed change as inherent to the vigorous development of language. Surprisingly, it wasn't a widely accepted view. One of the reasons Frank admired Ade was that he wrote his Fables in the vernacular; they were easygoing midwestern stories, laconic but biting, and in them he used such relaxed and vivid Americanisms as *bellhop, up against it, drugstore, third degree,* and *cold feet.* This unselfconscious new style signaled that the unique and respectable American voice hovered on the edge of the new century awaiting an explosion of popular acceptance. Frank wanted to be in on it.

When he called on Ade, it was ostensibly to sell him insurance; actually he yearned to meet and speak with one of his heroes. The columnist was eating a leisurely breakfast of fresh strawberries and cream, and paging through a newspaper, at 11:00 o'clock on a miserable February morning. The sight startled, then inspired Frank, and he decided on the spot that here was the life for him.

The kindhearted columnist was touched by the young hero-worshiper and bought a fire insurance policy, netting Frank 45 cents. He went back to the office to tell Charley that someday he would go to work for a newspaper. In a letter written to Ade many years later, he remembered that "your strawberries lured me away from trade."

But since Frank's salary was needed at home, he couldn't go prancing off on whim. He had to be able to earn a respectable wage. Yet he was determined to become a newspaperman, so whenever he could take a few minutes from selling insurance, he did what newspapermen do: he wrote. He wasn't interested in becoming a reporter because he knew most reporters reported—they didn't often create. Frank wanted to invent and experiment and write in his own voice.

He wanted to become a columnist like Ade—or, more exactly, like Bert Leston Taylor (B.L.T.) who "conducted" a special column in the *Chicago Journal*—"A Line-o-Type or Two." Unlike Ade, whose columns were entirely his own invention, B.L.T.'s staccato material contained unrelated verses, epigrams, comments on news stories appearing in other newspapers, parodies on social notes, and in a special "Poets' Corner" he published verses written by others, usually identified only by initials or aliases like "Dog-Daze." The format fit perfectly with Frank's goals. He set to work composing humorous verses and began submitting them to Taylor.

Much to his delight, his contributions began appearing regularly in "Poets' Corner." In fact, he wrote a series of poems, "Not Knocking Swinburne," "Not Knocking the West Side," and a limerick, "Not Knocking Phidias":

> *A sculptor there was named Praxiteles*
> *Whose critics would give him blamed little ease;*
> > *They claimed that his pieces*
> > *Were not up to Greece's*
> *High standard, but way down to Italy's.*

One afternoon Frank called on Taylor, bringing with him a newly purchased book of parodies on French ballades and rondeaux by Gleeson White. After introducing himself and disclosing that he was a frequent contributor to "Poets' Corner," Frank asked him if he was familiar with the book. When Taylor admitted he wasn't, Frank took out his pen and wrote on the flyleaf, "Yours truly, Franklin P. Adams," and handed it to him. It was a generous if calculated act, and B.L.T. took note and remembered it.

As with George Ade, Frank's intrepid enthusiasm had won him another helpful friend.

He continued selling insurance by day and writing verse at night. Brief as his poems were, he took pains with them. His education had stressed the formal rules and forms for poetry, and he made sure his own technique was as precise. In his poems there was always a rhyme scheme (he didn't approve of blank verse); if he was writing a rondeau, there were thirteen lines and two rhymes, and the opening lines occurred twice, once as a refrain. His sonnets, like Shakespeare's, contained fourteen lines in iambic pentameter. While his poems had to do lightly with love and other of life's amusing ironies, he was careful to maintain stylistic formality. Sometimes he worked on a single phrase for hours.

His work always pointed in one direction: the building of a reputation and body of work that would earn him a decently paid job on a newspaper.

After a while his friends encouraged him to publish a book of his poems. He thought it a good idea. A published author had a definite advantage in job interviews, especially when the applicant was barely twenty years old with the audacity to want his own byline. So Frank arranged for the Evanston firm of William S. Lord to print copies of a sixty-page book of his poems, which he titled *In Cupid's Court*. He didn't expect it to sell many copies, and it didn't. It was lighthearted and unremarkable, a collection devoted largely to poems about women and his mostly unrequited love for them. Titles included "On Julia's Birthday," "To His Edythe: Asking that She Skippe with Him," "On Returning Gwendolyn's Gloves." Many of the verses were tortuously written in old English, ("Goe! Litel rime!") but he took special care to include two straightforward poems dedicated to the men who had helped him. One was called "The Line-o-Type Man," and the other concluded:

Go all: from Deuce Sport to Main Squeeze—
Wife, Husband, Bachelor and Maid—
Stand in the salty, slangy breeze
And read the Fables of George Ade.

He carefully wrapped and sent two copies of the thin little volume to the Library of Congress in September 1902, hoping his next book would be published with somebody else's money.

Early in 1903 he started work at the *Chicago Journal*, former home of both B.L.T. and Mr. Dooley. George Booth of Detroit had purchased the paper in 1897, putting Willis H. Turner in charge of turning it into a scrappy, popular journal along the lines of William Randolph Hearst's *New York Journal* and Joseph Pulitzer's *New York World*. On the strength of the material he submitted to B.L.T., managing editor William McKay assigned him a daily weather column, which he wrote in a breezy, conversational style. The men on the entertainment desk rapidly discovered that he was a young man with considerable knowledge of the theater and an amazing capacity for aisle sitting. (They called it a "lead butt.") Frank volunteered several items for the "Around the Theaters" section and often condensed publicity handouts from theater press agents when space was short. He was eager to learn and scurried everywhere, even to the typesetting room, where he watched as men with special cuff-guards set up the copy for each day's paper. Sometimes he served as surrogate for critic Barret Eastman when more than one show opened the same night.

To his everlasting satisfaction, he never had to pay for another theater ticket.

Finally when his salary was raised to $25 a week, he was given his own column, "A Little about Everything." Preceding writers of the column included Willis Turner, B.L.T., and Mr. Dooley himself. Frank's diligence and his careful plans were paying off. But while he persisted with the proven format used by B.L.T. (who now wrote for the *Chicago Tribune*) and obviously imitated the way Taylor's column was laid out, his work displayed a refreshing intellectual wit and bite that clearly separated it from the other, homier rendition.

His sights had a new, special reason to be clearly focused on New York. And his apprenticeship had a little less than a year to run.

VII

Turn-of-the-century Chicago was the mother lode for American newspapermen. Its two dozen dailies carried stories written in a style at once maudlin, judgmental, heavy-footed, long-winded, and fascinating. Contents reflected the public taste, which ran to scandal and the dreadful outcome of pandering to human nature. This was the innocent age of melodrama, when good and evil were easily identified and there was never any question which side you should join. Daily papers, with their often smeared illustrations and gossipy, preachy "news," were ideal messengers to deliver information about the latest in human error. Since papers cost a penny or two a copy, most households bought at least one morning and one evening paper, often more.

Lincoln Steffens said that Chicago newspapers were "the best in any of our large cities." Focus on the wrenching contrasts between the lives of its snooty new millionaires (two hundred of them in 1893) and the miserable poverty of many of its people produced rich material and a dramatic tension that energized the writing. And with the development of this new urban journalism came its grand and unwieldy offspring, the new realistic literature.

According to long-time Chicago newsman Sherman Reilly Duffy (immortalized by Ben Hecht and Charles MacArthur in *The Front Page*), a reporter was regarded by polite society "a little below a butler and a little above a whore." The columnists were something quite different from the reporters, however. Every paper boasted several columns although only the most popular writers were identified with a by-line.

A senior columnist had been Eugene Field, whose column "Sharps and Flats" (named for a play of the time) ran in the *Chicago Daily News* until his death in 1896. Besides his columns and verses, Field wrote bawdy poetry for his buddies at the Chicago Club, corresponded in Latin with his father (a famous lawyer who'd defended Dred Scott), and in the *Tribune Primer* parodied the sugary lessons in McGuffey's *Reader*. The pieces were lunatic and hilarious. An example, titled "The Bad Mamma":

> Why is this little Girl crying? Because her Mamma will not let her put Molasses and Feathers on the Baby's face. What a bad Mamma! The little Girl who never had any Mamma must enjoy herself. Papas are Nicer than Mammas. No little Girl ever Marries a Mamma, and perhaps that is Why Mammas are Bad to little Girls. Never mind; when Mamma goes out of the room, Slap the horrid Baby and if it Cries, you can tell your Mamma it Has the Colic.

In a letter written to a friend before his death, Field asked, "Why cannot we do something toward making American literature better? I don't believe it would do any good to assail our contemporaries; the trouble would seem to be with the readers who tolerate the slop that is emptied out. . . .''

And, in a revealing aside, he voiced the midwestern insecurity that would later take Frank Adams to New York: ''But I am anxious that, if my work deserves recognition, such recognition should come from the east. . . .''

There was more than critical recognition that pulled Frank toward New York City. For nearly two years he'd been in love with a young woman who awaited him there. Part of the urgency of his ambition had to do with the plans he'd made to marry Minna Schwartze.

He'd met her in Chicago. She was a generously endowed showgirl, originally from a small town outside Cheyenne, Wyoming, and a member of the famed *Florodora* sextet when its touring company played Chicago in the spring and summer of 1902. The show wowed Chicago. And Frank.

Florodora was a precedent-setting musical comedy, the first block-buster Broadway musical. It had originally played in London, to mild success, but the American version, with its fast pace, lush costumes, fancy lighting, and flirtatious chorus girls was distinctly and refreshingly American. The show sailed into Chicago from an extraordinary run of 533 performances in New York.

The biggest hit in the show was the sextet. This famed group ended up numbering seventy or so young women who replaced the original six and then each other by the time the show and all its road companies closed. They mesmerized Broadway and permanently established the showgirl stage-door Johnny tradition. Their unforgettable number was ''Tell Me, Pretty Maiden,'' and they sang it with six young men while strolling along the stage apron, twirling their black lace parasols and flirting with the audience. They didn't even pretend to be part of the story but glanced from the corners of their eyes to the lucky gents in the first rows, smiled and winked invitingly over their shoulders as they sauntered off arm in arm with the chorus boys. The patrons in the two-dollar seats whooped and cheered.

A week before its Chicago opening, a piece about *Florodora* ran in the *Chicago Journal*'s ''Around the Theaters'' section, pitched to stir preopening excitement at the box office. Those were the days when newspapers unblushedly served as publicity agents. The piece described the musical's ''double sextet'' as having been ''imitated from one end of the country to the other.'' Further, the writer revealed that ''the six pretty maidens have received an immense amount of publicity. Everyone seems to have overlooked the six young men, otherwise known as the 'gentle strangers.' The girls have been given various tips that have won them fortune on the stock market and others have found wealthy husbands and retired from stage life.'' Not so the chorus boys, "for not one of them has succeeded in winning the affections of an heiress.''

When the show opened in Chicago, the *Journal* critic, Barret Eastman, could hardly contain himself. He raved, and, as far as Frank was concerned, he saved the best for last:

> . . . In the London company all the chorus girls were women of unusual height, and consequently, of unusual clumsiness and awkwardness. In repose, they were stunning. In action they were grotesque. The [American] species of chorus girl is quite another type. She is as stunning in repose as her British cousins, though not as overwhelming in extent, and in action she is light, graceful, and altogether fascinating.

The review in the *Chicago Tribune*, while not as exuberant, gave the show another fine review. After a column of encomiums about the splendid songs, the distinguished stars, and their beautiful costumes, Frank read that

> . . . In certain instances it would seem that fairness of face and form rather than vocal ability had been the standard applied. The six young women in the Sextet are a feast for the eye but less satisfying to the ear; in fact, it is the singing of their six male associates that alone saves the celebrated selection from vocal disaster.

Frank's unrelenting pursuit of his career ambitions was duplicated by a similiarly purposeful courtship technique. Despite an unprepossessing physique, a large nose, receding chin, and hopelessly bad posture, the grown-up Frank was popular with women. He had a deep voice and a way of saying ordinary things in unusual ways. Although he wasn't yet twenty-one when he spotted Minna, he pursued her with single-minded determination. She was several years older than he, but it was precisely this voluptuous womanliness that aroused him. His courtship was persistent, flower-laden, and romantic. He brought her poems he'd written for her and read them aloud in a passionate baritone.

She considered the situation. The *Chicago Tribune* review had implied, probably correctly, that she wouldn't get farther than she already had. As an aging chorus girl without much of a voice, she looked forward to a dwindling career even if she managed to keep her figure for a few more years. If a woman hadn't made a name for herself on Broadway by the time she was twenty-eight, she knew she'd better get married because the road ahead was rutted and all uphill. Besides, Minna was an intelligent Jewish girl whose parents had died years before; she needed the security of marriage. There were no respectable alternatives for a woman in her position. Without any millionaires around, as she'd hoped, Frank's future seemed promising, at least according to him. He was obviously talented and brimmed with persuasive plans. She was pleased and flattered by his attention. With him buzzing around her all summer, it was impossible to resist.

Florodora closed in Chicago on Saturday, July 19. The set was struck and loaded into boxcars in the middle of the night, and the exhausted cast boarded the railroad coaches early the next morning. After a journey of a day and a half, they reopened hundreds of miles away at the Manhattan Beach summer theater in Brooklyn. Before she left, Minna promised to marry Frank.

Next he had to figure a way to get himself to New York. It took longer than he planned. Confident letters went regularly to Minna with frequent plaintive responses. The months passed. After a year or so, his editor unwillingly assured him his reputation as a columnist was solid enough to win a like place in New York. McKay was loath to lose him and offered to raise his salary to $30 a week. But Frank was desperate to leave Chicago for the place O. Henry called "Bagdad on the Hudson." His departure came about ultimately because he persuaded his thrifty sixteen-year-old sister Evelyn to loan him $100. A large part of his lifelong affection for her rested on his memory that she was the one who enabled him to go to New York to become F.P.A.

CHAPTER TWO

New York, 1904–1917

. . . But there was only one place where one might live in a keen and vigorous way, and that was New York. It was the city, the only cosmopolitan city, a wonder-world in itself. It was great, wonderful, marvelous, the size, the color, the tang, the beauty.
—PAUL DRESSER TO HIS BROTHER THEODORE DREISER, 1898

The name of the American dream was New York.
—ALFRED KAZIN, 1984

I Frank Adams, twenty-two years old and ready to take on New York City in the fall of 1904, had been rigorously if conventionally educated, was clever, sure of himself, romantic, and determinedly ambitious. His friends were older than he, and for the moment he was content to seek advice and guidance from them; the woman he had chosen—Minna Schwartze—was older, too, and experienced. He was proud of her statuesque good looks and unselfconscious about the difference in their ages. In fact, he considered it a feather in his cap. She had had her pick, after all, and it was his arm she'd taken. Although he was the kid among their friends, he was precocious and determined to learn, which he did, as fast as he could. Also, wit was a great equalizer, and his sense of humor sparkled with the confidence and dash of an older man. He moved quickly to the center of any group, effortlessly popular with people he respected.

Frank used every facet of his charm as he acted out his carefully constructed plan. Nirvana beckoned, attainable if he took advantage of his opportunities. If they didn't come along unbidden, you were supposed to make them. Frank understood this and relished the chance. And his friendships were genuine, many of them lifelong.

He'd become known in Chicago not only by succeeding with his own column but by seeking—and securing—favor with the journalistic powers of that city. He'd courted all the important columnists (even John McCutcheon, who wasn't a writer at all, but a cartoonist who became famous drawing for the *Chicago Tribune* and illustrating books by George Ade). Frank visited them, sent them deferential notes, asked them to autograph their books or brought them copies of books he thought they'd like. He asked them what they thought of what he wrote and listened carefully to their responses. His was an ubiquitous but never obnoxious charm. He was invariably modest, intelligent, graceful. By acting as though he were part of this world he coveted, he became part of it. By pursuing connections within it, by assuming the manner and interests of the men he admired, his funny poems (carefully hand-written in green ink) appeared regularly in the columns that printed contributions. Later, when his daily offering in the *Chicago Journal* replaced B.L.T.'s, and indeed was its replica, the blatancy of the im-itation didn't bother the older man. He and Frank maintained a warm friendship until Taylor died in 1921. In 1914 B.L.T. called Adams "the most generous man I've ever known," surely a remarkable com-pliment from a person whose own extraordinary generosity had handed Frank his future.

In the summer of 1904, his editor wrote to Theophilus E. Niles, managing editor of the *New York Evening Mail*. Frank told McKay there was nothing he'd rather do than become famous in his hometown, but despite his best efforts, he kept hearing love and destiny calling from New York. Kindly, and with regret since the initials "F.P.A." had become a favorite with *Chicago Journal* readers, McKay sent a warm letter to Niles. In a few days the reply came. Steady work as a col-umnist—with a by-line—awaited Frank at the *New York Evening Mail*. It was an astonishing stroke, even given Frank's thorough orchestration. If he came to believe inordinately, even arrogantly, in his powers to manipulate fate, who could blame him? He was barely twenty-two, and life looked like something he could get his hands around and shape to his pleasure.

And how could he have claimed his ladylove with anything less than a job and a promising future?

At every step of his career, Frank was helped by others; to his credit, his was a memory for kindnesses received as well as for the details of history. He devoted much of his career to giving back the important assistance he'd received by helping other newcomers. He always remembered his friends, especially when they were down on their luck. And for forty years aspiring writers never had a warmer or more interested welcome than at Frank's overflowing desk.

II   Frank swept into New York City in October 1904. He rented a furnished room in a house on West Nineteenth Street, opposite a department store, ignorant of the pandemonium erupting there early every morning. The tumult made him even more determined to make good. A better address would mean a full night's sleep.

The *New York Evening Mail* and *Express* building was located in lower Manhattan on Broadway, a door down from the corner of Fulton Street. From the editorial office's tenth-floor windows, Frank could see north across the roof of St. Paul's chapel to the fork in Broadway, with Park Row jutting to the east. Park Row was famous for its array of newspaper buildings, standing shoulder to shoulder, facing City Hall Park. Once all of the city's major English language newspapers had been produced along this half-mile: the *New York Tribune*, the *New York Herald*, the *New York World*, the *New York News*, the *New York Evening Telegram*, the *New York Morning Journal*, the *New York Sun*, and the *New York Times*. A hundred yards south across Fulton Street from the *New York Evening Mail* was the *New York Evening Post*. Still facing the park in 1904 were Joseph Pulitzer's *New York World*, Charles Dana's *New York Sun*, and Whitelaw Reid's (once Horace Greeley's) *New York Tribune*. In 1894 James Gordon ("I Make News") Bennett's *New York Herald* had moved up Broadway to the block between Thirty-fifth and Thirty-sixth streets, to a new "magnificent Italian Renaissance building, richly adorned with marble, with arcades of polished granite columns . . . abounding in reminiscences of the palaces of Venice, Verona and Padua," designed (of course) by McKim, Mead and White. A dozen years later the *New York Times* moved uptown too, to its elegant tower building on Forty-second Street at the convergence of Broadway and Seventh Avenue. The site had once been called Longacre Square, then, inevitably and ever afterward, Times Square. (Times Square and Herald Square were known for the newspapers that had named them, even after the *Herald* vanished from the scene and the *Times* moved again in the 1960s and a chemical company took over what had been the Times Tower.)

The *New York Evening Mail* and the *New York Express* merged in

1882 when the *Evening Mail*'s owner, Cyrus W. Field, bought the *Express*. When he died six years later, Colonel Elliott F. Shepard, lawyer son-in-law of William H. Vanderbilt, took charge. His was an optimistic takeover despite the paper's circulation problems and a generally lackluster editorial policy. The *New York Evening Mail* had been lurching along, losing readers every year. Shepard reversed the slide by enthusiastically embracing many of the New Journalism techniques. "Yellow" journalism was a catchword personifying the no-holds-barred battle for the city's newspaper readers, waged by Joseph Pulitzer's *New York World* and its major competitors, the *New York Journal* of William Randolph Hearst and Charles A. Dana's *New York Sun*. The Yellow Kid was a cartoon character appearing every week in the Sunday *New York World*. In his ankle-length yellow dress, with his toothless grin and "What, me worry?" expression, the Kid predated *Mad* magazine's Alfred E. Neuman by sixty years and gave his name to twentieth-century popular journalism.

What characterized this style (and the *Evening Mail*'s circulation soared as a result of Shepard's adopting some of its features) were huge scary headlines and many photographs, often touched up or entirely faked by superimposing one upon another. Ersatz scientific articles described the stunning discovery of a living fossil (and interviews with the pith-helmeted discoverer) or the life story of "a medical miracle" like a recovered leper. Preoccupation with maudlin or perverted human behavior was integral to the yellow technique, as were exposes, contests, and frenzied crusades like collecting pennies from schoolchildren for some good cause. The *New York World* gathered $100,000 in this way to pay for the erection of a pedestal for the Statue of Liberty. Ostentatious displays of concern for victims and helpless types like wives of philandering or drunken husbands were continuously enlivening the front pages. Because of a new ability to reproduce color, the *New York World*, the *New York Sun*, and the *New York Journal* all had Sunday supplements featuring cartoons that evolved in a few years into comic strips. And with the advent of the yellow press came the birth of the sports section—and the sportswriter, with his slangy, man-to-man style—which legitimized leisure pursuits and did much to influence modern writing.

With it all came the perpetual competition for readers. Papers lowered their prices to entice customers. When the *New York World*'s circulation reached 100,000 in 1884, two years after Joseph Pulitzer purchased the paper with money borrowed from Jay Gould, he announced the feat by firing a hundred guns in City Hall Park. When the *New York Journal* lowered its price to 3 cents, the *Herald* went to 2 cents and bought a full-page ad in the *New York World* for six consecutive days:

The *Herald* at Two Cents
Cheapest Paper
In America

Then the *New York World* lowered its price to a penny.

Ultimately the *New York World* won the battle for circulation and became the most profitable paper ever published.

When Frank Adams arrived at the twelve-story *Evening Mail* building, he went to work for a crisp Republican paper with an upstanding and (mostly) dignified editorial outlook. Its feature pages catered strongly to women's interests since females were known to be free in the afternoons to cut out recipes and study fashion drawings, if they weren't lallygagging by visiting each other or shopping. For their husbands, men who were actively concerned with important matters of politics and commerce, the political cartoons of Homer Davenport appeared on the first page of every edition. Davenport's well-known drawings of Uncle Sam set against various drooling or otherwise unsavory figures (labeled "The Trusts," "The House of Morgan," or "Crocker" of Tammany Hall) invariably lambasted the Democrats, especially whichever of them was foolishly running for president.

Frank was fortunate to have a by-line awaiting him. As in Chicago, reporters rarely were well known or respected enough to sign their stories. Theirs wasn't an admired profession. Charles W. Eliot, president of Harvard (or some graybeard like him), is supposed to have described reporters as "drunkards, deadbeats and bummers."

Newspaper editors took advantage of young people who dreamed of writing by hiring them as "spacemen" and paying them a few cents for each published inch of their work. The neophytes spent their days and nights tramping around the city on story assignments. If it turned out there was substance in what they discovered, the information was taken from them by a rewrite man who wrote the story for inclusion in the paper, received an admirable salary, and rarely left his comfortable desk except to dine at Rector's, Sherry's, or Delmonico's. (H. L. Mencken called rewriters "literary castrati.") The hapless spaceman was paid for only those published stories actually written by him. Since he was forced to relinquish the interesting news, not much of what he was able to keep for himself was published. It often happened that a young man spent an entire week chasing a story, buttonholing witnesses and following up leads, to end up by getting paid four or five dollars. Journalism wasn't a career for heads of families. Because the rewrite men were sacrosanct on big papers, there was little chance of replacing them.

One of the reasons a newspaper's style was readily identifiable was that most of the news was written by the same one or two people. While this method of operating was undeniably unfair to up-and-coming journalists, it cut costs and helped boost profits. But the way for newcomers was exceptionally difficult, especially in New York.

The movement of opinion from the front pages was gradual. Much of what made the dailies snappy was the intrusion of colorful opinion in the news columns. It wasn't unusual to read on the front page about the hysterical assassin whose lips quivered from guilt and terror, only to discover, often much later, that the unhappy person so described had never been arraigned, much less found guilty. In the press, innocence was never presumed. Terror and shame made a better story, especially when the offender groveled and carried on.

Once an effort was made to make news objective, room for opinion, reflection, and frivolity became available inside the paper, where book and drama reviews had always resided. Of course, it was customary for newspapers to reserve a place for editors to publicize their opinions—on the editorial page—but they rarely signed their names unless they owned the paper. Feature writers and drama and music critics often wrote under by-lines. They claimed special, unvarying page locations and demanded serious attention. They were personages. But until Frank's arrival there wasn't any such thing as a daily literary column.

The halcyon days of the newspaper columnist hadn't begun in New York at the turn of the century. Famous names like Don Marquis, Heywood Broun, Grantland Rice, and Walter Winchell still hovered unknown and uncelebrated on the horizon. When Frank arrived in town, his became the groundbreaker, the column that defined and legitimized the technique. He was the right man in the right place.

For a couple of months after his first column on October 21, 1904, he carefully followed the format established by Bert Taylor in Chicago. He included a few gentle puns ("Cotton is the root of boll weevil"), pseudoserious remarks ("If you don't register, you lose the moral right to talk politics"), and comments on the weather. He dropped some names, fancifully assuming the insider's connection with wealth and power: "Reg Vanderbilt has moved to Portsmouth, R.I. What is New York's loss is Portsmouth's gain." But he talked about nobodies, too. "Charley Fairbanks was a pleasant caller here Thursday. Come again,

Charley.'' It was an inventive trick. He set a democratic, unintimidated tone by giving equal space to the famous and to the unknown. His readers could identify with both varieties of person. It was a chatty, easygoing, thoroughly charming column, and within a week it gained the important right-hand space on page 6, the editorial page. It stayed there until Frank left the paper.

The first day it appeared, the column was unimaginatively headed ''Local News.'' That name was quickly replaced by the shamelessly plagiarized ''A Line or Two in Jest'' (B.L.T.'s column was ''A Line-o-Type or Two''), which in turn became ''A Manhattan Bargain Counter.'' Finally Frank's editor christened the column ''Always in Good Humor,'' and the name stuck.

Young and unpracticed as he was, Frank already had an audacious vision for his column. He planned to shape it with the participation of his readers, somehow to make it into dialogue. He sensed there would be interest in such an approach if readers helped him write the column. Also, and important, conversation was his strong suit. B.L.T. used contributions from readers, and Frank liked the idea, as far as it went, although he was determined to stamp his own personality on the technique in a way that B.L.T.—who served more as editor and observer than participant—didn't. Frank remembered how he had delighted in reading the daily papers in Chicago, how he and his mother had laughed with Mr. Dooley, feeling as if his words were meant to tickle *them*. That was the peculiar intimacy afforded by a daily newspaper column. If the reader could respond, then the column could be like a real conversation. It was an unusual concept, but he wasn't able to fashion it overnight. There was a good deal of bumbling to get through first.

III Designing the column wasn't the main focus of Frank's thoughts those early weeks in New York, important as it was. He and Minna were scurrying to get married. First they had to find a place to live. Fortunately the Indian summer weather held, and the couple explored potential neighborhoods in the pleasant afternoons after the paper had gone to press.

In Manhattan huge apartment buildings were a new phenomenon. Most young couples lived in rooms or apartments in the three- or four-story attached brownstone houses that filled the city.

Minna and Frank admired the apartment building called the Dakota without dreaming of moving in. It was an elegant structure of ecru brick, mammoth, with gables and spiked turrets, polished mahogany stairways, brass elevators, and eighteen-foot ceilings, only twenty years old when they started looking for a place of their own. Of course, the rent was out of their range, intended as it was for wealthy families. It stood majestic and singular, with vistas of undeveloped land sweeping into the distance from its location on the northwest corner of Seventy-second Street and Central Park. The wealthy people who lived there in its twelve- and fifteen-room apartments kept their private carriages and horses in a special livery stable just up the street. A quarter of a mile west from the Dakota, another magnificent apartment building, the Ansonia, had recently been completed and looked like a giant wedding cake on upper Broadway, with its granite frosting of ormolus and swirls, round towers, gargoyles, cupolas, and porthole-looking upper windows. Opera singers lived there—Caruso kept an apartment for the winter seasons—and outrageous rents ranged from $125 a month for a five-room apartment with one bathroom and a servant's toilet, to $625 for sixteen rooms, four bathrooms, and two servants' lavatories. While Minna and Frank strolled past extravagant buildings like these and dreamed of the day when they'd be able to afford to live in them, they looked with more seriousness at furnished rooms in houses closer to Broadway and Forty-second Street, then the northern boundary of the theater district. Frank was determined to live uptown, on a shady sub-urban street away from the predawn clatter and confusion at Siegel Cooper's department store.

Finally they selected a flat in a brownstone at 247 West Fiftieth Street, a couple of blocks from the Hudson River. It was a quiet street where children rode tricycles and rolled hoops on the sidewalks, watched by mothers and nannies who pushed babies like royal personages in tall prams. The setting seemed to Frank to provide both stability and se-renity, resembling as it did his boyhood neighborhood on Chicago's Twenty-sixth Street. He could picture his children playing here. He and Minna paid a month's advance rent and moved in their belongings.

Frank used some of his new pull and arranged to have Mayor George B. McClellan perform the marriage on the morning of November 15, a Tuesday. Like his father, Frank picked his own birthday to get married on. He was twenty-three. Moses had been a worldly and traveled thirty. Frank felt at least as mature.

After the ceremony the bride and groom walked arm in arm down the wide steps from City Hall to the park. Minna took a tablecloth from the hamper she'd brought, and they spread it festively on the grass. The temperature was forty-five degrees, with a skittish wind that caught at the corners of their tablecloth. But the sky was clear, and they wanted to have a picnic. Besides, Frank hadn't dared ask for time off, even to get married. He thought it might remind his editor how young he was. So he and Minna were content to huddle together on the grass with their coats on and feed each other lunch. Between giggles and murmurs, they admired the recently built federal post office across the lawn and looked at the expensive new *New York World* Building, with its imposing parapet and swollen turret that resembled a golden crown. After a while Frank got up, brushed the crumbs from his trousers, kissed his wife, and went back to the office. Carefully Minna folded the tablecloth and wrapped the leftovers in a napkin, then boarded the cable car at the corner for the ride back to Fiftieth Street.

He didn't mention the momentous ceremony in his column that evening. But the poem he printed, his own "To Phyllis," was flagrantly romantic. Minna knew he'd written it for her. Significantly, he placed the verse at the top of the column, in the place of honor, even above the announcement of the winners of the limerick contest.

> *So when the lyre strings I smite,*
> *I feel thine eyes to grow more bright.*
> > *Glow with a mist-pervading ray.*
> > *That lights the traveler on his way.*
> *Sweetheart, for others I must write:*
> > *I SING FOR THEE!*

IV The life of the young Adams couple sparked and bustled. Often they went to the theater. Frequently Frank received free tickets from producers who wanted him to mention their plays in the column. Since orchestra and box seats cost $1.50 or $2.00, free tickets were a bonus to the penny-pinching journalist and his bride. Even at this early time, he wrote about what he did in the evenings, where he ate, what he saw, whom he'd been with. Acquaintances learned to look in the paper after a visit with him.

The Broadway scene was spectacular. In 1904 there were nearly fifty theaters in the district, as well as half a dozen vaudeville houses and several Yiddish playhouses. During the season three or four shows opened every night, sometimes more. Hits could cost as little as $3,000

(*Florodora* had cost an astonishing $8,000). It was the heyday for theatrical entrepreneurs and eager actors and actresses who swept up and down the avenue, hailing one another and behaving with grandiose, often eccentric manners.

The respectable Charles Frohman ran the Empire Theater, at Broadway and Fourteenth Street—the "star factory." He produced plays from England mostly by Shakespeare and by the new playwright George Bernard Shaw—except when the prolific American dandy William Clyde Fitch offered him one of his. Frohman wielded a paternalistic stewardship, and his stars usually went along with whatever he required of them, even including accepting the imposition of his moralistic philosophy on their romantic entanglements. Actors yearned to see their names in lights on the Empire Theater marquee. They were discreet if they went against his wishes. He put great store in the way his actors behaved and didn't hesitate dictating to them. He knew best. "Never engage a star besmirched by scandal," he cautioned and couldn't forgive his darling Billie Burke when she ran off with the arrogant and ill-bred Florenz Ziegfeld.

Rector's, the elegant "lobster palace" decorated entirely in a lush green-and-gold approximation of the Louis XIV fashion, sported the city's first revolving door, braved initially by Gentleman Jim Corbett and followed by the rest of Broadway. There David Belasco, forty-six, dined at an honored table downstairs. He was unmistakable in his peculiar outfit: the black suit and stiff collar of a Catholic priest. His reputation as a man of the world and a womanizer was widely known, as was Frohman's personal conservatism. Broadway assumed that Belasco's latest lovely female star was his sexual companion as well.

Joe Weber and Lew Fields, the irrepressible, disheveled and entirely lovable team of comics known as "Mick" and "Myer" to their fans, formed a vaudeville stock company in a theater that became Weberfield's Music Hall, at the corner of Broadway and Twenty-ninth Street. There somebody caught a custard pie in the face for the first time, producing a huge laugh as it always would. Star variety performers were paid lavishly to entertain, treated with generosity and respect by these two gifted American gentlemen. In return, the headliners gave all they had. Every dog act, every wobbly tenor and ingenue, every baggy-pants comic and top (or bottom) banana wanted to play the Music Hall. It was tops during its lifetime and became a glorious Broadway legend.

One afternoon Lew spotted Lillian Russell (the "Golden Beauty") at the track picking horses by shutting her eyes and piercing the program with her hat pin. "Why not use a fork," suggested Lew, "and get the one, two and three?'' When she played the Music Hall, Joe and Lew paid her $1250 a week for 35 weeks and bought all her costumes. This kind of generosity was unheard of in those pre-Equity days when actors furnished and maintained their own props and costumes, never received pay for rehearsals and could be fired any time, anywhere, sometimes on the road without warning, recourse, or return fare.

Frank (and indeed all of Broadway) was heartbroken when Weber and Fields broke up. In the column Frank encouraged mending of their rift, but nobody could persuade them to reconcile. Joe and Lew went off separately, and the Weberfield's Music Hall closed its doors forever.

New York's first subway, the West Side IRT, opened a few days before Frank and Minna were married. (It had a convenient station located a block from the Adamses' new home on West Fiftieth Street.) Builders boasted that the train would whisk passengers from City Hall to 145th Street—a distance of about thirteen miles—in less than half an hour. Everybody was excited. While modern electric trains ran regularly on lines elevated above Sixth, Third, Ninth, and Second avenues, these trains were affected by vagaries like the weather. They were loud and unsightly. Grit and soot wafted through the New York air, causing pedestrians to choke and rub their eyes and curse the els. People who lived along the routes of the els in second- and third-floor rooms girded themselves not only for horrific noise but for the scrutiny of passengers riding past their windows, who were sometimes stuck there at eye level for minutes at a time. Underground rapid transit seemed the obvious answer, and as soon as the technology existed to burrow through the granite on which the city stood, subway plans were made. The city fathers resented that Boston had beaten them to it, so nothing would do but that their subway be the longest and most remarkable in the world.

August Belmont's Interborough Rapid Transit Company opened the city's subway system on October 27, 1904. Steel-framed wooden cars were painted flaming red. The celebration greeting the achievement was gargantuan, immodest, innocently self-congratulatory, and chauvinistic, granddaddy to the Charles Lindbergh welcome and the ticker-tape parades for World Series victories and for astronauts. Tugs, fireboats, and ocean liners clogged the harbor, spewing water and blaring their foghorns. Church bells and clarions chimed and tinkled and clanged, New Yorkers from the Battery to Harlem shouted their approval. Bigwigs donned striped trousers and top hats for the first subway ride, Frank Adams among them. After an interminable ceremony of logrolling speeches at the City Hall station, concluding with a solemn benediction from an archbishop, Belmont presented Mayor McClellan a mahogany case that held a solid silver controller. He thought the mayor would pose for photographs and then hand the cumbersome object over to a bona fide motorman, who'd take the eight-car train on its way. Belmont didn't expect McClellan to take him seriously.

The pink-cheeked mayor took the train smartly from the station, laid on the juice, and ran it straight through to 103rd Street. Belmont's general manager stood apprehensively behind him, poised to push the mayor aside if he lost control. Frowning with concentration, the inexperienced but determined general's son took the sharp curves at what seemed like breakneck speed (the train was designed to race along at 30 mph before blood started spurting from people's ears). In fact, many of the men who'd been honored with standing room in the first car had some white-knuckled moments as the mayor acted out their fantasies. They were greatly relieved when at last he relinquished control and was seen moving among them, grinning and slapping people on the back.

The next day Frank's column was full of comments about the new transit system. In a regular feature called "Snide Lights on Literature," in which his jokes had classical or intellectual references, he inserted a topical anecdote:

> Jean Valjean was groping about in the sewers.
> "Well," he said, "I'll wait till the subway's
> completed and eliminate eighteen chapters."
> Which is but one of the subway's advantages.

Further along he commented that "subway scenery, however, is not the kind that will warrant the addition of observation cars."

He noticed right away that the air in the tunnels was foul-smelling, so he immediately launched a campaign to improve subway ventilation. It was, of course, a lost battle, but he devoted many columns to its waging. Regularly he issued a subway air report, predating by seventy-five years the weather bureau's solemn rating of aboveground air. The major difference was that his was supposed to be funny:

> Brooklyn Bridge: GOOD
> Fourteenth Street: FAIR
> 145th Street: BAD
> BOIL THE AIR!

His efforts on behalf of the lungs of the subway riders continued for several years, unrewarded and unsuccessful but appreciated nonetheless by his fans. Other crusades of lesser social value but which he waged relentlessly in the face of public servant indifference had to do with demands for crisp bacon, the display of house numbers on lamp-posts (instead of hidden behind growths of ivy or worn away entirely), and street cleaning with dry brooms (wet ones merely redistributed dirt).

He complained indignantly when inconvenienced, on his own and his readers' behalf:

> Since the letter-carriers have been given Sundays off, the openings of the branch offices Sunday mornings is a farce. At one branch office last Sunday 28 people in succession were told that there was no mail for them—not true in one case. Why not inform the public, Mr. Postmaster General, that it is useless to call for mail on Sundays, or close the p.o. altogether?

At twenty-three he was already a curmudgeon.

V   Frank and his colleagues spent time every morning reading and clipping newspapers from all over the country. Scores of papers arrived at the *New York Evening Mail* offices with each postal delivery. Many small-town and rural publications covering huge geographic areas arrived weekly or twice a month. The exchange editor's task of reading them and finding out what people were saying in other places wasn't as monumental as it might seem since in those days papers rarely numbered more than six or eight pages. There were no elaborate classified advertisements or international news sections then, and most papers, except for the models in New York, Chicago, and St. Louis, rarely ran illustrations. Frank could easily page through a few of the important ones as soon as he arrived at his office. And the exchange editor could bring others to his attention.

It was important for Frank to keep up to the minute. In the column he liked to include gibes at other papers, point out foibles in grammar, spelling mistakes, convoluted diction, or silly headlines. He thought such carelessness was laughable and viewed his role as a teacher who gently (or not so gently) poked fun when syntax went awry. Apparently his readers, who'd been educated in the same meticulous way, approved.

> "Addick clings to hope," says a contemporary. This doubtless got past the proofreader. It should have read "dope."

Or, in a format to be duplicated years later in *The New Yorker*'s newsbreak columns:

TWO HEARTS THAT PARSE AS ONE
William Sprouse and Nancy Roberts was seen going west Sunday evening.

—Braymore (Mo.) Bee

As the months passed, the top of Frank's rolltop desk became cluttered with clippings and newspapers, notebooks, and bits of paper, half-finished verses and cascades of mail from readers. As he worked, he smoked big black cigars and ashes fell everywhere, including all over his clothes, speckling them with little brown holes. His was an untidy mien, although he was unexpectedly fastidious, as when he compulsively scrutinized the column over the linotyper's shoulder to catch last-minute mistakes, or displayed an intense concern with its cosmetics, how it looked with different sized type, boxes, italics, printer's symbols, its paragraphs and verses clustered with an eye to attractive arrangement. He always filled his fountain pen with green ink and wrote his copy painstakingly with a distinctive wedding invitation handwriting.

Years later when he had his own office, he left his mail piled for days outside its closed door, indicating to visitors that he was elsewhere. But when his easily recognizable desk stood against the wall in the corner of the city room, he encouraged visitors, despite the signs tacked to the wall behind it: "Out to Lunch" and "Tell Him No." (The mail-outside-the-door ploy never worked anyhow because later when he didn't welcome drop-ins and kept his door shut, he could be heard bellowing on the telephone inside, so nobody was fooled.) In 1904 and 1905, he was establishing his readership, so he actively sought mail and visitors. In November he published a gag submitted by somebody called "Veritus":

Dear F.P.A.: I wish to correct the impression you gave your readers that the Hotel Astor's architect was Art Nouveau. I understand it was Al Fresco.

And on Thanksgiving a fan brought him a "delightful mince pie," which he gratefully noted in the column. Clearly he was inviting new friendships and, more important, contributions. He started inserting reader inventions within his own material, slowly at first, Space was too short for articles or essays, but the format was ideal for jokes and humorous verse. In order to attract first-class submissions, he took pains with his own material, displaying an elan and confidence essential to the new genre—sort of a vaudeville patter for newspaper readers. His years of serious study at the Olympic Theater had paid off. Whether his wisecracks were corny, tortured, lunatic, or sharp, he was absolutely unselfconscious in delivering them. This boldness defined and set apart the authentic comedian. He often chose unexpected cultural or intellectual subjects, and as a result he became known for his sophistication. He was a man of the world.

From his lengthy poem "The Life of Verdi," he included the following couplet:

> *Ah, he yearned for fame and glory,*
> *And so he wrote Il Trovatore.*

In the same opus, he carefully summarized the plot of *Aida*:

> Aida was a lady slave
> Fair passing all description.
> To Rhadames her heart she gave—
> He was a young Eygptian.
> But Rhadames was loved in turn
> By Egypt's sovereign's daughter.
> Her heart for him began to burn
> More warmly than it oughter.

The biography of Verdi was greeted enthusiastically so he wrote other stories and verses about operatic composers. He disclosed the little known fact that Georges Bizet weighed 14 pounds at birth "which is the reason for the plural of his name."

F.P.A.'s following grew. And in the summer, editor Niles rewarded the popular new columnist with a week's vacation. Frank was delighted. Most of his colleagues had to toil for more than a year before receiving such recognition. The benefit signaled his value to the paper and his acceptance as a full-fledged member—even leader—of the elite corps of columnists.

Frank and Minna took their long deferred honeymoon during a week of throbbing ninety-five degree New York heat. They journeyed blissfully to a resort hotel in Center Lovell, Maine. Frank went fishing every morning, and Minna spent her days rocking placidly on the big front porch, making friends with the other wives and thinking about what to have for lunch.

Frank took an extra week and telegraphed columns to the *New York Evening Mail*. Life in the wilderness was idyllic and restful, but by the time two weeks had passed, he was impatient to get home. As soon as they returned, he set about getting back into the city swing. This included life as a fan of the Chicago Cubs and, to a lesser extent, the New York National League team, the Giants, housed just north of Harlem at the Polo Grounds. Baseball was a passion with Frank, as it was with many men of his generation. A relatively new sport—at least its organization into two "major" leagues was recent—it offered an exciting opportunity for identification with the strong, talented players. Sophisticated understanding of the complicated rules and vernacular were requirements for fans, who liked as well as anything to second guess the team managers and each other, to follow the new sportswriting in the papers, and to argue about the plays and players in the peculiarly intimate, wearying game. In that age of reverence for rugged male pursuits, baseball engendered team spirit, obsessive competitions, and emotional advocacies. Frank spent many hours with his friends at the ballpark and usually bet on the outcome of the game, often as much as a dollar. (Gambling for him would always be a temptation, with at least once truly sobering results.)

And he was the author, in July 1910, of a poem that gave a phrase to the language:

> *These are the saddest of possible words:*
> *"Tinker to Evers to Chance."*
> *Trio of bear cubs, and fleeter than birds,*
> *Tinker and Evers and Chance.*
> *Ruthlessly pricking our gonfalon bubble,*
> *Making a Giant hit into a double—*
> *Words that are heavy with nothing but trouble:*
> *"Tinker to Evers to Chance."*

The poem was reprinted all over the country and later in dozens of anthologies. Letters about it poured in. To those who were curious about his use of the word "gonfalon," he suggested a visit to the dictionary. (The word was a noun, defined as a kind of streamer-laden banner, but few dared question his use of it as an adjective.) Some of his friends like B.L.T. and Grantland Rice, among others, submitted additional verses, and he printed many of them, but it was F.P.A.'s original that people remembered. "Tinker to Evers to Chance" became as well known to baseball fans as "Casey at the Bat."

His sincere enthusiasm for the sport put him even more solidly at the center of what he admired. With his cigars and his "so's yer old man" baseball talk, he was undisputedly One of the Guys. He sat happily in the catbird seat.

Soon after returning from vacation, Frank began a regular Saturday feature. He called it "The Gotham Gazette." It was a down-home parody of rural newspapers. Editor Niles, obviously delighted with his rising star, centered the copy on the first page of the special Saturday second section. Soon he made room for it at top center on Saturday's editorial page, where it remained for several years.

The Gazette featured short essays written by imagined local celebrities like Euphemia Hemans Simpson (her name was a play on the word "euphemism," a literary device on which her fudgy writing depended), fictional valedictorian of the local high school, who wrote verses about patriotism and the future with solemn fervor. The Gazette also printed social notes from all over and news of the elaborate goings-on in spas like Newport, Rhode Island, where the arrivals and departures of Reggie Vanderbilt and his chums were breathlessly remarked upon. President Teddy Roosevelt's family, and dignitaries like Senator Chauncey Depew and Mayor McClellan were a focus of the "Local News" section. The Gazette slogan was "Genial, Glittering and Gorgeous," and in the fourth week of its existence, Frank proudly displayed in it a letter from William Allen White, the real-life small-town editor from Emporia, Kansas. Tongue in cheek, White predicted that "if hustling will make a good newspaper in Gotham, bro. Adams will make it, [since] Gotham has long been a newspaper graveyard and such brilliant men as C. Dana, J. B. Pulitzer and W. C. Bryant—the well-known poet—have sunk money in the business there without receiving adequate returns." He complimented Frank and wished him well.

Frank had written the older man with characteristic boldness, enclosing copies of several columns and the first couple of Gazettes. He'd asked White to comment. The charming response was unexpected and gracious. Once again Frank had dared to go after what he wanted, and the effort had paid off. He and White remained friends, corresponding and visiting over the years.

Frank was invariably impatient with anyone who was reticent or insecure, preferring instead somebody who recognized what he wanted and went after it, as he did. Tact and good manners weren't high on his checklist. He was direct, honest, said what he meant, and did what he intended to do. He sought this forthrightness in others, including Minna, who "gave as good as she got," according to one of their friends. Certainly his no-nonsense nature was as crucial to his reputation as was his talent.

VI

Large numbers of educated New Yorkers read "Always in Good Humor" and talked about it. They scanned it on their way home from work or sitting in the parlor before dinner. Often they sent in their own ideas—poems, jokes, punch lines, responses to Frank's comments—and waited excitedly to see if F.P.A. would print them. Americans had always cherished the notion of writing letters to the editor, but such letters were hardly exercises in whimsy. Frank challenged his readers to top his gags, to dare to be playful. As a result, there grew an unusual relationship between column "conductor" and reader, a precursor to the intimacy later established between the radio phone-in show host and listener. Like the radio program, the column invited gripes or asides, but it was different because of the iron control Frank maintained as editor. His careful stewardship produced a variety of techniques ranging from subtle to sandbag. Yet within this large category of acceptability, nobody was permitted to say anything that offended Frank's taste. His stamp was unmistakable, even in the material he didn't write.

While his style appeared effortless, he worked hard to maintain the appearance of spontaneity. Under a grumpy headline, "Tonight We Will Stand on the Sixth Avenue El and Pay 5 Cents," Frank addressed "Any lady who gives up her seat, and who says 'You are the mysterious editor of the *Gotham Gazette*,' we will give a sweet smile and the other ticket to the theatre. We will be wearing a red geranium on the left lapel. Is or is not courtesy Dead?"

And like an exasperated teacher he snapped at "F.G.": "No, 'Hampshire' and 'camp fire' do not rhyme. The discussion is closed."

Of course, the readers whose work Frank published formed a proud contingent of special fans. Some of them didn't yet know they were going to be famous. When they submitted material, they hoped desperately for the miracle of recognition. Unlike magazine editors, Frank either accepted or rejected their stuff right away. If he didn't print whatever it was the day he received it, he usually didn't print it at all.

By encouraging and rewarding humor, Frank became well known among a small band of American wits who were making efforts to reintroduce it as a respectable tool for use by thoughtful people. Most popular literary taste in the first years of the century ran to sugary tales celebrating Christian precepts, virginal brides, and patriotic morality. Pussyfooting publishers thought "naturalism" too stark and embarrassing for contemporary audiences. In fact, the publisher of *Sister Carrie* was so ashamed of its vigorous realism that he had the few hundred copies his farsighted editor, Frank Norris, persuaded him to print hidden in a warehouse. *The Little Shepherd of Kingdom Come* and *Rebecca of Sunnybrook Farm* were the fashion. In 1906 *Huckleberry Finn* was forbidden to children at the Brooklyn Public Library.

It wasn't a healthy time for laughter. The prevailing geniality wasn't wit, and it couldn't identify and make fun of pretension. America was undergoing a period of cultural self-righteousness, producing a lot of stuffy writing. Intellectuals took themselves too seriously. Frank's column helped to turn public taste because he and the writers he encouraged weren't so serious; they wrote funny stuff. And many of them went on to become widely read.

One of Frank's most diligent contributors was young Louis Untermeyer, who toiled daytime in his father's jewelry store and wrote poetry at night. In order to disguise his identity (although he admitted his father probably didn't read "Always in Good Humor"), he called himself Daffydowndilly. One of his contributions, titled "Useless Verse," addressed the Mary Sunshine aspect of contemporary taste:

> *Father's down with meningitis,*
> > *Mother has a case of gout—*
> *Brother Charlie's face a sight is,*
> > *He has measles—and no doubt*
> *Cousin Bill is surely dying*
> > *(He has had a fearful fall)—*
> *Ah, but what's the use of crying?*
> > *It's a good world after all!*

> *Critic spare your righteous curses*
> > *For tho' your rebuke is meet,*
> *Our great public likes its verses*
> > *Sugar coated, smooth and sweet.*
> *As for me, I'm not denying*
> > *That such stanzas bore and pall.*
> *Hang it, what's the use of crying,*
> > *It's a good world after all.*

Amazed at his own audacity, Untermeyer, who wanted to become a poet—and the host of a salon—called on Frank one afternoon and invited him and Minna to dinner. Such a brazen invitation was precisely what Frank admired, and he happily accepted. They established a long and easy friendship. Untermeyer and his wife, Jean Starr, a full-time poet, entertained other of Frank's regular contributors, and in fact their home was headquarters for a coterie of them. Lawyer Newman Levy described his first evening at the Untermeyers' when he met Frank and the others as if "a stagestruck youngster had astonishingly found himself in the taproom at the Mermaid tavern." Later, guests at what became regular Sunday evening occasions included a dignified young man named Walter Lippmann; Amy Lowell, who smoked cigars and thunderously quoted her own poetry and that of others; the already famous Vachel Lindsay; unknown but erudite Deems Taylor; others who were aspiring writers, and still others, legendary performers like Laurette Taylor and Minnie Maddern Fiske, to whom Frank dedicated an adoring verse:

> *Staccato,hurried,nervous,brisk,*
> *   Cascading,   intermittent,choppy.*
> *The brittle voice of Mrs. Fiske*
> *   Shall serve me now as copy.*
>
> *Time was, when first that voice I heard,*
> *   Despite my close and tense endeavor,*
> *When many an important word*
> *   Was lost and gone forever*
> *Though unlike others at the play,*
> *I never whispered: "WHA'D'D SHE SAY?"*
>
> *Somewords she runstogetherso;*
> *   Some others are distinctly stated*
> *Somecometoofast and s o m e t o o s l o w*
> *   And some are   syncopated,*
> *And yet no voice—I am sincere—*
> *Exists that I prefer to hear.*

Contributors entertained by the Untermeyers in later years included lyricist Howard Dietz, who signed himself "Freckles" (a vice president of Metro Goldwyn Mayer, and author, with Arthur Schwartz, of many Broadway and Hollywood musicals); Morrie Ryskind, who was to write for the Marx Brothers and twenty years later was coauthor of *Of Thee I Sing*, for which he won the Pulitzer Prize, then moved to Hollywood to become a sword-waving fighter of communists; Ed Anthony, "Edar," a gangling young man whose adult life was spent as the respected publisher of *Collier's* and the *Woman's Home Companion*; Bob Simon, for many years *The New Yorker*'s music writer; "Smeed" (Deems Taylor), who, in the mid-1920s was commissioned by the Metropolitan

Opera to write its first American opera (*The King's Henchman*, with libretto by Edna St. Vincent Millay—"Nancy Boyd" to F.P.A. fans). But in those early years, all of them were still stretching and seeking and concocting their bright verses under F.P.A.'s ever-watchful and not much older eye.

One of the contributors, Adelaide Hahn, busy earning her Ph.D. in classics (she was professor of Latin and Greek at Hunter College for thirty years), telephoned Newman Levy, who signed himself "Flaccus" (Latin poet Horace's last name), and suggested that F.P.A.'s contributors form a club. The idea of establishing a group had been discussed before. Somebody had suggested an annual contributors' dinner, and plans had whizzed along until too many people wanted to come.

Then the question of eligibility arose. What if your only contribution had appeared in 1905? Would that qualify you for membership? Frank was uncertain. And what about those who'd been unsuccessful but still sent stuff in regularly? A disgruntled contributor, one of the first, "Veritus," wrote:

> I hereby resign as a contributor to your column and desire to say in parting that in suppressing my contributions you have gained but a Pyrrhican victory—it will cost your paper dear in lack of circulation. . . . I propose to form a club of Rejected Contributors, and we will have a banquet in the Bronx Park, with overflow into Central park and I invite you not to appear there.

Frank's heading for the paragraph was "I Accept."

In an effort at democracy, he announced that "eligibility is not determined by publication. All contributors, successful and futile, qualify." But a mountain of requests for reservations followed, too many to verify or accommodate. It became a nightmare of record keeping, so the project was tabled.

But later, after Hahn called Levy, they met with Frank and promised to make all the arrangements. A meeting was finally held in a public room of a hotel on Columbus Avenue. Membership was restricted to people whose contributions had been printed. The group named itself the Contribunion, and its first act was to initiate a dinner party to fete itself.

The celebration became a boisterous annual event in the room at the head of the stairs in Sheffel's Hall, a saloon located at the corner of Third Avenue and Seventeenth Street. Frank gave his blessing but never attended. He thought his presence might inhibit his proteges, but he was there in spirit. He was the Boss who wielded unmistakable authority.

He decided to reward the best of the year's contributions. At first he wasn't certain what the prize should be. He thought a gold watch, suitably engraved. Others disagreed. "It's no incentive for me," Edna Ferber wrote him. "I already possess two watches. One is the gun-metal sort that's worn about the wrist, and the other a from-gold one I chuck in my pocketbook. Make it a cash prize. That's something I'm not overburdened with and will enhance any home." And Jeannette, wife of Deems Taylor, recently fired from his newspaper job, thought there wouldn't be room on a watch to engrave, "To Deems Taylor, who used to conduct a column on the *Press*, for the best contribution to Always in Good Humor for 1913." (Frank had already printed a "situation wanted" ad for Taylor set in a box with an "At Liberty" heading, describing a "versatile and sober writer" who was a "swell dresser, with considerable experience." Jeannette wrote Frank that, "I shall probably be able to send you quite a number of contributions now. My husband . . . says he doesn't need his good ideas anymore.")

On December 5 Frank announced that "the year's end is imminent. The prize offer of a gold watch, suitably engraved, stands. Nothing yet has surpassed—or such is our opinion—'The Study Hour'—the joint offering of Flaccus and Baron Ireland. And unless that is beaten, each of these gentlemen is to receive a watch, fitly graven." (Baron Ireland was also known as Nate Salsbury.)

The ceremony awarding the watch became the high point of the annual dinner. Newman Levy remembered many years later that winning the watch rivaled winning the Nobel Prize, then admitted proudly to having received the honor twice. Everybody wanted to win. The festivities invariably buzzed with anticipation, and following the announcement of the award by a representative sent by Frank, cheers, rowdy toasts, and banging of cutlery ensued. Losers determined to do better next year and swallowed their pride in congratulating the delighted winner. It was assumed that maintaining one's poise and behaving graciously was required by the Boss. (Not everyone was able to manage suitable esprit. In 1914 when Levy was returning from Europe on an ocean liner, he sat on a deck chair next to Edna Ferber and introduced himself: "Hello, Miss Ferber. I'm Newman Levy." She had been unable to attend the dinner, so she looked at him coldly. "I don't believe it," she said. "Let me see the watch.")

One year Frank sent Robert Benchley as his emissary. Benchley was fresh from Harvard and unknown to the Contribunion sophisticates. In Boston his reputation as an after-dinner speaker had begun to percolate. At the dinner after the Harvard-Yale game, with big shots from both schools in attendance, he'd posed as interpreter for a "distinguished professor" from China whose speech supposedly outlined the differences between American and Chinese football. Unsurprisingly, the differences were all weighted against Yale. Benchley nodded pleasantly to the Oriental "professor" after he'd finished speaking (he was Benchley's laundryman; his "speech" consisted of him cursing in Chinese while maintaining a dead pan expression). Benchley told the audience that "Professor Soong is amazed at the restraint displayed by the Yale men in their tackling of the Harvard runners. In the game as *he* knows it, the idea is to tackle a runner and get him down that way, but Yale seems to pursue the moderate policy of letting a Harvard man run until he trips himself."

Frank had heard about Benchley from friends in Boston and wanted to present the young man as a surprise gift to his group.

That year, as always, the Contribunion gathering was hilarious, with speakers interrupted rudely by the wits at the crowded tables, who heckled and yelled. Into the scene stepped Benchley, introduced by poet Clement Wood, as "The Bringer of the Watch." He was a tall, inept-looking young man whose abstention from alcohol set him apart from the audience, which quieted: "Give the kid a break." (Few of them were much older than he was.) He cleared his throat several times, then began, "Ladies and gentlemen, we are gathered here for the purpose of presenting a watch. It seems appropriate, therefore, to give a brief history of the watch industry in the United States." He removed a typed manuscript from his pocket. The dog-eared document was about two-hundred pages thick, and with its appearance a damp unhappiness settled into the room. "Who *is* he?" they asked one another. Oblivious to the whispers, Benchley continued with increasing self-assurance and a bore's iron insensitivity. Not until a minute or two had elapsed and he started misquoting poetry and throwing around inappropriate Latin phrases did anybody catch on. "Allowance for my figures must be made *ad valorem* and not *per capita*," he said. As soon as the snickers started, the jig was up. Everybody began to laugh and bang the tables. Somebody threw a half-eaten roll. The entire Contribunion membership had fallen into the trap expertly set by this innocent-appearing young man. By the time Benchley presented the watch to Deems Taylor (for a poem about the sinking of the *Eastland* in Chicago harbor), the announcement was anticlimactic, something that had never happened before and never would again. Benchley's achievement became legendary. (And he became the humorist's humorist: When he praised a James Thurber cartoon appearing many years later in *The New Yorker*, Thurber—not known for his humility nor for giving compliments—remarked truthfully that there was no more valued praise than Benchley's.)

His "History of the Watch Industry" evolved into the "Treasurer's Report," a performance he gave on Broadway, on the radio, and in the movies. It was the sketch that made him famous.

VII Probably no endeavor attracted Frank so much as playwriting. The fascination was unsurprising considering the endless hours he'd spent in darkened theaters as a child. That bespectacled boy, grown-up, was a compulsive theatergoer who attended plays two and three, sometimes four times a week. And when he and his friends weren't talking about baseball or whether the Ivies could throttle the Big Tens, they talked of plays, actors, playwrights, and who was doing what in the theater. Everywhere he looked, people he admired (and some he didn't but envied anyway) were writing plays, acting in them, or making plans centering on them. Inevitably, success in the dramatic arts constituted "making it" for many of the young people who whooped into New York City just in time for the new century.

That such geniuses of prose as Mark Twain and Bret Harte had collaborated for the stage—with gruesome results—didn't serve as a deterrent. The lesson was to tailor the work for the medium. Such care didn't look impossible to a man with an editor's eye.

So Frank considered writing a play. His natural prudence prevented him from jumping foolishly into something without proper credentials. But he had the editor's gift of crossing out his favorite sentence if it didn't fit, and he believed this ability, along with his good sense and technical skills, was the necessary element in conjuring a play of his own. He also relished a healthy opinion of his capacity. After all, he was twenty-seven years old and had yet to fail at anything. Memories of his father's limping business and dependence on Clara's inheritance continued to rankle. Perhaps because of that unsettling picture, Frank was driven to succeed. Yet his ambition wasn't unwarranted or incautious. He'd proved he could write; people—strangers as well as friends—told him how they laughed at what he wrote and exerted great effort to qualify their own work for his selection. His large following consisted of many of the most intelligent, talented people in New York. And he wrote rhymes. Poets were heroic in that Edwardian day of obsequious veneration of order. He made his living determining what the public liked and giving it to them in a style he dictated. If he'd invented the literary newspaper column, why couldn't he write something equally special for Broadway? The endeavor would enrich his reputation and his pocketbook. Perhaps he could strike upon an additional ennobling and profitable career. Of course, he couldn't give up journalism, at least until success in the theater was assured. But becoming a playwright was an idea too seductive to ignore.

While he was musing on the possibility, opportunity presented itself, for once without his orchestration. A Chicago acquaintance, theatrical manager Harry Askin, wrote him a tantalizing letter.

Askin headed the Chicago branch of the theater trust. At that time of trusts and trust-busting, regional monopolies of road theaters existed; the largest and most famous was "the syndicate," headed in New York by Abraham Lincoln Erlanger and Marc Klaw. Like any monopoly, it set its own prices, decided what plays to produce, where, and with what casts. Nontroublemaking employees were favored at every level. The syndicate came close to absolute control of what the national public paid to see, and it imposed relentless punishment on actors and managers who dared independence. In an exhausting battle beginning around the turn of the century, only Mrs. Fiske and her manager-husband Harry (also publisher of the *Dramatic Mirror*, forerunner of *Variety*) successfully battled Klaw and Erlanger, and the crusade cost them greatly.

Stultifying and resented as it was, the syndicate was reality, and Frank didn't dare challenge it. When it came to his future (and his bank balance), he was wary. It flattered him that Askin had contacted him, and if his first play were to be produced under the iron hand of the syndicate, that would have to be satisfactory. He could take a stand for the abstract principle of liberty after he'd made a name in the demanding new field.

Askin's letter arrived in February 1909, and opened with the enticing proposal that Frank collaborate on a musical comedy with the famous short-story writer O. Henry. To demonstrate his seriousness, Askin had picked the story, "To Him Who Waits," running in a current issue of *Collier's Weekly*. The manager was eager to create work for a little-known Chicago actor, apparently under his contract. John E. Young was "really a sensation," Askin said. "We want to get him a piece that will suit him. It must be a modern character as he is a nice-looking fellow, quite a fast talker, natty, dances very well, sings excellently and is in every way very clever." The story, Askin said, "fits Young to the ground."

He left the task of contacting and persuading O. Henry to Frank, who'd never met the celebrated author but had heard rumors about his failing health and precarious financial condition. He thought the forty-six-year-old man might welcome an infusion of income, particularly if he wouldn't have to spend much energy in its earning. He might be persuaded to leave most of the work to another younger, peppier fellow and merely lend his considerable name to the collaboration. Frank thought the idea mutually propitious. Always starstruck but never intimidated, he had built his career on a foundation of contacts with successful writers. He rushed uptown to call on O. Henry on the same afternoon he received Askin's letter.

O. Henry, who lived in a room at the Hotel Caledonia at 28 West Twenty-sixth Street, turned out to be in worse shape, physically and financially, than Frank had anticipated. Letters and bills were piled so high on the table by the front door that the slightest jolt sent them cascading to the floor. William Sydney Porter had written over 250 stories in eight years, becoming famous and admired after serving time in a southern prison for embezzlement during his incautious youth, a shameful episode he obsessively concealed. He never permitted photographers to take his picture, a mysterious rule to most acquaintances who were unfamiliar with his background and knew only his public personality. He was immensely gregarious and enjoyed smoking cigars, drinking whiskey, eating large meals, and hanging out agreeably with his friends, while procrastinating good-naturedly about writing the stories that supported him and his family. His second wife lived in Asheville, North Carolina, with his daughter, where he journeyed periodically to dry out and work.

Not only did Porter agree to work with Frank on a show, but it was his friend, A. Baldwin Sloane, whom Askin had suggested write the music. Sloane's career had faltered since his last hit, in 1903, *The Wizard of Oz*, for which he and Paul Tietjens had written the words and music. Sloane was the author of several variety show ballads, including "When You Ain't Got No Money, Well, You Needn't Come Around." Recently he'd written the music for *Tillie's Nightmare*, a show that had closed after a few unhappy days on Broadway, even though the song "Heaven Will Protect the Working Girl" made a modest splash. ("You may tempt the upper classes / With your villainous demi-tasses, / but Heaven will protect the working-girl!")

At first Frank was blissful. He and Porter, friends at first sight, agreed to cooperate by discussing each other's ideas and contributing equally to the project. Frank was eager to learn from the master storyteller, who seemed as enthusiastic about the project and as eager to please Askin as he did. The partners met every afternoon, outlining scenes and making notes, blocking and hammering their ideas into shape. Almost immediately they threw out the suggested story, which seemed to them an unlikely candidate for dramatization. (Its plot focused on a taciturn man who, on being jilted, becomes a hermit—hardly a role for the "natty dresser" Askin had described; Frank and O. Henry wondered if the enthusiastic producer had read the story. Later they wondered unkindly if he could read at all.) Instead they decided to make up a new if unlikely plot about an anthropological expedition sent to Central America to substantiate the theory that North American Indians were descendants of the Aztecs. O. Henry called this "aztechnology," and until Askin heard about it, the title of the opus became *The Enthusiaztecs*. But Askin sneered that the title sounded both highfalutin and amateurish, like an extravaganza produced by the seniors at Lincoln Memorial High School. The collaborators, properly chastened, settled on a new title, *Lo*, taken from Alexander Pope's ironic lines:

> *Lo, the poor Indian! whose untutored mind*
> *Sees God in clouds, or hears him in the wind.*

Askin was delighted with the new name. "You can advertise it easy, and it looks good in type," he wrote.

But the idyll at the Hotel Caledonia soon palled. Being writers of words, they naturally considered lyrics more important than music, and both supposed the librettist wrote verses to which the less important composer fitted tunes. Unfortunately, this wasn't the case. "Most of our songs were constructed to fit tunes the composer had already written," Frank said later. Much of the music for the songs was lifted directly from the score of *Tillie's Nightmare*, which had passed before the public eye too quickly to have left an impression.

The work of fitting the words to the music was especially difficult for Frank because perfect meter and rhymes were an obsession. In addition, Askin ruled the struggling librettists with a heavy hand all the way from Chicago. His decisions knew no appeal. He told them, correctly, that they were inexperienced. "Believe me," he said repeatedly, "I've been in this business 27 years and I know." Without a theatrical credit between them (somebody else had dramatized O. Henry's story "Alias Jimmy Valentine") and working hundreds of miles from management, neither Frank nor O. Henry was in a position to argue. So they gave in and did what they were told until they despaired, seeing little invention or pep or hope left in the material.

What made the ordeal worse was that "Always in Good Humor" was Frank's livelihood, and he couldn't give it short shrift, no matter what other important work he was doing. The sparkle in the column had to be maintained even when his concentration jumped and hovered elsewhere. As he watched his cherished playwriting fantasy dissolve, he knew he had to keep the column sharp so he could come back to it without its having lost its snap. It might turn out that it was his destiny, not Broadway.

He had few moments for reflection and slept badly. Every night a player piano across the courtyard from the Adamses new apartment on 116th Street demonstrated its volume and endless repertoire. Often Frank slept in the living room. He was grumpier than usual and snapped at Minna, who disliked it and told him so. It was a bad time.

In April he received unrelated bad news from Chicago. Moses Adams had died, alone in a rented room, on Saturday, April 17. His body wasn't found until Monday morning, when the boardinghouse operator, noticing she hadn't seen the old man for several days, unlocked his door and entered the room. Moses was buried a few hours after his two-day-old corpse was discovered. There were no rituals at a funeral parlor, no opportunity for condolence calls or leisurely good-byes. Frank didn't have time to get to the funeral, although he took the first train to Chicago on Monday, as soon as he heard the news. (He'd once quipped in the column, "It takes only eighteen hours to get to Chicago. But what's the use?") His sister Evelyn arranged for Moses to be buried next to Clara at Rosehill Cemetery. The funeral was simple and without eulogy or ceremony. The mourners consisted of the dead man's daughters and some of his wife's relatives. Moses hadn't any friends left. He'd waited for another chance to reestablish his business, but it never came.

While in Chicago, Frank met with dapper actor John Young at Askin's office to talk with him and the manager about the show. They planned to open it on the road and, after a brief tour of midwestern towns, bring it into Chicago. If it did well there, they hoped to move it to Broadway in the spring of 1910. Frank planned to return to Chicago during rehearsals in the summer to tinker with the book, if necessary. He gave Askin the manuscript, then hurried back to New York to await instructions.

Askin rejected the draft. "We need comedy," he insisted. "Laughs is what we want, all the time." He said the first scene was wrong: "How come it's an interior?" The second act was worse. He concluded the letter by accusing the inexperienced collaborators of missing the boat in all kinds of obvious ways, especially in omitting sufficient laughs and jokes. And he announced that he'd hired another writer to redo the book. Frank and O. Henry waited for the new material. The subsequent outline was acceptable to the producer, but when the new writer submitted his dialogue, Askin—who certainly had a firm grip on what he wanted—threw it out and ordered Frank and O. Henry back to work on their version. They were both relieved and angry. The endless project became a nightmare. Neither of them had ever worked harder or more conscientiously on anything. Frank was awed by O. Henry's effort, appreciated his tireless commitment and duplicated it. They spent every night together at the Hotel Caledonia, frantically revising, rejecting, adding and subtracting, patching, editing, and figuring out. At last they sent the final rewrite to Askin, no longer apprehensive, and too exhausted to celebrate.

But Askin demanded that Frank return to Chicago for more show doctoring before the opening. He obeyed, hurrying back to work with the cast during final rehearsals. When Frank tried to polish a line of the soprano's solo, Askin prodded him, saying, "Don't bother. Nobody'll understand what she says, anyhow."

Finally *Lo* opened in Aurora, Illinois, on August 25, 1909, for a one-night stand. Frank was present. "With two exceptions the acting was mediocre," he reported without further elaboration.

The small-town audience enjoyed the performance, and Frank was mildly pleased, though it was hardly a night of triumph. Askin collared him afterward and ordered him upstairs to his hotel room. "You have to fix up that rotten second act," he said. Frank did as he was told and spent the night reworking the faulty scenes, presumably to extricate more laughs, but the revisions were never incorporated. The play went on to Waukegan and to Janesville, Wisconsin, without change. Frank was baffled but silent and returned to New York.

Lo played Milwaukee for the Labor Day week, opening Sunday night and closing the following Saturday. The run was unphenomenal and offered little competition to Milwaukee's other late summer amusements, the Wild West show and fireworks exhibition, Fraser's Highlanders at the Hippodrome, an Irish picnic at Schlitz Park, and a Knights of Columbus outing in Pabst Park.

Frank was disappointed and embarrassed to read at his desk in New York that the *Milwaukee Journal*'s drama critic thought *Lo* "the usual musical comedy of the uninspired sort, presented in the usual way by people of average talent."

Relief followed when Frank discovered that nowhere had the program mentioned the names of Franklin P. Adams and O. Henry. Apparently Askin hadn't wanted to muddy the waters of his own and his protege's fame, which was fine with Frank. He read the rest of the review: "You could not find much fault with *Lo* if you tried," it said, "and you could not bestow much praise on it justly. . . . The old ingredients are served strictly according to the standard dramatic cookbook. There is about the usual investment in scenery and costumes. The music is the usual jingle, only not quite so good as what it is an imitation of."

It was too bad about *Lo*, for its failure ended forever any hope of a Broadway career for Frank. Ironically, it deserved better treatment, not from the reviewer, who was probably fair with what he saw, but from its creators. Their inexperience had intimidated them, and they had not trusted their own ideas and gifts. They had given in too easily to the producer.

Realizing the hopelessness of promoting the show, Askin abandoned it. For the rest of the Milwaukee engagement the *Milwaukee Journal* contained no mention of *Lo* and no advertisement for it. It staggered on in a series of one-nighters in small towns and villages offering little more than railroad depots and two-story hotels, but on the night of December 5, in St. Joseph, Missouri, it closed for once and all. And it never made Chicago.

Frank learned of the last performance from a stray newspaper paragraph (he never heard from Askin again) and morosely visited his collaborator bearing the news. They shook hands, went for drinks, and toasted each other in a valiant effort at stiff-upper-lipping it. Yet the debacle represented a rite of passage for both men. O. Henry, sick and burned out, borrowed from Frank for his daughter's schooling; he died that spring. A humbled Franklin P. Adams helped with the funeral arrangements, which included a memorial service at the Little Church Around the Corner in Greenwich Village.

Despite its failure, Frank was always proud, if not of the product, of the collaboration. Asked to submit his biography to *Who's Who* four years later, the first accomplishment he listed was the musical play he'd written with O. Henry. Long afterward when everybody else had forgotten about it, or perhaps had never known of it, the listing persisted. There were other events in his life he included in the annual biography and later removed (he was listed in the reference book for forty-four straight years), but the sentence about *Lo* never varied and remained.

The experience saddened and humiliated him, and he never forgot it. It taught him to respect and adhere to the limitations of his talent—an

important if painful lesson—and he never reached again for the gold
ring.

VIII   In June 1911, Frank began a breezy personal memoir written in the style of Samuel Pepys, the seventeenth-century
British diarist. His intention was to include the journal
entries within the regular column every other day for a
month or so. He named it "The Diary of Our Own Samuel Pepys" and
inserted its first grumpy sentence on a Wednesday morning: "To breakfast, where was a canteloupe. Wretched, it being the season's first."
The tone was set for twenty-seven years.

At first the paragraphs appeared every few days. "Whether it was
exciting fun to write about myself or it automatically took care of a
certain amount of space—or both," he said, "I continued." It was a
guileless exercise, boring and fascinating at the same time, sprinkled
with old Briticisms like "bespeaks" and "betimes" and "betook."
Despite its preciousness, his fans welcomed the account of everyday life
as observed by a self-proclaimed ordinary fellow.

After 1922 Frank permanently retired Saturday's "Gotham Gazette" in order to run the Diary. "I did it solely to get a day off," he
claimed, and printing it regularly on Saturdays "proved better than the
two-or-three-days-a-week method, for those who didn't like it knew
which day not to read that part of the paper, while my adorers preferred
the wholesale scheme." Reading the Diary became a Saturday morning
treat in many homes, as much a part of New York City life as the
crowded subways it endlessly denounced.

Frank's personality guardedly revealed itself in the succinct paragraphs. He told when he got a haircut and whether the results pleased
him:

Saturday, January 25.
Home, and fashioning some verses, and thence to my barber's
to be trimmed and he asketh me something, and, understanding him
not at all, what with his accent of Palermo, I did say, Yes, whereat
he took a bottle and poured its contents upon my head, and then I
did know it for olive oil, by its odour. And he did rub it into my hair
till that I did feel like any head of lettuce and was minded to ask
him to pass the salt and vinegar, but did not.

He described his reactions to plays and playwrights, actors and actresses, books. He reported reading mostly popular fiction, titles and authors forgotten almost as soon as he had laid them aside: Harry Leon Wilson's *Bunker Bean* and *The Boss of Little Arcady*, Gilbert Cannan's *Round the Corner*, Henry Harrison's *V.V.'s Eyes*, L. J. Vance's *Joan Thursday* ("a great book"). When he commented that he'd read *The Sweetest Sweetmeat*, by Fannie Hurst, "misliking it greatly," she wrote him and, in a sense of fairness, he quoted her rebuttal: " '. . . Yet did not Mr. Pepys the elder himself mislike many of the tayles and plays of the great Shakespeare?' " He commended Hurst's spunk in speaking up but didn't like her book any better.

Friends and acquaintances mentioned in the Diary were some of the new century's most celebrated or controversial people:

Wednesday, May 22.
 With Mr. Theodore Dreiser the great tayle-writer to luncheon, and he tells me of many things that have happened to him in Germany and in England and fills me with a great lust to travel.

Thursday, May 15.
 To luncheon with Jack Reed the poet and he told me of the four days he was in prison in Paterson, and of the horrible uncleanness, and of one man 80 yrs. of age and ill that was imprisoned for six months for begging five cents. Also he told me how great a man is Bill Haywood, and it may be as Jack saith. Also he told me that the Industrial Workers are sorely misjudged and that the tayles in the publick prints of their bloodthirstiness are lies told by the scriveners. And out of it all I wish I did know how to appraise what is true and what is false, but I am too ignorant, and ill-fitted to judge truly.

December 5.
 . . . To Leroy Scott's for dinner, where was Max Eastman, who told me how the great combined press is seeking to put him in gaol with Art Young. But I doubt they will do it.

Monday, February 9.
 To dinner, and met Mistress Ida Tarbell, who told me of many ways in which a journall might be made interesting, and some of her notions not bad neither.

Tantalizing as these descriptions were, he never waxed serious for long enough to probe and question topics or attitudes. That wasn't his purpose. It was sufficient for his readers to know that F.P.A. and his companions addressed such matters; you didn't have to know what they said. That might be boring.

In 1935, when Simon and Schuster published a two-volume compilation of the Diary, Frank reedited the material and admitted his own latter-day frustration with some of what he had written. He footnoted the entry telling of his meeting with Ida Tarbell, famous muckraking reporter for *McClure's* magazine, whose comprehensive *History of the Standard Oil Company* was a basic reference. He complained that his account of the conversation was "the most conspicuous exhibition of bad reporting that even I have made. The readers of the newspaper that employed me were entitled to know some of the things that so wise and informative a woman as Miss Tarbell might say, especially on one of the few subjects that I really care about." Then he got funny again, because in 1935 he was still F.P.A., and he didn't want to reveal a passionate concern about anything. "It is possible, however, that she said that a newspaper might be made interesting if it denuded itself of features. I might have thought it expedient to suppress this."

There was no way Frank was going to be serious for long, even twenty years later. His persona wouldn't accept it, nor would his readers.

The Diary went along year after year, describing Frank's ups and downs, how he spent his days, whom he saw, the food he ate, the funny things people (including him) said, what he hated, and what he enjoyed.

He appeared to play tennis more frequently than did even Bill Tilden, though with more modest result. And his readers sympathized when he suffered from tennis elbow:

Friday, December 19.
This afternoon the osteopathist did pummel me and pound me, but truth to say, I find my arm no great deal improved, nor can I lift anything of any considerable weight without pain.

His trips to the dentist were chronicled, as were his head colds and when he came down with the ague or the flu. He bought a bicycle and told of riding it to work. He complained about the traffic and wished he could purchase an automobile, but declared the expense too great.

During the summers he journeyed to the Polo Grounds with his friends Grantland Rice, Damon Runyon, and, when he was in town, Ring Lardner. Often he bet gleefully against the Giants. He reported the extent of his winnings and losses, perversely giving the figure in shillings. He described apartment life, the windows that rattled and kept him awake, the indifferent elevator and hall boys and the "proud, imperious" telephone operator, the slovenly janitor who couldn't be found in February to fix a broken window but glad-handed him at

Christmas. He talked about married life as one who'd been wedded a thousand years, unsentimentally and with easy affection. Minna, whom he invariably called "my wife" (although everybody else he mentioned precisely, sometimes including middle initial), was somebody who fixed his breakfast when the cook was away, whose abandonment of him for the seashore during the summers forced him to purchase expensive and often unpalatable meals in restaurants. He reported when she bought the latest fashion in ugly hats and hobble skirts, and told of reading to her when a passage pleased him, and of his delight in making her laugh.

With its unpretentious, subjective view of the times, the Diary was uniquely successful. He'd initially thought that the idea of a parody of Pepys was original with him, but he was wrong, as he admitted: American newspaperman Edwin Emerson, Jr., had written a similar journal during the Spanish-American War, and British essayists and journalists had often attempted a similar exercise. But where the others had failed and been forgotten, Frank succeeded. Perhaps the Diary's long popularity came because he never fancied it something more than it was. He evidenced irritation often, and contentment, but rarely outrage and never despair. These limitations became the Diary's strength. His concerns were those of a conventionally educated middle-class person, and they reflected the interests and inclinations of his readers. His intellectualism was predictable and mildly liberal, though he preferred describing the menu and the identity of his companions to disclosing the content of serious dinner table discussions.

He told of supporting "My Lord Theodore" when, in 1912, Theodore Roosevelt bolted the Republicans to found the Bull Moose Party. Frank described a rally at Madison Square Garden where the candidate's arrival caused "such a noise of cheering as I never had heard, long and loud, and enduring three-quarters of an hour, which I deemed somewhat silly . . . but him I did admire greatly and shall be proud to cast for him next Tuesday." Yet when next Tuesday arrived, he failed to mention the outcome of the election or his reaction to it, instead choosing to describe going home on election night "by electric-car [where was] seated behind me as pretty a lady as I have seen, with her black hair parted on the side, and a fair voice." (Her name was Hilda Gaige, and she popped up frequently for several weeks after that first sighting.)

One morning the *New York Evening Mail* quoted "a tired-looking middle-aged woman" on its front page. She'd testified at the New York State Labor Department hearings investigating the causes of a laundry workers' strike, saying, "I was a piece worker and I worked anywhere from eleven to sixteen hours a day. The most I ever got in one week was $19.30. That was the week before Christmas and I worked 90 hours to get it.'' Inside, on page 8, Frank's Diary entry for the day said, ''At my labour all the day, with great content to myself, and read this night Laurence Hope's 'India's Love Lyrics,' which seem to me over-ardent and over-scented with musk and suchlike heavy odours.''

He wasn't heartless or unaware. His job was to entertain, and he never forgot it. Because he cultivated a detached, ironic manner, his popularity grew. And lasted.

On the rare occasions when he voiced an opinion, it rarely involved anything controversial. After the Triangle Shirtwaist factory disaster in 1911, Frank told of attending a meeting of the Women's Trade Union League: ''It is inevitable many will rise to call the indignation against things hysteria. Perhaps it is. It is due to hysteria after the Iroquois fire that the theatres in Chicago are the safest in the country, and it was a variant of hysteria that led to the document signed by John Hancock and his hysterical accomplices.'' His detached remarks hit exactly the tone his readers expected and wanted. He was concerned, but his concern wasn't unseemly; good people would get together and something would be done.

He spoke to his readers as a stern but fair father, concerned with his own affairs but interested in what the children were up to. For example, he supported female suffrage and admired the men who marched up Fifth Avenue with the women. (''Far from being weak brothers,'' he said, ''we believe they showed unusual strength of conviction.'') But he was too busy ''scrivening'' to join them. And when King George's son and daughter-in-law, the Duke and Duchess of Connaught, came to town with their daughter, the Princess Pat, they were feted and fawned over. Frank chided the silliness, caught the sons of the revolution with their hypocrisy showing:

> *When Freedom from her mountain height,*
> *(Ah, did you see the Duke last night?)*
> *Unfurled her banner to the air,*
> *(Bow low! Salute the ducal pair!)*
> *O hail Columbia, happy land*
> *(I saw a mortal shake his hand!)*
> *Land of the brave, land of the free,*
> *Sweet land of [laughter] liberty!*

Like Pepys, he was a man of his time, and therein lay his success.

CHAPTER THREE

The *New York Tribune*
World War I
The *Stars and Stripes*

MOMUS: *Thy wars brought nothing about;* [*to Mars*]
Thy lovers were all untrue. [*to Venus*]
JANUS: *'Tis well an old age it out,*
CHRONOS: *And time to begin a new.*
—JOHN DRYDEN, *Secular Masque*

The world must be made safe for democracy.
PRESIDENT WOODROW WILSON,
APRIL 2, 1917

I "Always in Good Humor" continued to attract attention and, in fact, its presence in the *New York Evening Mail* greatly broadened the newspaper's appeal. Editorial focus had narrowed considerably since the first days of Frank's tenure. The publisher directed the editors to bear in mind that readers bought the paper on their way home from work, when their primary concerns were ball scores and race results, not weighty matters. So three-inch headlines (GIANTS THROTTLE CUBS) and box scores invariably squeezed nonsporting matters to the bottom of the front page or to the inside, especially during pennant races. The *New York Evening Mail* viewed its role as one in which it whipped up and selectively served the public's curiosity. Like William Randolph Hearst's *New York Journal*, the *New York Evening Mail* offered surrogate vitality and appealed to interests requiring little intellectual effort. These ebullient afternoon papers left serious news coverage to their august morning rivals. People were known to study the editorial and financial pages of the *New York Times*, the *New York Tribune*, and the *New York World*, savoring second cups of breakfast coffee while doing so. But when Joe or Charley got home from work, he wanted his supper. He didn't have the time or energy to pore over complicated details, so the *Evening Mail* didn't provide them. The paper was designed for reader enjoyment.

As was "Always in Good Humor." Yet within the *Evening Mail*, the column was untypical. For while his purpose was to delight and amuse, F.P.A. never talked down to his readers. Within his self-imposed limitations—no passion, no evidence of vulnerability or serious commitment—he challenged his readers, striving to stimulate them. He presumed their intelligence. Elaborate parodies of Horace presupposed years of training in Latin. In addition, familiarity with literature was a prerequisite for the enjoyment of much of his intellectually biased nonsense. Given the accepted profile of afternoon paper readers, it was startling that the column was popular, but it was, and not only as the most popular column in the *Evening Mail*. It was the most popular newspaper column in New York.

His province was the city, and he prowled it, on the lookout. "Mark Twain, as everybody knows, used to do a good deal of his work in bed," he said. "But he has nothing on Mr. H. L. Lind of 2209 Seventh Avenue, whose announcement reads: 'I also retire and repair baby carriages.' " He spotted a sign in a tailor's window at Morningside Heights and 123rd Street: "Uncalled for Men's Suits."

"One knows so many," he sighed.

He ran a series called "Impossible Story Beginnings: " 'Your teeth,' the dentist was saying, 'seem to be in perfect condition. I can find nothing to do. Good morning.' " And, poking fun at the boxer with grandiose ideas of invincibility, " 'I'm not at all sure of defeating him,' the pugilist said. 'He is a good fighter and I may have trouble.' "

Infrequently he was charmed by the work of the children of contributors:

> From a contrib comes a poem on a wedding written by a ten-year-old niece of the bride. The epithalamium is too long to print in full, but we append one couplet, describing the bridesmaids:
>
> *Some had pug noses while others had Roman;*
> *And each had blue ribbons tied round their abdomen.*

In 1911 Frank's second book of verse, *Tobogganing on Parnassus*, was published by Doubleday, Page and Company. He dedicated it to "Bert Leston Taylor: Guide, Philosopher, but Friend." (Ironically, people were now referring to Taylor as "Chicago's F.P.A.") *In Other Words* followed the next year ("To the w.k. [well-known] human race this book is hopefully dedicated"), *By and Large* in 1914, and *Weights and Measures* in 1917. All of the poems and paragraphs in the books had first appeared in the column.

Because the *Evening Mail* was where F.P.A. held court, other gifted young writers gathered around him, printed first within his column and then next to it or on other pages with columns of their own. Grantland Rice's column first appeared on the *Evening Mail*'s sports page in 1911. Frank welcomed the Tennessean to the paper—he'd been a longtime contributor. (Frank told how "Miss Florence Davenport Rice, whose father, Old Grant Rice, uses a typewriter, approached our shrine yesterevening and evinced surprise that we employed the o.f. [old-fashioned] fountain pen. 'You don't work, like Daddy,' said Florence. 'You only just write.' ")

Cartoonist Rube Goldberg (another steady contributor) fashioned a daily cartoon, also on the sports page. One afternoon a small photograph of Goldberg replaced his customary drawing. Under the picture of the cartoonist was the announcement that he'd inherited $15 million worth of California property. The item told how he'd bound his possessions to the roof of his automobile with a rope made of neckties and dashed off for the West Coast. The paper wished him well but tut-tutted the unseemly avarice forcing the departure and ruining the young man's promising career. Frank reported gleefully a few days later when a newspaper in New England earnestly reprinted the hoax. (It was the time for hoaxes. A couple of years later, H. L. Mencken wrote an entirely fraudulent and very boring article about the history of bathtubs for the *Evening Mail*. He fabricated names, dates, and absurd facts and wasn't found out for years. Any history of plumbing that mentions the purchase of the first "stationary" bathtub by Cincinnati millionaire Adam Thompson in 1842 has been taken in by this hard-to-kill tall tale.)

Newspaper people enjoyed horsing around. When an advice columnist began appearing on the same page with F.P.A., he and his contributors teased and chortled. Her name was Laura Jean Libbey, and the *Evening Mail* billed her as the author of *When His Love Grew Cold* and of "Forty Other Novels of Which Over 5 Million Copies Have Been Sold." One afternoon, in answer to a letter from "Outraged Reader," Libbey's response included the following indictment:

The wicked novel and the naughty play would never see the light

if authors and authoresses alike allowed the parental instinct to influence their genius. My mother was critic and censor in the days
when I was doing my best work. When she did not approve it was
enough for me to destroy my most carefully planned dramas and
novels.

A few weeks later, responding to "Perplexed," Miss Libbey advised:

One cannot use too much judgment in the selection of a sweetheart.
No man loves a girl the better for seeing her divide her smiles between
a rival and himself. The spirited man quits the field without ado in
favor of the other fellow. It is always the best of the two the girl
loses.

F.P.A. and his contributors didn't take such sentiments seriously.
In a December column, Frank printed the following exchange:

Dear Miss Libbey: [The letter has been turned over to us.] I am a
young lady of education and my friends tell me I am pretty and
attractive. I am deeply in love with a newspaper paragrapher who
is unaware of my very existence. What shall I give him for Christmas
so that he may know where I stand?

Answer: Try first to stifle your love. If this is impossible, send him
a 1911 motor car, a deed to a country house or a few nicely engraved
government bonds. If he is still obdurate, ask for a change of venue.
He is not worth your affection.

F.P.A. ran a contest to name a collection of Miss Libbey's columns.
Ideas poured in: "Yearned Increments," "Hearticles of Faith," "Love
Lorgnettes," "Libbey's Extract of Grief." After a few months her
column quietly disappeared.

Evening Mail publisher Henry Stoddard appreciated Frank's importance to the paper. He knew that his star columnist's contributors
were young men and women fresh from the hustings, many of them
tomorrow's important journalists and writers. He knew too that the
presence of "Always in Good Humor" added class to his paper and
attracted not only literate readers but other gifted writers as well.

A good example was the nineteen-year-old ribbon salesman from
Paterson, New Jersey, who began submitting material to Frank in 1908.
His name was George Kaufman. He inserted an *S.* so he too would have
three initials, just like F.P.A. Kaufman's wisecracks and epigrams

quickly dominated the other submissions, and for a period of three years, it was a rare week that the column didn't include several contributions from G.S.K. His unmistakable style was ironic, succinct, acerbic. At first he yearned endlessly to win the coveted position at the top of the column and, knowing Frank's obsession with typeface and his desire to vary the appearance of the paragraphs, submitted gags with whole sentences written backward or with every other word printed upside down and, once, memorably, in mirror writing. Sometimes Frank printed Kaufman's gags in agate type, so small you needed a magnifying glass to read them. Undaunted, G.S.K. countered by suggesting that Frank "run the column all the way across the page [which] would give you more space at the top for those that want it." As he gained confidence, his outlook broadened, and he addressed less parochial issues, though he was careful to select topics that would appeal to Frank and were in fact clearly imitative:

> Sir: I would like to drop something hard, heavy and harmful on the joker who hands out that "fine weather for ducks" rigamorole every time it happens to rain a little.
>
> You wouldn't call the subway a Bronchial Tube, would you?
>
> Two of the syndicates that bid for the Cubs have withdrawn their offers. One might almost refer to them as rescindicates. In fact, one did; and G.S.K. are his initials.

Or, following editor Niles' short-lived experiment with moving "Always in Good Humor" from its customary right-hand position to the center of the page:

> Sir: I am glad to see the Column back in the corner again. I turned, absent-mindedly, to the Usual Place on Thursday, and read half-way through Altman's advertisement before noticing my error.

According to Kaufman's biographer, Howard Teichmann, many "American boys from eighteen to twenty-two study under professors. Kaufman did his college years under the blue pencil of F.P.A."

Although Frank was eight years older than Kaufman, the two young men looked so much alike they might have been brothers. Each was thin, round-shouldered, had a large nose and wide, thick lips. Each of them hurried ahead, with face in advance of feet in a gawky, unathletic stride. Kaufman's hair exploded from his scalp, as did Frank's, except his was beginning to run to thinness in front. Their backgrounds were remarkably similar: Both were from "out there," George raised in Pittsburgh instead of Chicago; both had dynamic, intellectual mothers and charming fathers who were business failures. George's grandfather had been a rabbi. He had no older brother, while Frank didn't have a younger one, so once they'd met and discovered their identical interests, it was inevitable they'd hook up together. Their friendship lasted fifty-two years. Frank took George under his wing and gave him the advice and counsel that various older friends had given him, mixed with heavy doses of hard-won, unique perspective.

They worked together on George's writing, going over it painstakingly, rewriting, polishing, throwing it out and starting again. Because George was stagestruck, Frank advised him to go to acting class, which he did at night at the Alveen Drama School. Much to his delight, he landed a job in a summer stock company in Troy, New York, abandoned his unfulfilling career as a ribbon salesman, and hurried off to meet his destiny in upstate New York. Unfortunately, the vision didn't match the reality, and the company folded after only a week. ("Last Supper and original cast wouldn't draw in this house," he telegraphed his father.) Next George signed up for a Sunday morning playwriting course at Columbia University. Afterward he often dropped in on Frank and Minna in their sunny apartment overlooking the Morningside Heights campus.

After lunch he and Frank went for long walks to discuss his future.

When grocery store tycoon and press lord Frank Andrew Munsey offered Frank the senior columnist job on the *Washington* (D.C.) *Times*, Frank refused. He couldn't picture himself leaving New York. But he immediately thought of George. The young man was gifted, Frank said. He was witty, disciplined and bright, perfect for the job. Munsey took Frank at his word. He hired Kaufman with the knowledge that he'd never worked on a newspaper. Frank wasn't apprehensive about George's inexperience. Kaufman was a perfectionist and a workaholic, just as he was.

So Kaufman went to Washington, where he lived and worked for a year. He played poker at the National Press Club and wrote "This and That" in the *Washington Times*, a column in which the format, style, and point of view was interchangeable with "Always in Good Humor":

> It is our case-hardened belief, apropos of the Newport gem thefts, that anyone who can afford to own a hundred thousand dollars' worth of jewels can afford to have them stolen.

Two men were killed yesterday in the construction work at Panama.
One was an Englishman, the other a laborer.

Legend goes that after a year Munsey saw George working at his
desk. "What's that Jew doing in my city room?" he's supposed to have
said. The story is probably apocryphal, since F.P.A. was a Jew too,
and Munsey had offered the job to him first. True or not, George was
back in New York in December 1913, once again without employment
or prospect. "Always in Good Humor" printed the announcement:

Sir: A gr-r-eat colyum conductor is AT LIBERTY meaning . . . but
doubtless you've guessed it, despite the adjective. *I have been
canned.*
Regards to Deems Taylor.

—G.S.K.

Frank responded:

Welcome back to the contrib leadership, old friend. The *Washington
Times* erred in canning you, but to err is inhuman, and newspapers
are only that, after all.

George didn't have long to wait before Frank was able to help him
again.

After *Evening Mail* editor Niles retired, Frank felt himself ethically
freed from his carefully maintained loyalty to the paper. He'd worked
there for ten years, and during that time Niles had shown him impeccable
kindness and tolerance. It was Niles who had given him his first chance
in New York, had stood with him while he learned and experimented,
and had provided unwavering support. With him as his editor, Frank
had never considered leaving. But although he maintained an easy relationship with publisher Henry Stoddard, Frank didn't feel the same
abiding affection for him. So when Niles retired, Frank, who was thirty-
three, began to look around. It didn't take long before Ogden Mills Reid
of the *New York Tribune* approached him with an offer. Frank was
elated. The *New York Tribune*, with its deep news coverage and thoughtful editorials, was superior to the *Evening Mail* in every way. It would
earn its reputation among newspaper people as the best written paper
in America. Publisher Reid coveted Frank, and to get him on his staff,
he promised a special bonus (though, as it turned out, the opportunity
materialized after more than a year and a half had passed): In addition
to writing his daily column, Frank would take over as managing editor

of the proposed Sunday *Tribune* magazine. The assignment was a plum. And Frank jumped at it.

His final "Always in Good Humor" column appeared in the *Evening Mail* on December 31, 1913. There was no mention of his departure. But clever Frank included a camouflaged message by spelling out "Read the Tribune" with the first letter of every line in his translation of Horace.

THE MONUMENT OF Q. HORATIUS FLACCUS

Horace: Book III, Ode 30

AD MELPOMENEN

Exegi monumentum aere perennius

Regalique situ pyramidum altius.

Reader, the monument that I've
Erected ever shall survive
As long as brass; and it shall stay
Despite the stormiest, wildest day.
Though winds assil, yet shall it stand
High as the pyramids, and grand.
Eternally my name will be
Triumphant in posterity.
Recurrent will my praises sound;
I shall be terribly renowned.
Born though I was of folk obscure,
Unknown, I spilled Some Lit'rature.
Now, O Melpomene, my queen
Entwine the laurel on my bean!

—F.P.A.

Frank's replacement at the *Evening Mail* was George S. Kaufman. With acquisition of the built-in stature of "Always in Good Humor," Kaufman was launched. He toiled there for a year, then, slightly in advance of the *Evening Mail*'s final collapse, changed venue, first to assist Heywood Broun at the *New York Tribune* (at Frank's suggestion, of course). Next he became third-string drama critic at the *New York Times*. A year later, when Kaufman married Beatrice Bakrow, Frank was their best man. His promising young friend would become America's most prolific and successful playwright, working with some of the best-known figures in popular culture—Edna Ferber, Marc Connelly, the Marx Brothers, Irving Berlin, Abe Burrows—and in his version of the Adams/Kaufman scenario, his own protege, Moss Hart. He never forgot his debt to Adams.

At the *New York Tribune*, Frank changed the name of the column from "Always in Good Humor" (an obvious misnomer) to "The Conning Tower." It made its first appearance on Thursday morning, January 1, 1914.

And with him to the *New York Tribune* came Grantland Rice, whose column, "The Sportlight," appeared for the next several decades in the center of the sports page.

Since the *New York Tribune* was a morning paper, Frank's schedule changed. To his everlasting joy and relief, he didn't have to get up early anymore. The horrific battle with the morning subway rabble was memory. For Frank, an unreconstructed night person, stopping at the office after dinner or a show was no inconvenience. His deadline, once noon, now was midnight. So he'd amble into the office around eleven in the morning, open his mail, and go over the contributions. After marking and editing the ones he wanted to use, he went downstairs to the composing room, where he gave them, with instructions, to the typesetter. Then he went back to his big new desk with its new typewriter, which he learned to use, but unwillingly. Both the desk and the typewriter were gifts from the publisher and indicated the esteem with which he was welcomed. He worked on his own verses and paragraphs for an hour or two, then went back downstairs to check on the proofs for the next day's column, stopping to chat with his friends along the way. He proofread the galley, then measured it to see if the material as typeset was sufficient for a column. He needed enough stuff to measure four inches across and run the length of the page. Considerable material was required. He usually had a supply of fillers to cut out and paste onto the proof when necessary. Then he was finished in time for a leisurely lunch and a stroll up Broadway before he returned to the office for work on the following day's column. There was ample time to visit with friends and to keep up with other newspapers and magazines, to peruse and discuss the current political and theatrical scene. He loved his life.

Every night, high above Broadway, the *New York Tribune* announced itself as F.P.A.'s new home in a huge, lighted sign. Frank steered Minna by the first night it appeared, and her mouth gaped. His name in lights fulfilled the promise he'd made her a dozen years before. It was a thrilling moment for both of them.

And in June 1914, he received an honor of great personal significance. The University of Michigan awarded him an honorary master of arts degree. Frank, always disappointed about not having finished college, was delighted. He went to Ann Arbor for the commencement exercises. The award lauded him as "a keen and original commentator upon the life of the great metropolis [who has] charmed thousands and secured wide recognition as a literary man." The commendation was almost as satisfying as an earned degree.

II

Before Ogden Reid decided to commit the *New York Tribune* to the ambitious new weekly Frank would edit, he watched with frustration as his editors pasted up a series of unsuccessful Sunday feature magazines. One used the *New York Tribune*'s state-of-the-art ability to reproduce drawings and photographs and was called the graphics section. It contained photos of charmingly posed pets and children, publicity shots of actors and actresses, bucolic scenes in Central Park or the Tuileries. There was nothing vital or imaginative about it, so it floundered, as had its predecessors. Reid was heavily embroiled in a contest for Sunday readership and the resultant advertising revenues; he felt he needed a magazine to complement the rest of the Sunday edition, which was fat and readable, containing as it did separate sections devoted not only to expanded coverage of current events but also to sports, society, books, theater, real estate and finance, the funnies, and "Women's Chief Business"—which became the "*Tribune* Institute," with articles about planning meals and teaching efficiency to scrubwomen.

It was the idea of Reid's wife Helen, a gifted business manager and promoter, to offer Frank the opportunity to design a popular magazine insert. She argued that not only could Frank reach well-known intellectuals and persuade them to write timely articles for the magazine but he would lend a lightness and wit to the enterprise differing considerably from competitive publications. She was right.

Once on the *New York Tribune* staff, Frank turned to his column, which, except for its new name and expanded size, was identical to "Always in Good Humor." (With seven instead of eight columns per page, Conning Tower space was greatly enlarged, and a different column was due every day, including Sunday.) His readers and contributors loyally followed him to his new home. He invited a group of Yale undergraduates to write the column for the St. Patrick's Day number, and several from the Columbia School of Journalism followed a couple of months later.

In July, a young drifter cum playwright, enamored of a woman named Beatrice Ashe, submitted an F.P.A.-influenced poem called "Speaking, to the Shade of Dante, of Beatrices":

Lo, even I am Beatrice!
  That line keeps singing in my bean.
I feel the same ecstatic bliss
  As did the fluent Florentine
Who heard the well-known hell-flame hiss.

Dante, your damozel was tall
  And lean and sad—I've seen her face
On many a best-parlor wall—
  I don't think she was such an ace.
She doesn't class with mine at all.

Frank put the valentine at the top of the column. It was a rare occasion when this particular lovesick playwright attempted humor in public. His name was Eugene O'Neill.

Setting up the new magazine took longer than anybody anticipated. Frank planned it with characteristic thoroughness. He studied the competition, talked to his friends, and drew up and rejected dummy copies. Finally the project was ready. Initially, his staff numbered two people: Arthur Folwell, a former editor of *Puck*, and artist William Hill. Deems Taylor, who'd finally landed a position as assistant editor of the Western Electric house publication, joined Frank's retinue after a couple of months, as did promising young artist Rea Irvin and Columbia University senior Irwin Edman. The most important addition to the staff, however, was Robert Benchley. His presence lifted the magazine to memorable heights.

Frank's friend and contributor Earl Derr Biggers, who wrote for the *Boston Transcript*, had been a classmate of Benchley's at Harvard. Biggers lauded the young humorist as "the funniest man alive" and insisted that Frank hire him. The reason for his enthusiasm was, at first, obscure. Since the halcyon days as president of the Harvard Lampoon and third-from-the-left "chorus girl" in the Hasty Pudding show, Benchley's career had lurched and sputtered. He'd been fired from his job as editor of the house organ at the Curtis Publishing Company. Lately he'd been engaged with a paper company in Boston, organizing employee bowling teams and outings. Since Frank's favorite candidate

Kaufman was ensconced elsewhere, and because Biggers swore he wasn't exaggerating, Frank wrote Benchley and offered him a job without having met him. (His hilarious speech to the Contribunion occurred a few weeks later.) Frank told Benchley to drop everything and offered him a spectacular $40 a week. When the young man hesitated, Frank telegraphed that "your future hangs on the result" and rushed off to Boston to reel him in.

Benchley met Frank and Damon Runyon, who'd come along with Frank for the Harvard-Yale game, Saturday morning at breakfast at the Copley Hotel. In their first conversation, Adams and Benchley discovered shared reverences, especially for George Ade. The young man invited Frank to spend Saturday and Sunday nights in his wife's bed. (She was in the hospital, having recently given birth to Nathaniel.) The young father joined the *Tribune* staff in New York a few weeks later, there, along with Adams, Folwell, and Hill, to father the Sunday magazine's first issue.

The eight-page, newspaper-sized weekly represented an ambitious enterprise because of its outspokenness and broad selection of subjects. Its outlook was, like Frank's, progressive, lively, and up to the minute. Issues contained articles written by important men like New York governor Charles S. Whitman, presented "in a spirit of fairness [since] this paper has consistently opposed many of the Governor's acts and policies"; U.S. commissioner of immigration Frederic C. Home, who wrote admiringly of Robert La Follette, calling him "The Little Giant of the U.S. Senate," predicting that his "fight to drive privilege out of politics will be intensified on the floor of the Republican national convention, at the door of which privilege lurks." (Frank wasn't keen on La Follette's style. In the Diary he was "deeply disappointed that La Follette must speak in such a manner of an evangelist and employ many gestures and cause his voice to tremble and such like theatrik ways.")

Sing Sing Prison warden Thomas Mott Osborne wrote a thoughtful critique of John Galsworthy's play *Justice*, from the standpoint of an experienced prison reformer. He called the drama a masterpiece, adding in sentiments expressed by other reformers seventy years later that "we need to learn a man should come out of prison a better and not a worse man than when he went in, and that any system that does not accomplish this is a disgraceful failure. Punishment is revenge and the law should mete discipline."

Frank generously offered writers a wider audience than they usually addressed. George Kaufman appeared several times. So did John Reed.

Walter Lippmann and others were regularly reprinted from the pages of the *New Republic*. In April, excerpts from Amy Lowell's address to the Authors' League were published. Max Eastman, socialist editor of *The Masses*, wrote an essay that challenged newsstand operators Ward and Gow for refusing to carry his publication.

Alice Duer Miller authored an angry, often sarcastic column, "Are Women People?", containing feminist comments on news stories, the battle to win women their right to vote, and the even more bitter struggle for equality.

But serious as these and other articles were, at the heart of the Sunday magazine was its humor. This sensibility presented itself in its drawings and cartoons, in the regular last-page story by Montague Glass, which eavesdropped on dialect conversations between Luis Birsky, a real estate salesman, and Barnett Zapp, a blouse manufacturer.

Rea Irvin drew a weekly cartoon series, "This Day in History," commemorating the anniversary of events like "The day Queen Elizabeth lost her collar button" and "The day the American cocktail was perfected." Themes and cartoons much like Gluyas Williams' "The day the bar of soap sank at Procter and Gamble" appeared many years later in *The New Yorker*. And, one Sunday in 1916, Irvin etched—on a photograph of a slum street—the profile of an eighteenth-century dandy with ruffled cuffs and shirt: a young Eustace Tilley, without monocle.

William Hill, whose black wash drawings resembled Charles Dana Gibson's, took an entire page every week to observe and comment upon the city scene, for example, "The upper West Side discovers Greenwich Village," in which each of the several illustrations depicted the superior sophistication of Village types, such as when the aghast "Mike the waiter sees a man put ice and three lumps of sugar in his Chianti," and a hopelessly bored saloon pianist plays "A Perfect Day" for the matron sitting at a table next to him, dabbing at her eyes.

And Arthur Folwell parodied a famous poem every week in his illustrated series "Movies That Might Have Been."

Robert J. Wildhack wrote and illustrated a biting series of verses called "How to Make Money." L. M. Glackens' bold drawings included numbers and arrows pointing to components that proved the point of the accompanying verse, a technique used much by Benchley in later years. Among the various methods of making money suggested were Selling Phony Gold Mines, Counterfeiting, Short-Changing, Marrying It, Strike Breaking, and Child Labor:

Take a child of eight or nine
To your factory, mill or mine;
Take his sisters and his brothers—
If they sicken, there are others;
They are human? Yes, but then
They are cheaper far than men.

If humor was at the heart of the magazine, Robert Benchley was the heart. At first he wrote book reviews. Volumes he selected had titles like *Pettingill's Perfect Fortune Teller and Dream Book.* "In this latest addition to the Elite Library series," said Benchley, "Mr. Pettingill has fulfilled the promise given in his earlier works, viz., *The Book of Riddles and 500 Home Amusements* and *The Fireside Magician, or the Art of Natural Magic Made Easy.* Here is the same easy style and analytical mind, with perhaps a more mature touch, which serves to lend authority to his exposition. . . . The tone of the book is frankly fatalistic, almost depressingly so, and there runs through it a note that is reminiscent of Freud in its insistence on the significance of dream stimuli. In fact, in its first editions, Professor Pettingill's work antedates that of Freud although the latter has never made any public acknowledgment of his indebtedness."

Spalding's Official Baseball Record Book was an annual compilation of box scores and batting, pitching, and fielding records. Benchley called the latest one of a "stirring series, [although] the insertion of the names of other characters . . . would have served to conceal the sameness of the incidents."

In his review of *The Young Lady's Friend* (originally published in 1836), Benchley announced that "eating with your knife is not unladylike." Writing about the 1916 edition of *The New York City Directory*, he spoke of it enthusiastically as "a fairyland for browsers," but when it came right down to it, he admitted the work was "disappointing, even artificial because of its superficiality of treatment."

After a few issues he abandoned the popular book reviews and instead wrote essays about whatever caught his fancy. He quickly established himself as a likable fellow much like anybody's brother-in-law, somebody perplexed and captivated by everyday situations and incidents. His sense of wonder held to ordinary things, as if he were seeing them for the first time. He probed, reflected, and reexamined, all the while making unusual, slightly akimbo observations. In his review of the mystery melodrama *Lost in New York* he bragged that he'd caught on early in the evening: "To begin with, it was too elegant a home for any strictly honest person."

Upon the discovery of an ancient skull shaped (in Benchley's singular vision) like a foot, he mused, "Did Prehistoric Man Walk on His Head?" In "Do Jelly Fish Suffer Embarrassment?" the soft-hearted Benchley asked, "How often have you wondered this? Did you ever stop to poke fun at them for being so flat and wobbly? Did you ever twit them for not knowing how to speak French? Or ridicule them for not wearing cool summer underwear? . . . On the other hand, it has been argued that jelly fish have no real sense of shame or they wouldn't behave as they do. . . . No good can come of plaguing jelly fish."

When Frank took the month of July off for a trip to California, he left Benchley and Taylor in charge of the magazine. Gaily they sent the Adamses off with a stack of presents they brought to the train—a croquet set, a sandpile bucket and shovel, an album of gag photos.

The group had a good time in the Boss's absence. On the first Sunday he was gone a special page appeared: "Our Own Science Page." An article, "Efficiency in the Household," parodied the *Tribune* Institute. ". . . Let us housewives begin by taking up all the floors in the house," it said. "With no floors, countless steps could be saved, and there would be the decided advantage of having the whole house thrown open, with one room being as easy of access as another. Any one working in one of the upstairs chambers, for instance, could reach the kitchen in no time if there were no floors intervening."

"Items of Interest" included little-known facts:

Soft coal is much better than hard coal as a stuffing for sofa cushions.

For the boy of five, a gold fish muzzle makes a pretty toy.

Old electric light bulbs make excellent Chianti bottles.

And, later in the month, "Our Own Home Magazine Page" provided an advice column offering homemaking tidbits:

Dear It Has Been My Experience: I used to suffer from nose-bleed until I discovered the following simple remedy: Drop a heaping tablespoonful of Portland Cement up each nostril and hold the head back until it has hardened.

The editor of the feature "Among the Shops," unearthed hard-to-find bargains like "hand-laundered crab-nets," "dainty hand-painted china ear muffs," "hand-carved cornerstones."

In later months Benchley essays included "Celebrating Chewing

Gum's Fiftieth Birthday'' and ''Well, What's Good Today, Otto?''
about a tour of restaurants with a board of health inspector. (''As the
manager is dressed, so the food is inclined.'')

With the inspired lunacy, the overriding element of Benchley's
personality was his strong impulse for decency and fairness. He sided
with the underdog, the harassed, the well-meaning person in a world
run amok. His expert shots were invariably aimed at self-righteous
people who took themselves seriously and acted as if they thought they
were better than everybody else. This integrity was basic to him, the
main reason for the love he engendered. Unlike many of his contemporaries, who cultivated their gifts with acerbic distance (H. L. Mencken
was a prime example), there was nothing misanthropic about Robert
Benchley.

He went on to write for *Life, Vanity Fair*, and *The New Yorker*,
journeyed to Europe, where he played with the legendary Gerald Mur-
phys and their friends, to Hollywood, where he wrote and starred in
short movies and appeared as third lead in others. But he never wrote
the long book he wanted to, or anything that he was really proud of,
quitting writing entirely a couple of years before he died. He had a
curious marriage. His wife and family lived in Scarsdale, New York,
he in New York City and in Hollywood. Sometimes he didn't see them
for months at a time. When in New York, he was a regular patron of
Polly Adler's well-known pleasure house, and he maintained relationships with a series of beautiful young women. Yet he cared deeply for
Gertrude and spent time every summer with her and their boys at their
place on Nantucket. From his teetotal origins, he became somebody
who was drunk much of the time. In fact, alcoholism contributed to his
death at the young age of fifty-seven.

He was kind, generous, gentle, haunted. And twentieth-century
American comedy owes its soul to him.

III

Although for many years Americans referred condescend-
ingly to Russia as ''the sleeping giant,'' in 1914 the U.S.
could have answered to the same title. National energies
had long been associated with the steady push westward,
the breaking and settling of the frontier, the domestication of what was
left of the Indians (and their impossible conversion from hunters and
nomads into farmers), construction of cities and railroads, the awesome

efforts of immigrants endlessly arriving on both coasts. Foreign entanglements were of little interest to Americans who felt safe behind thousands of miles of oceans. They were too busy to pay much attention to foreign affairs, anyway. Even though their relatives lived on other continents, they were content when the national press sensationalized, ignored, or patronized disputes between other countries. It was a self-centered viewpoint. People often sent money to relatives in the old country, but they didn't necessarily feel any connection with how things were over there.

One of the curious aspects of American feeling was its strong anti-German bias. Germans made up the third largest American ethnic group, behind the English and Africans, so it might have been expected that strong defenses of the German position vis-a-vis the English and French would be promulgated, that debates and emotional confrontations would take place on a large scale. This didn't happen. Americans hated the "Huns." Everyone wanted to show what America meant to him, and it almost always meant English culture, tradition, and language. People rushed to change their German last names to acceptable English translations. Muller became Miller. Austerlitz, Astaire.

In the *New York Tribune* magazine, Frank published a series of articles about German military training, written by somebody identified only as a son of a former major in the German army who'd spent some years as a cadet at the Prussian military academy at Potsdam. The biased essay was subtitled "The Prussian Officer—Autocrat and Slave," and paragraph headings included: "Money or no money, an officer must pay his debts or kill himself"; "To the German civilian an officer is a divinity"; "Dueling among officers is not only legal but encouraged." Propaganda like this circulated nationally.

When, on May 7, 1915, the Cunard Liner *Lusitania* was torpedoed by a German submarine off the coast of Ireland, killing twelve hundred passengers (including hundreds of Americans, Charles Frohman and Alfred Vanderbilt among them), outraged cries reverberated throughout the land. It didn't matter that the British Admiralty, with its First Lord Winston Churchill, and the American State Department had acted deliberately, challenging the Germans to sink the ship by cramming it with arms for the Allies as well as innocent passengers. The fact that the *Lusitania* was a munitions transport ship was kept from the public until well after the war. The incident was widely reported as evidence of German inhumanity, pointing up the differences between the honorable Allies and their crazed adversaries, who senselessly murdered women and children. An article in the *New York Tribune* magazine pointed out that "the captain of the submarine that sunk the *Lusitania* was probably once a normal, good-hearted German youngster, but eight years of training in one of Prussia's military academies got to him."

As a liberal editor of a widely read progressive newspaper, Frank directed much of his effort toward maintaining a balance in the opinions he presented. He reprinted a rabble-rousing essay from the *New Republic*, ostensibly focusing on "preparedness" but in reality demanding commitment to solution of social problems having nothing to do with waging war:

> What do they mean when they shout "preparedness"? Are they willing to unify and socialize the railroads and the means of communication, to regulate rigorously basic industries like steel and coal mining; are they willing to control the food supply and shipping and credit; are they willing to recognize labor as a national institution? . . . Are they willing to end the destruction of national vitality through unemployment, child labor, overwork and poverty? . . . [Or] do they mean simply a little preparedness, a better . . . line of military defense, and all other things left to drift?

After the sinking of the *Lusitania*, American sympathy was aroused and intervention on the side of the Allies was assured. The national press proclaimed the bloodthirsty nature of the enemy and stirred readers to a state of frenzy. Who cared that the royal families of Europe were all related to one another and that the Kaiser was the King's first cousin? The Kaiser stood for inhumanity, depravity, decadence. Germans, Austrians and Prussians were Evil. Their allies, the Turks, were known to eat babies. The English and French were Good; hot-blooded Italians were Good too, once they'd got around to deciding whose side they were on. Russians were Good (the nice if henpecked Tsar was yet another cousin of King George) until they deserted the Allies to become Godless Communists, thereby betraying Christianity and Colonel Blimp in a single stroke. But that came later.

In April, 1917, the U.S. declared war on the Central Powers, led by Germany. At the behest of President Woodrow Wilson, historians fell in line and became propagandists. Textbooks and pamphlets were produced eagerly reinterpreting history to fit the goals of the War Department. In his widely read essay on a new and enlarged understanding of the Monroe Doctrine, Cornell Professor Carl Becker argued that what had once been a policy to protect America and its neighbors from invasion by foreign powers should be expanded to one which guaranteed America's ideological interests, wherever they were threatened—even in distant places. (Much later Professor Becker changed his mind and despaired that making the world safe for democracy had actually meant making it safe for dictators.)

In 1914, as one of several acts assuring America's intervention on the side of England, British agents had cut the transatlantic cables between Germany and the United States. The result of this action was that only English wires transmitted war news to America. Unsurprisingly, this copy was heavily slanted in favor of Great Britain. Despite this, there were early efforts by some American newsmen to remain neutral, or at least fair. A group of them (from the *Chicago Daily News* and the *Chicago Tribune*, the *New York World,* the Associated Press, and *Collier's*, and *World's Work* magazines) slogged along with the German army in its spring campaign and reported in a joint communique that they'd seen no evidence of atrocities. Their view wasn't popular.

The following year there were five hundred American newspaper reporters in Europe. By mid-1917 there were many more. But they were hamstrung by the mountains of red tape and the fearsome scope of the war and its rigorous censorship. Despite the restrictions on their ability to gather news, they had the best reputation of any group of journalists. Newspaper historian Frank Mott claims that "the American people were better informed of the progress of the war than those of any other country in the world."

Well informed or otherwise, the home front went beserk. As soon as war was declared, it became treasonable to criticize the government or to call for discussion of the German position. The U.S. Post Office refused to deliver newspapers it suspected of subversive opinions, and many publications went bankrupt as a result. Federal agents hauled people to jail for obstructing recruiting efforts or for preaching disloyalty. Pacifists and socialists were thrown into jail because of their "subversive" opinions.

Hundreds of public schools banned the teaching of German and destroyed copies of works by Goethe, Nietszche, and Schiller. Some orchestras were forbidden to play music by Wagner and Beethoven. Vigilantes calling themselves "four-minute men" interrupted movies to harangue audiences on topics ranging from "The Deceit of Germany" to "The Inherent Brutality of the Germanic Tribes." Bolsheviks, thought to be equally untrustworthy, were hounded and jailed in a brutal crusade begun by President Woodrow Wilson's attorney general, A. Mitchell Palmer, a Quaker who ran amok.

It wasn't the First Amendment's finest hour.

IV Publisher Ogden Reid was unhappy with the *New York Tribune* magazine after a year and a half. Not noted for his sense of humor, he felt that the publication had become too big for its britches, that some of its most uproarious features too obviously ridiculed the rest of the paper he'd inherited from his father. Ersatz reportage and ridiculous advice to wives were not his idea of fun. Besides, he felt that the terrible war in Europe demanded seriousness of purpose, and the magazine remained unreconstructed despite its large number of solemn articles (too many of them left-wing, another matter that increasingly irritated Reid). Despite warnings, the approach of Frank and his staff remained irreverent. Reid thought reverent commitment appropriate. So he ordered the magazine dismantled.

The last issue appeared in June 1917. Twenty years later Frank remembered the magazine's year and a half as the most fun he'd ever had. He was acutely saddened when it ended. He shook hands with his young staff and did what he could to help them find work elsewhere.

As always, he rebounded quickly. The air around him throbbed with the excitement of a country readying itself for war. Such activity and purpose invariably produced frenzied gaiety, and Frank wasn't immune. He went back to "The Conning Tower," pulled a few strings, and awaited his country's call. In October, the thirty-five-year-old columnist was commissioned captain in the army by President Wilson, via the U.S. mail. He was filled with patriotic fervor and looked forward to serving overseas. Before shipping out, he told of "coalless Mondays" in New York, when householders went without heat for the war effort, as yet an unremarkable sacrifice since fall temperatures hovered pleasantly around seventy degrees. To save coal during the winter, the theaters closed an extra day a week but gave additional matinees. He reported that chorus men's names and ages were printed in theatrical programs, sometimes followed by their draft numbers so that audiences could assess who was doing whose bit for Uncle Sam. Many rushed to enlist. Still, American military action was little more than an inspiring idea. Martial music swept people into paroxysms of idealism and speech making, but few knew what war was really like. Only older people remembered the Civil War, and sometimes it seemed that nobody but Teddy Roosevelt and William Randolph Hearst had been affected by the war with Spain. By 1917 Europe had struggled for three years through one bloody battle after another, but in America there was a bellicose patina obscuring the reality. Inexperienced Americans couldn't picture the horrors of stalemated modern warfare. They expected glory.

Frank reported in a burst of exuberance how "some fellows even refer to us, as they grip us by the hand the day or week or the month before we embark, as You Lucky Guy. Which we are.'' At thirty-six he was old but eager, a happy participant in the swelling national commitment. He awaited his orders impatiently.

Finally they came. Minna joined the Food Administration, and Frank left for Europe. (During his absence, someone named Frederick F. Vandewater appeared in the *New York Tribune* as his surrogate.) When Frank arrived in France, he was quickly sent to Paris, where a new publication was being distributed to American soldiers. It was called the *Stars and Stripes*, and plans called for a staff made up entirely of enlisted men. In charge was Major Frederick Palmer, formerly with *Everybody's* magazine, then with the Associated Press. He'd been the only American correspondent named to accompany Lord Kitchener's forces in France, but since dozens of other journalists ignored official sanction and went along too, the honor was hardly important. Palmer wrote the U.S. Field Service regulations dealing with newspaper coverage of the war and was chief American censor. He appointed Lieutenant Guy T. Viskniskki publisher and managing editor of the *Stars and Stripes*, but once Private Harold Ross came along, Viskniskki's authority was in jeopardy.

Ross, a rumpled twenty-five-year-old Pfc. from Salt Lake City, had ideas of his own about the identity of the editor. A high school dropout, he'd worked on several papers in America's Far West, including the Denver *Post*, the *Salt Lake City Tribune*, and the *San Francisco Call*, as well as the *Atlanta Journal*, the *Hudson* (New Jersey) *Observer*, and the *Brooklyn Eagle*. Ambitious, if curiously footloose, he was so eager for the top job on the armed forces newspaper that shortly after he learned of its existence, he went AWOL and hurried to Paris to claim the position. With his tiny portable typewriter in one hand and a battered duffle bag in the other, he reported to Viskniskki, who was a veteran of service with the army corps of engineers in Puerto Rico during the Spanish-American war. Despite the older man's experience and important civilian position with *McClure's* syndicate, Ross wasn't intimidated.

Viskniskki liked to throw his weight around and was nonplussed at the upstart competition—a Pfc., no less. From time to time, he threatened humorlessly to have Ross arrested to hamper his trouble making. But he didn't bargain on Ross's tenacity, talent, or capacity for making loyal friends. Ross skillfully persuaded the staff of his expertise and inexpendability, receiving first their admiration, then their backing, and finally the appointment itself, when the others went on strike to demand it. Upon learning that the paper wasn't going to be put out unless Ross was at its head, the brass promoted Viskniskki to major and transferred him to Germany. A victorious Ross took over the paper, outranked by almost everybody on his staff.

They were a talented group of individualists. Corporal John T. Winterich, a New York newspaperman, wrote the headlines and was the second person appointed. Advertising manager Bill Michael was a foot soldier happily transferred from the trenches around Paris to the *Stars and Stripes* office, which at first occupied two crowded rooms on the second floor of the Hotel St. Anne. Pfc. Hudson Hawley, Yale '14, barely five feet tall, was a displaced machine gunner, formerly a reporter with the *Hartford Times* and the *New York Sun*. For a harried few weeks, he tried to write the entire paper by himself.

To round out the staff, from Tennessee in February came cavalry Lieutenant Adolph Ochs, who administered the office and was listed as the paper's treasurer. New officer-in-charge was Mark Watson, popular editor from the *Chicago Tribune*. His assistant, later to become FDR's press secretary, was infantry Captain Stephen T. Early of Washington, D.C. Other additions included Sergeant Alexander Woollcott, from Phalanx, New Jersey, and Hamilton College in New York; Lieutenant Grantland Rice of the 115th Field Artillery; cartoonist Albian A. Wallgren, a marine private from Philadelphia; Private George Boas, who would head the postwar philosophy department at Johns Hopkins University, and in March, Captain Franklin Pierce Adams. (Frank's arrival, on the Sunday preceding Easter, was a day of heavy shelling. He referred to it as "Bomb Sunday.")

Words on Taking a New Job

When I was a civilian in the typing days of peace,
I spilled a column daily, sans vacation or surcease.
I whittled many a mournful wheeze and many a halting rhyme
To cop the fleeting jitney and to snare the elusive dime.
I justed by the carload and I frolicked by the bale,
When I used to write a column on the
New
    York
        Mail.

The years continued flitting, as the years are wont to do,
Until one New Year's Eve I went and shifted my H. Q.
I wrote a ton of trifles and a mass of metric junk
To give me daily ammunish for my Barrage of Bunk.

Oh, many a paragraph I pulled and many a sassy squib,
When I ran a daily column on the
New
    York
        Trib.

Goodbye, O dull serenity! Ye days of peace, farewell!
I went—oho!—to fight the foe and hear the shot and shell.
Yet once again I find that I must hurl the merry josh,
Though I now command a column set against the beastly Boche.
But the grandest, proudest job I've ever had among the types
Is this job to run this column in
THE
    STARS
        AND
            STRIPES!

                                —F.P.A., 1918

Initially it was difficult for Ross to gather an appropriately experienced editorial staff because, when he requisitioned enlisted men from other outfits, company commanders often refused to permit the transfers. At first the newspaper was officially designated part of the U.S. Signal Corps. Military protocol dictated that each service branch jealously protect its men from intraservice kidnapping. Officers were unwilling to permit the lowly Signal Corps to raid their ranks for appropriately qualified journalists. The problem came to an ultimate solution when, after considerable negotiation—and information that the paper's circulation would soon be greater than that of the *New York Times*—the *Stars and Stripes* was reassigned. It came to rest under the auspices of the general staff, a place of great importance, with authority superseding all other military branches. There it stayed for the duration.

The *Stars and Stripes* developed into a lively eight-page newspaper of conventional size and format, with an editorial policy devoted to concerns of American soldiers and heavily censored but well-written news coverage. It offered a large variety of short stories, poems, letters to the editor, and columns. Regular features leaned on heartwrenching (and good-for-circulation) crusades and human-interest stories that echoed those in the yellow press. One campaign devised by Ross helped servicemen to adopt war orphans and detailed the procedure wherein any group or person within the American Expeditionary Force (A.E.F.) could sponsor a child for a year by spending a mere five hundred francs.

The Red Cross supervised the project, distributing photographs of the children and overseeing correspondence between orphans and soft-hearted new stepfathers. By the time of the Armistice, more than thirty-five hundred such children had been helped.

Every issue of the paper contained a sports page with, in its early numbers, articles and columns about the upcoming baseball season.

The weekly paper cost 10 cents, expensive in that day of 3-cent newspapers but necessary because Ross didn't want his paper to take on the tacky character of a barracks handout. Bill Michael hustled advertisers to help defray the cost of production and to increase the paper's resemblance to the hometown press. Fatima cigarettes regularly bought space, as did several Paris bistros and clothing stores. Punchy headlines, clear photographs and cartoons, and interesting, well-written stories quickly earned popularity with the doughboys, as did its policy, captured in the not quite true slogan, "BY Enlisted Men FOR Enlisted Men." Mail for homesick soldiers was irregular and heavily censored when it came; and even the lucky ones who received papers from the States yearned for news, not only from home but from the front. Nobody knew what was going on even a few miles away. Besides, by the time the stateside papers had been delivered, even their wildly distorted or blatantly untrue war coverage was old hat. Ross maintained rigorous standards, both in the quality of the writing and in the accuracy of the news he was permitted to print. In a few months his paper resembled other American papers and outclassed many.

Frank's participation was intense but short-lived. It was soon apparent that trench warfare didn't provide the best setting to read or polish contributions for a column like his, called "The Listening Post," in the *Stars and Stripes*. Nobody except Frank had time to hone elaborate rondeaux or translations from Horace. Besides, Ross was already publishing submissions from enlisted men in other parts of the paper, notably in columns called "The Army's Poets" and "Where It Comes From," which contained letters, often long ones, from soldiers and the editors' responses to them. Most important, Frank's brand of frivolity and understatement was out of step. It wasn't that jokes weren't circulating. Black humor and offbeat jokes were expected by-products of war. But Frank's fastidious humor skidded badly overseas. It didn't translate in the war zone.

Despite his misgivings, Frank was game. When he saw he'd have to write most of his material himself, he did. He produced ten columns between April 19 and June 14. It wasn't his best work, but it was characteristic. On censorship:

> *Ride a cock-horse to a certain British suburb,*
> *To see a Fine lady ride a fine horse.*

On Tennyson, "whether he likes it or not":

> *A certain distance,*
> *A certain distance,*
> *A certain distance onward!*
> *Into the eastern sector*
> *Rode a certain percentage of the* —— *Division.*

On the endless Parisian muck and rain:

> It occurs to us why baseball never has been the national pastime of France. The double-headers would pile up so that when a sunny afternoon came along there'd be about thirty-two games to play off.

And,

> *Bill's fighting for his country,*
>   *He rises to explain;*
> *Lorraine is where he's fighting—*
>   *With the accent on the rain.*

Uncharacteristically homesick, he needled a Chicago paper:

> "Michigan," observes the *Tribune,* "won the most points and was declared the victor." Which proves that things have not changed much at home. The winners of the most points still are returned the victors.

Not everything was bleak and thankless, however. There was a regular poker game in Montmartre and welcome partying when Heywood Broun brought his bride, the Adamses' old friend, journalist Ruth Hale, to Paris. Frank had been best man at their wedding. He called them "the clinging oak and the sturdy vine." Their buddies celebrated the popular marriage by buying the couple many dinners and bottles of wine in Left Bank hangouts. The pair spent the rest of their unusual honeymoon scurrying to various European battlefields to observe and report on the war. And despite what turned out to be the impossibility of transplanting "The Conning Tower" to the *Stars and Stripes,* Frank and Ross became friends, both of them sensibly avoiding embarrassment about F.P.A.'s lack of success. Instead, they established a lifelong relationship based on gruff affection and a remarkable, shared reverence for language and its forms.

Camaraderie on the *Stars and Stripes* was something the members of its staff would later remember and cherish. But the relentless boredom of life behind the front lines and especially the feeling of being hopelessly beyond the center of things sapped Frank's enthusiasm. He was a big-city, peacetime newsman, uncomfortable with the role of morale booster. Disapprovingly he contemplated the dog-loves-soldier story "Verdun Belle" by the clever but wet-eyed Aleck Woollcott and knew he couldn't write such stuff, even if he wanted to. Back on the *Trib*, he and Benchley would have had a great time with such muck. But Benchley and most of Frank's fans were thousands of miles away.

War was hell, and Frank's hell had the unique component of his sitting without prospect or plan behind a desk miles from where interesting things happened and people were in danger. The situation filled him with feelings of futility. No soldier was happier when the war and his service in it ended. Once sentimentally patriotic like everybody else, Frank found that his experience had made him cynical. Many years later when Woollcott hosted a popular radio program, "The Town Crier," Frank wrote that when Aleck talked about the war, he was "still too sentimental about that silly, boring, rotten conflict that made nothing safe for democracy, nor was it a war to end wars."

He was transferred to the U.S. Army Intelligence Division under Colonel Palmer in Paris for the summer and fall of 1918, then shipped back to the States. Woollcott, with characteristic elan, arranged for the gang at the *Stars and Stripes* to be "hired" by the Paris office of the *New York Times*, then fired as soon as their discharges came through so they could all go home on the same ship.

Frank, thirty-seven, returned to his Tower on January 19, 1919. He hadn't been thrilled by the war or his performance in it, but as usual he had the last word:

> *I didn't fight and I didn't shoot.*
> *But General, how I did salute!*

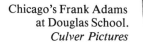

Chicago's Frank Adams
at Douglas School.
Culver Pictures

New York's Newspaper Row
in the early 1900s. Left to right:
City Hall, the World Building,
the Tribune Building, and the
Times Building. *The New
York Public Library Picture
Collection*

Minna Schwartz's bridegroom, bright
new columnist for the New York *World*.
Culver Pictures

At the top of the *World* in 1924.
Culver Pictures

George S. Kaufman, Marc
Connelly and Lynn Fontanne
at a rehearsal of *Dulcy*.
Culver Pictures

Robert Benchley: The heart
of the Algonquin set.
Nikolas Muray

Heywood Broun: The conscience of the Algonquin set. *Culver Pictures*

Edna Ferber, prolific author, Frank's friend and counselor. *The New York Public Library Picture Collection*

Dorothy Parker, whom F.P.A. "raised from a couplet." *Pinchot*

Frank and Edna St. Vincent Millay on a hot summer afternoon in Maine. *Photo courtesy of Timothy Adams*

Alexander Woollcott, owlish, perverse, at the center of the Round Table. *Vandamm*

Frank's lifelong friend, Harold Ross, founder of *The New Yorker* and probably the best magazine editor who ever lived. *Nikolas Muray*

Alice Duer Miller at Barnard, class of 1899. *The New York Public Library Picture Collection*

Frank and Esther, fascinated with each other. *George Eastman House*

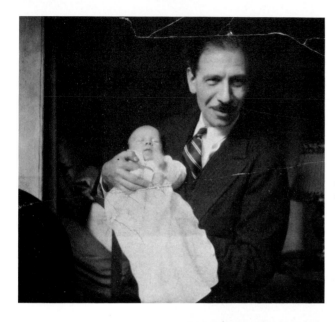

A first-time father at 45.
*Photo courtesy of
Timothy Adams*

Lyons Plains, the house
in Connecticut where
Frank and Esther moved
their family in 1937.
*Photo courtesy of
Timothy Adams*

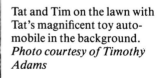

Tat and Tim on the lawn with
Tat's magnificent toy auto-
mobile in the background.
*Photo courtesy of Timothy
Adams*

F.P.A. at his cluttered desk at the *Herald Tribune*, in 1935.
Wide World

Panel of the second broadcast of "Information Please." From left to right: Marcus Duffield, F.P.A., Paul de Kruif and Lewis Hacker. *Culver Pictures*

Showing only an echo of his fabled charm, a very sick F.P.A. toasts starlet Diana Lynn with a paper cup at an actors' shindig in 1948. *Culver Pictures*

PART TWO

CHAPTER FOUR

The Twenties

Nothing is more responsible for the good old days than a bad memory.

—F.P.A.

I The 1920s burst into America like revelers at a New Year's Eve party. Capitalism, heroism, invention, old-time religion, romance, grit, and the Republican Party were monuments to the American dream. Busy for a century and a half *becoming*, after the Great War the country regarded itself as *finished*, and just about perfect. Anybody could do anything, and even the women could vote. The war heard the last gasp of the stodgy Victorians on both sides of the ocean. Here came the new decade, all decked out with ribbons, spangles, and a brass label proclaiming itself "Made in the U.S.A."

Prosperity resulted from the know-how of American businessmen, so their government avoided interfering with them. Regulations that might have required fair recompense and protective safety measures for workers went unenacted. Businessmen decided what was best for their employees. At U.S. Steel, that meant a twelve-hour day, sometimes seven days a week, at wages amounting to less than the minimum standards set and then ignored by the pussyfooting U.S. Department of Commerce. Abundant natural resources were noted and exploited joyfully as an endless treasure, a gift from God to his favorite sons. Sunshine and optimism ruled the day.

The continent was settled at last, and great-grandchildren of immigrants claimed its riches. They reacted against foreigners who unrelentingly demanded entry, space, schools, and jobs. "Old" families wanted American abundance protected. All the poor people of the world

113

seemed to covet it, yearning for absorption into the United States. And who could blame them? The United States was thought of as the end of the rainbow by both its residents and others who longed for a new start in a young country unscarred by centuries of war and poverty.

But where would it all end?

Many Americans resented the streams of newcomers. Each of them appeared to have endless numbers of odd-talking relatives awaiting permission to enter. In 1923 immigration was drastically curtailed. Then Congress defined acceptable immigrants through quotas ("good" immigrants were from western Europe, undesirables from everyplace else). Growing America, desperately in need of cheap labor, had opened its doors to immigrants who hungered to work at any task for any wage. Grown America, with abundant native-born labor—consisting of large numbers of children—discriminated among points of origin and closed itself to most of the world's population.

In 1919, Europe agonized over the catastrophe of hubris that had robbed it of a whole generation of young men. But United States participation in World War I had lasted only a year and a half. There wasn't any permanent damage to the nation's youth, and the politicians boasted it was good old American know-how that had saved Europe. The United States ended up paying the Allies for most of their war costs. American bankers knew their function as the world's bank would enrich and empower their country. The way was clear for an explosion of patriotic materialism. Salesmanship was king.

Except for a loss of humility, the country hadn't strayed far from its beginnings. In 1630, Puritan John Winthrop's "City on the Hill" was a showplace honoring divine order. In it, he said, the rich wouldn't "eat the poor, nor the poor and despised rise up against their superiors." Since then the *Arabella*'s mission into the wilderness had evolved to become a race for God's major blessing: prosperity. Americans in the 1920s credited themselves with innate superiority and the wonderful ability to understand and act upon God's plan. They knew God wanted you to make money, and if you were poor, it was your own fault. Never before was avarice so celebrated, or the idea of liberty so clearly defined as the freedom to get rich. Even Woodrow Wilson announced that every man had his price and admitted he hoped his was high enough so that nobody ever offered it.

The times jangled with booming real estate development, goods produced by ever-expanding smokestack industries, history's first unemployment figures, union dues and strike busting, Model Ts, short skirts, rolled silk stockings, radio programs, the reborn Ku Klux Klan, movies and airplanes, and flappers who smoked. Bad speller Scott Fitzgerald came to town, decorated his wall with 122 rejections, then authored a best-selling novel celebrating American youth. He and his bride prepared to be twenty-three forever. When the Black Sox scandal hit the World Series in 1919, the game staggered, and heartbroken fans thought it might not recover: "Say it ain't so, Joe." But in 1920 the thrifty Boston team unwittingly saved the game by selling Babe Ruth to the Yankees for $100,000, and the glory years began.

It was the time for Prohibition. In New York City the Volstead Act forced posh establishments underground, often literally, into the basements of staid-looking brownstones. Prohibition brutalized once elegant Times Square, and it never recovered. In June 1923, receivers auctioned the silver and glassware from once peerless Delmonico's, favorite of Enrico Caruso, David Belasco, and Jenny Lind. In two days the sale brought $22,000. The sixteen crystal goblets used exclusively by John D. Rockefeller when he'd dined there "almost daily" were sold for a disappointing $26.

Devastating as Prohibition was to Times Square and its legitimate cafes and restaurants, nobody took it seriously. Who wanted to celebrate an anniversary or impress a best girl without a bottle of champagne? People could get a drink whenever they wanted one. The whole idea was preposterous.

Sixty percent of the national electorate elected Warren G. Harding president. (The wife of a stock broker casting her first ballot in the 1920 election remarked, "I don't see why they gave women suffrage, it only makes twice as many votes to count.") Election polling places had been in unsavory places like backrooms of saloons; after 1920 they were moved to schoolrooms and churches so as not to offend delicate sensibilities. At the same time, more women than ever before pursued postgraduate programs at American universities, even though their chances of marriage and motherhood decreased drastically with every year of college. In the 1920s more Ph.D.s were awarded to women than in the self-congratulating 1960s.

Along with Scott and Zelda, other gifted youngsters clamored into New York. They found work with the newspapers and on the new slick magazines. Before the war the *Saturday Evening Post* was the only national publication with a circulation topping one million. While it remained in the catbird seat for another forty-five years, other magazines like *Life, Judge, Vanity Fair, The New Yorker, Collier's, American Mercury, Cosmopolitan, Ladies' Home Journal, Smart Set, Woman's Home Companion, Liberty, McCall's*, and *American* captured the country's imagination and made way for blockbusters like Luce's *Life* and the Wallaces' *Reader's Digest*. The slick magazine represented a flamboyant departure from its parent, the small circulation weekly: It was cheap, easy to read, often beautifully illustrated (covers suitable for framing), and sturdy enough to save from one week to another. It offered deeply researched series, as well as serialized novels and short stories. The magazines mixed fiction and nonfiction, so the public felt itself entertained—often with fine new writing—*and* well-informed. Burgeoning numbers of magazine readers became multimillion dollar markets for abundantly produced new consumer products. Advertising agencies prospered. For the first time Americans went into debt to buy goods on the installment plan.

Prolific, energetic writers were essential to the popular new medium, which voraciously devoured material. Writers leaped at the chance to write for the good money and recognition that magazines offered. It was an opportunity for them in much the same way early radio and television represented training and enrichment for other generations of new, ambitious writers.

The Equity strike of 1919 changed much. Actors, organized at last, sought half pay for rehearsals when they exceeded four weeks, full pay for extra performances during runs. When these diminutive demands were rejected, the actors struck. On August 7, 1919, Frank Bacon, star of the Broadway hit *Lightinin'*, closed his show and the casts of fourteen other plays walked out with him. Ed Wynn, in *Gaieties of 1919*, refused to appear onstage, as did John and Ethel Barrymore, their uncle John Drew, Marie Dressler, Al Jolson, and Eddie Foy. Bacon and his cast rented a stagecoach and drove around town with a big sign: ''Lightnin' Has Struck!'' The public supported the actors and by the time the strike ended a month later, forty shows had been shut down and sixteen more hadn't been able to open. Benefits to support the strike were given at the Lexington Avenue Opera House and at the Astor Hotel, where John Drew and Ethel Barrymore led the Grand March and even Mary Pickford and Douglas Fairbanks came from Hollywood to lend their support. The strike cost the producers $500,000 a week and in the end their losses amounted to more than $2 million. Finally producer John Golden called an emergency meeting and invited playwright Augustus Thomas to serve as a mediator. ''For God's sake, get in here and help us back-pedal,'' pleaded Golden. The producers gave in on every point, even to agreeing to full pay for rehearsals after four weeks.

Five years later in one season 228 new shows were produced on Broadway. That year playwrights replicated the actors' action by forming a group of their own, the Dramatists' Guild. It provided playwrights with desperately needed minimum guarantees and protections, hammered out through negotiations with mostly reluctant Broadway producers, who were rarely able to agree on anything, as they'd demonstrated in the Equity strike. Ziegfeld hated the Shubert brothers so much he refused to sit at the same table, even when his interests were involved.

By 1920 hundreds of young writers had swooped into Manhattan, fresh from the war in Europe. The time was ripe for an American literary explosion, both in print and on stage.

II In 1920, thirty-nine-year-old F.P.A.'s unique fame soared, more than the sum of its parts. Fifty years later Groucho Marx remembered that "in those days we all tried to get a piece into his column. When I finally got a little piece in it, just a little one, not more than an inch, I thought I was Shakespeare." Morrie Riskind, who, with George S. Kaufman, wrote the scripts for the hilarious Marx Brothers movies, said, "It would be almost impossible [now] to realize the influence Frank Adams had in New York at that time. If Frank recommended a book, people bought the book. If he recommended a show, you went to see the show. He had a tremendous influence. It was the thing everybody read. You could become well known just by getting your name in there." And after nurturing by F.P.A., a grateful John O'Hara dedicated his first novel, *Appointment in Samarra*, "To F.P.A."

Yet the popularity of "The Conning Tower" with Broadway and the literati didn't explain the fact of F.P.A. as a household word. His published ruminations remained continuously witty and topical but didn't put him in the same league with humorists George Ade or Finley Peter Dunne. But his fame was greater than theirs. Since many thousands more people read the column regularly than contributed to it, self-interest didn't explain more than a few dozen readers. His renown sprang from an intangible something that transcended his work, most of which was, after all, no more than momentarily interesting. F.P.A.'s stature was the consequence of a combination of propitious but uncontrollable circumstances. Wide new fascination with what he was interested in magnified the importance of his opinions in subjects that included sports, popular expression of the language, current plays and their actors and writers, books and authors, the escalating cost, perplexities, and inconveniences of urban living, nostalgia and the sharing of memories, like loving descriptions of childhood bicycling outfits or recitations of the lyrics to Gay Nineties' songs. Frank, by being himself, was recognized and esteemed as the intellectual's Everyman.

Unlike prewar America, which had galloped along without much self-awareness, after the war the country's curiosity about itself exploded in narcissistic profusion. Nobody could get enough gossip. Manhattan proclaimed itself the center of interest, and Frank was on the front lines, commenting on life there with sharpness and humor. But "The Conning Tower" wasn't a conventional gossip column, which was why it was impossible to duplicate, although it was widely imitated. F.P.A. never told or cared who was after somebody else's husband, or which spouses were being unloaded for how much money. Society weddings didn't interest him. There was never an element of prurience in his interest in other people. He was too well-mannered for that. And a desire to preserve his dignity prevented him from probing into somebody else's life. The kind of gossip he engaged in was extremely personal, having to do with his activities, his reactions to whatever captured his attention. What he wrote was extremely individualistic and self-centered. Day after day he showed how clever, or how grumpy and long suffering, or what a good friend, or how boorish or funny he was. Readers knew what he was reading, what he thought about, what his friends were doing and saying. His was an extremely subjective rendition, flattering to his readers because he gave them his most prized information: gossip about himself. Certainly it took a peculiar arrogance to assume people wanted to know about him, but that characteristic is invariably present in people who write publicly about themselves, from Benjamin Franklin to Eleanor Roosevelt. And the assumption, boldly made, was correct. He presented a continuously updated autobiography, not just in the Diary, but in every epigram, every verse, and every paragraph he wrote. His readers felt as if he were involving them in his life. Such trust and respect were much more valuable to them than endless conjecture about other people, no matter how glamorous they were.

In addition, "The Conning Tower" provided a how-to primer for the up-and-coming sophisticate. F.P.A. and his clever friends showed what the good life consisted of and that, democratically, it lay within the grasp of all. Post-World War I Americans nursed an intellectual inferiority complex, even while they strutted and bragged. Across the country an intense desire for self-improvement swelled, so it was important to know what books to read and what to think about them, what sports successful men followed, what professional teams they rooted for, what topics civilized conversation included. If Frank had been born twenty years earlier or later, it's doubtful that anybody would have heard of him, for his personality adroitly dovetailed with the mood and manners of that time, and no other.

F.P.A. expressed a confident, selective memory and intelligence with which to define the past and invent the present. While his most recent birthday qualified him for status well along in the middle-aged category, he wasn't stodgy. He enjoyed himself more than ever. He jumped around, mentioned this, hurried there, poked at this, and scorned that. His running commentary bobbed along, and by midmorning cosmopolites were heard to ask each other, "Have you read F.P.A. yet today?"

During the first part of the decade, contributions rarely made up more than half the column, often less. And F.P.A. favored his own epigrams and paragraphs more often than his verse, which was far more difficult to write—and time-consuming. Sometimes he claimed that the pressures of a daily deadline prevented him from taking special pains with his material, but the claim was transparently self-serving. He didn't mean for anybody to believe it. His readers knew the limits of his talent as well as he did, because he told them about it. When he talked about lending his fountain pen to Edna Ferber, then Zona Gale (author of the Pulitzer Prize winning novel, *Miss Lulu Bett*), and finally to George Ade, the poem was more wistful than funny, and concluded:

> *And so, fair fountain pen of mine,*
> *Thou canst achieve the mighty line.*
> *Perhaps, if such a thing can be,*
> *The difficulty lies with me.*

He knew his was a minor talent. He was able to appreciate the giants of classical and romantic poetry, and he had the critical honesty to perceive his slightness in comparison. But few wrote better light verse than did F.P.A., whose efforts often sparkled with the irresistible wit of the self-deprecator:

> *My desk is cleared of the litter of ages;*
> *Before me glitter the fair white pages;*
> *My fountain pen is cleaned and filled,*
> *And the noise of the office has long been stilled.*
> *Roget's Thesaurus is at my hand*
> *And I'm ready to do some work that's grand. . . .*

All of the proud ingredients mine
To build, like Marlowe, the mighty line.
But never a line from my new-filled pen
That couldn't be done by a child of ten.

Frank's Conning Tower persona was indistinguishable from the personality his friends knew; in both cases he was a wisecracking curmudgeon, an urbane tastemaker, a desirable dinner companion. He spoke and wrote with brilliant precision but unadventurously, without the embarrassment of untidy passion. With characteristic lack of insight, he mused that his short attention span and jerky style sprang from early and frequent attendance at vaudeville shows. As far as he was concerned, the fact that the column jumped from one thing to another was the result of instruction in that darkened schoolroom where the goal had been to grab the audience, dazzle them, and depart before anybody was able to reflect on substance, or lack of it. He ridiculed bores and never questioned why he so desperately feared being one himself. To prevent that fate, he didn't address any subject long enough for anybody to get glassy-eyed. He couldn't risk committing himself to something at which he might fail. *Lo* had been a catastrophe, and he never forgot the debacle or the pain it had caused him. So just as the variety act had ended with a ''wow'' finish, Frank wrote with an eye to the surprise ending, the twist, the punch line, intent always on pleasing his audience. He admitted that this style prevented him from being a Serious Writer—he invariably capitalized the phrase to show how amusing the idea was—but rationalized that he didn't want to be one, anyway. Revealingly, he felt it necessary to defend his style when nobody was criticizing it. He said, ''A desire for brevity tends to the jettisoning of unnecessary words.'' He thought, correctly, that many contemporary magazine pieces, novels, and speeches were too long and flowery. ''Underwriting is not so great or so common a literary sin as overwriting,'' he said ponderously, and it was a valuable lesson to his contributors and readers, many of whom became better writers than he was.

Often he was hilariously dogmatic. He never allowed himself or his audience to forget that he was, above all, a technician. ''Maybe I don't know good acting from bad,'' he said, ''but no commentator on matters of the theatre is a better speller than I am.''

In May 1920, Frank's heading for the following contribution was ''Quaint Doesn't Describe It'':

dear F.p.a.
have you seen

the may number
of the   dial?

there are
some poems   by
e. E.   cummings
which run   just
like
this

    and

         this
    and   this
few caps
    queer spac
ing
    and
   Everything

perhaps   they mark
the advent   of
a new School
of   poetry

rather quaint—
what?

The Dial was foremost among the "little magazines" of the 1920s. It had been founded in 1840 by the Transcendentalists. Margaret Fuller and Ralph Waldo Emerson were its first editors. The publication had traveled from Boston to Chicago and ended up in New York, where, in 1920 with Marianne Moore as editor, it started on its most distinguished—and last—nine years. By that time most of its pages were devoted to cultural and artistic criticism, but every issue presented a large amount of modern and experimental poetry, fiction, and excellent reproductions of paintings and other artwork. Despite its controversial reputation, the magazine was widely read and respected, although outspoken young poet William Carlos Williams seemed to agree with F.P.A. and his fans when he denegrated it in 1921: "If there is a loonier pack of nitwits in the world than you fellows who are making The Dial, they are not advertising it to the world as you are. This is the brazenest kind of prostitution, because it is colossal affectation. The Greenwich

Village brand of moral and spiritual and artistic degeneracy. You are not discovering new worlds, but only helping to ruin the beauty in this." But unlike F.P.A., Williams rethought his position. When he accepted the 1926 *Dial* award, he admitted it was "an epoch-making event for me, it put me on my feet." T. S. Eliot thought *The Dial* dull, that "there is far too much in it, and it is all second rate and exceedingly solemn." But it was *The Dial* that first published "The Waste Land."

In his continuous battle against the "new" poetry, F.P.A. gleefully quoted the president of Union College: "The important thing for most of us," he'd said, "is not to express ourselves too freely, but to cultivate ourselves to the point where we shall have something worth expressing."

"This sounds like a vicious thrust at the poetry of Mr. E. E. Cummings," said F.P.A.

He continued ridiculing the perplexing new poetry. A tongue-in-cheek thrust at Ezra Pound called him obscure, superegotistic, and pedantic, made fun of his "foolish affectations of indentation."

But it was Eliot for whom he saved his most disgusted parody:

AFTER READING THE WASTE LAND

I read "The Waste Land" riding
Down in the subway last evening.
Darn good, swell stuff, I said at times,
But I like rhymes.
I'm a conservative goof,
Aloof
From the poems amorphous.
I went to the orifice.
Terrible, rotten stuff, I thought Eliot's poem.
"Oh, the moon shone bright on Mrs. Porter
And on her daughter."
That's his impression.
O the moon shines bright
On the daughter of Officer Porter
Is charming Kitty.
Gentle sir, my heart is frolicsome and free—
Hey, but he's doleful, willow, willow waly!
Why do I always sing that going up the escalator?
City Hall Park
After dark.
He loves me; he is here!

Fa la la la!
Fa la la la!
Thought for ballade's refrain:
"Why should it get the Dial prize?"
They said Sir Kay the Senesch al
Nothing at all.
Tit willow, tit willow, tit willow.
Blah   blah   blah.

F.P.A. dismissed twentieth-century poetry because it didn't adhere to the rules he knew. His mockery, while amusing, demonstrated his rigidity, not a good thing for somebody who was supposed to be up to the minute. But he wasn't alone. Others shared his distrust of the curious new directions and excesses of the postwar decade, like Robert Frost, who said that "writing free verse [was] like playing tennis with the net down."

Heywood Broun's three-times weekly book column resided on the *New York Tribune* editorial page next to "The Conning Tower." When Scribner's published F. Scott Fitzgerald's *This Side of Paradise* in the spring of 1920, Broun was one of the few reviewers who wasn't rhapsodic about the new writer. He thought the book greatly overrated. "The enthusiasm leaves us not only cold but puzzled," he said. "Although its style makes no appeal whatsoever to us, we have not sufficient faith in our ear to be surprised when many other critics say that it is monstrously well written. We are puzzled chiefly because so many reviewers find this novel of Princeton life by a young graduate . . . sensational. . . ."

Frank shared Broun's opinion that reaction to the book missed much wrong with it. They became a two-man minority vote. F.P.A. aimed his remarks at Fitzgerald's cocky sloppiness; he called the book impudent and verbose, belittled Fitzgerald's idiomatic English. He gleefully listed spelling errors and mistakes in meaning:

Ashville	(Compton) McKenzie
Collar and Daniel's	Fanny Hurst
"First-Year Latin"	Lorelie
Mary Roberts Rhinehart	"Ghunga Dhin"
cut a swathe	flambuoyant
(Swinburne's) "Poems	flare (for flair)
and Ballades"	Gouveneer Morris
"Jenny Gerhardt"	Christie Mathewson

inexplicably (for inextricably) confectionary
Mont Martre Lyoff Tolstoi
tetotalling juvenalia
Samuel Johnston forborne
Celleni
stimulous
born (for borne)

Both Broun and Adams missed the lyricism that defined Fitzgerald's artistry. It was an oversight shared by many critics, most of whom didn't discover the incipient poetry either. They were interested in the young writer's titilating pictures of youth in the "raw." In this first novel Fitzgerald's gifts barely escaped annihilation under its mountains of overstatement and sophomoric attention to the energetic sexual adventures of the eastern college set. Much of the book read like a first draft. The rapture needed toning down; the technical carelessness indicated schoolboy haste and lack of concentration. F.P.A. was correct to point out the sloppiness.

He wasn't malicious. He wanted proofreading standards met and had no axe to grind with the young author. And he kept his readers' attention on the book for months (six months after its appearance, he said that "familiarity with an author's work is not essential to an editor. The 'Metropolitan' 's blurb about Mr. F. Scott Fitzgerald calls his novel *The Other Side of Paradise*").

Fitzgerald wasn't amused. He was badly hurt by the criticism, but it didn't take him long to forgive Broun, who was lovable and gentler than F.P.A. Scott took Heywood to lunch and told him it was a pity he'd reached the age of thirty without ever having tasted life. Broun laughed and agreed. But Fitzgerald nursed a grudge against F.P.A. for the rest of his life. Years later he still referred to Frank as "that horse's ass."

Tellingly, F.P.A., who was put off by Fitzgerald's self-conscious exuberance, missed the book's ominous importance to his own career.

With *This Side of Paradise*, youth suddenly discovered itself. Young people celebrated their youthful condition, not as a training ground for adulthood, but as a unique and interesting state in itself. Frank didn't sense this happening. There was no precedent for it. In failing to identify and adjust to the definitive style of the decade, and indeed the century, he lost ground. While he'd never claimed avant-garde status—he was up to the minute but never on the cutting edge—always before he'd attracted new readers every year, young people who wanted to emulate their elders by reading what they read and behaving as they did. In the Jazz Age, named, of course, by Fitzgerald, young people turned their backs on their elders in order to make up their lives as they went along. The old ways weren't their ways. F.P.A.'s currency brought him thousands of readers and made him famous. But although 1920 found him prosperous and admired, almost exactly mid-course in his career, there were clues to the impermanence of his status, the reason that, years later the people who'd heard of him thought him long dead. When "The Conning Tower" ended in 1937, F.P.A. was forgotten with brutal speed. As long as his views represented the current fashion, he sparked along effortlessly. But popular tastes swerve unpredictably. F.P.A. demanded adherence to various sets of rules. Modern and unstuffy as everybody knew he was, these values were leftover Victorianisms. In the 1920s most of his contemporaries shared them. But a new group of young people not so eager to be nurtured by the old ways was coming up. They wanted to experiment with new forms, new subjects, and new ways of looking at life. And nothing becomes passe so quickly as veneration for outmoded rules, or conventions that have lost their purpose.

As early as 1921, F.P.A.'s standing as arbiter and mentor to youth began to erode. He was wise to reemphasize contributors and to permit them to speak for the new era. But his own loss of currency would prove fatal.

Fortunately, the slide took a long time.

III

Nothing so closely defines the popular notion of the New York literati during the 1920s as the Algonquin set. To people born during the Depression or World War II, something magic and vanished clings to the idea of that fabled group. Nor does the phrase call up merely an image of sparkle, sophistication, and humor, although these qualities are boisterously present. The sense of the phrase holds a special aura of elegance—glamour with a bite. Americans aspire to a particular "with-it" humor, at once cutting, brilliant, and peculiarly democratic. You don't have to be rich to get a laugh or be laughed at. And in the group called the Algonquin Round Table, the essence of American urban humor was personified for the first time.

There were numerous famous precedents. Great Britain had its traditions: King Arthur's group, of course, gave its name to the American version—but the most celebrated English group was the bunch at the Mermaid Tavern in the seventeenth century. Theirs was a lively group that met to exchange quips, plays-on-words, insults, and bawdy stories, to shout with laughter over glasses of stout. Founded by Sir Walter Ralegh, members of this jubilant group of professional writers included John Donne and William Shakespeare.

"Can-you-top-this?" conversation has been an art form wherever English is spoken since long before the days at the Mermaid. No other language holds within it the opportunity for so many applications, so many variations on an idea, word, or phrase. English abounds with homonyms, synonyms, and antonyms, oxymora and onomatopoeia, chances for puns and rhymes and palindromes and double entendres, gags and twists of every stripe and color. For people gifted with verbal agility, large vocabularies, acuity, brains, and nerve, English has always been a perfect plaything. And a particularly American preoccupation with competition set the stage for the word games of the Algonks.

No lunch club has ever been so envied, admired, or criticized. Commentators, notably Edmund Wilson, found the group provincial, self-centered, and tiresome. "I was sometimes asked to join them," he said. (By whom?) "But I did not find them particularly interesting. They all came from the suburbs and 'provinces,' and a sort of tone was set . . . deriving from a provincial upbringing of people who had been taught a certain kind of gentility, who had played the same games and who had read the same children's books—all of which they were now able to mock from a level of New York sophistication." While he clearly intended to deprecate the group, a trace of sour grapes wafted from the comment, as well as the faint specter of a little boy who'd been left out of other children's games. Wilson was in the minority, anyway. The Round Table was widely admired.

It all started as a practical joke.

Publicist John Peter Toohey arranged a meeting with *New York Times* drama critic Alexander Woollcott (lately with Adams, Ross, and Rice on the *Stars and Stripes*, and, in 1920, George Kaufman's boss). He hoped to persuade Woollcott to mention his obscure client, playwright Eugene O'Neill, in Woollcott's Sunday *Times* feature column. O'Neill hadn't been faring well as far as publicity was concerned. When his father, well-known actor James O'Neill, died in August 1920, the obituary in the *New York Tribune* noted that "of his two sons, the elder, James, has attained success as an actor, and the younger, Laurence [sic], has fared equally well as a play writer."

Woollcott was a strange bird whose self-importance and unctuous sentimentality might have excluded him from sophisticated company except that his no-holds-barred reviews wielded great power. And his hilarious diatribes—in print and at the table—were unexpected, irreverent, fearsome. These verbal gifts made him an awesome companion and a great extemporaneous monologist. He was known to have made and broken reputations with a single sentence. He was short and fat, a self-defined rascal and bon vivant. He confided to his friends that he'd had mumps as a young man and was impotent as a result. But impotence was a condition known to most men at one time or another and didn't explain Woollcott's soft shoulders and hips, his grating contralto. One of his biographers, Howard Teichmann, feels he suffered from a hormonal imbalance that kept his voice nasal and thready, prevented any but wisps of whiskers, and transformed his libido into an irresistible sensual urge for sauces and rich desserts. His sexual preference, if any, was unknown even to his friends. He surrounded himself with actresses and other glamorous women, all of whom doted on him, but had a longtime crush on definitely heterosexual Harpo Marx. As if to compensate for a lack of physical muscle, his was a spectacularly unbenign demeanor. Behind his rimless prismlike spectacles, his light eyes were huge and unblinking. He was catty, ruthless, often sentimental, loyal, clever, in turn sly and heavy-handed, unable to write an understated sentence. Wolcott Gibbs, who wrote a Profile about him in *The New Yorker*, said he was "one of the most dreadful writers who ever lived"; yet his friends numbered almost as large a group as did his enemies.

Toohey asked press agent Murdock Pemberton to introduce him to Woollcott so Toohey could beat the drums for his client. (Pemberton's first job in New York, at the *Evening Mail*, had come at Frank Adams' recommendation.) Such meetings between press agents and drama critics often took place in those days of relaxed attitudes about professional ethics. Pemberton invited Toohey and Woollcott to lunch at the Algonquin, for all to see.

As might have been expected, Woollcott was in an expansive mood and spent most of the luncheon recounting his adventures in the army and with *Stars and Stripes*.

He breezily dismissed mention of Toohey's unknown client and wouldn't be deterred from endless recitations of war stories starring himself. Toohey and Pemberton sat silently, nodding and murmuring at appropriate intervals, unable to do anything but react. When lunch finally ended, they walked disconsolately back to Pemberton's office, swearing to each other never again to undergo such a frustrating experience. They became suddenly cheerful when the idea of planning and implementing a grand revenge occurred to them. They'd throw a lunch "honoring" Woollcott the following week, at the same place. Invitees would include theatrical writers and newspaper people—sharp professionals temperamentally unable to permit Woollcott's grandstanding. Frank Adams, of course, was high on their list. He was one of approximately thirty people who showed up.

The "program" Toohey and Pemberton distributed consisted of a lengthy list of titles of after-lunch speeches on various war topics, each more boring than the next. The alleged speakers were all named Alexander Woollcott, and the name was misspelled in every conceivable way. He was known to be particularly sensitive to this error.

The morning of the luncheon, Toohey and Pemberton met with Frank Case, manager of the hotel, and decorated the dining room with bunting and a huge green sign imitating the insignia of the newly formed American Legion, which read:

A.W.O.L.COT—S. J. KAUFMAN POST NO. 1.

S. J. Kaufman, no relation to George, was a columnist Woollcott despised. He called him a "leech."

The carefully planned joke backfired because the ever-vain Woollcott was delighted to be center of attention. He reveled in the occasion, topped every insult, unembarrassedly told heroic stories about his adventures "over there" and definitively earned his status as star of the proceedings. The party was uproarious. Prohibition was in effect, so no spirits were served. For once that didn't seem to make any difference. Honored guest and other participants were never so funny.

Woollcott enjoyed himself to such an extent he suggested his friends join him for lunch at the Algonquin every day. Situated on West Forty-fourth Street, the hotel was only a couple of blocks from his office at the *New York Times*, and indeed occupied a central location for most theater people. The offices of *Vanity Fair*, where Robert Benchley was managing editor, Dorothy Parker drama critic, and Robert Sherwood drama editor, were just up the street. Newspapermen who worked downtown, like Frank, could hop a subway, and often did. He and many of them met daily deadlines, so rarely made the lunch more than once a week, usually less frequently. Mostly Frank showed up on Saturday, when he had no Sunday column to prepare.

Woollcott always presided. He became the titular head, the chief blackballer, the setter of the tone. F.P.A., six years older than Woollcott and much older than everybody else, was The Elder. Members liked and respected Frank, who felt no compunction to be center of attention. By remaining silent much of the time, he was assured of an appreciative audience whenever he spoke. Algonks looked up to him not only because he was the boss and conducted "The Conning Tower" where many of their remarks were repeated—and credited—but also because in a flagrant world of braggadocio, hyperbole wasn't his style. Gruff and rude as he often was, he seemed a more modest and agreeable companion than was Woollcott who, surprisingly, regarded Frank as an equal and often turned to him to help settle an argument.

Other Algonks were some of the brightest and most entertaining of New York's youthful literati. With the quickly growing fame of the group, manager Case perceived its importance to his hotel. Every day he reserved a round table for the friends in the center of the Rose dining room. He may not have guessed that a legend was being created, but he enhanced and enlarged upon the image at every possible occasion, with a press agent's flair hidden within his discreet, almost professorial demeanor. Invitations to luncheon were at once impromptu and ironclad. Somehow there was never room for a bore more than once. When confronted with one—and they all agreed what was deadly and who was its embodiment—the group closed ranks quickly, and there weren't any extra chairs.

Over the years the group grew to include, besides Woollcott, Adams, the brothers Murdock and Brock Pemberton, and Toohey, playwright Charles MacArthur, who with Ben Hecht wrote the screenplay to *Wuthering Heights*; Herman Mankiewicz, screenwriter of *Citizen Kane*; Arthur Samuels, of *Harper's Bazaar*; composer and critic Deems Taylor; Heywood Broun, who, besides writing prolifically for the *New York Tribune* and the *New York World*, was founder and first president of the American Newspaper Guild and in 1930 Socialist Party candidate for Congress; Howard Dietz, who with Arthur Schwartz wrote countless popular songs including the first "Dancing in the Dark," a waltz; artist Neysa McMein, whose magazine cover paintings fetched thousands of dollars each, more than was paid to any other female artist, and whose studio was an unofficial clubhouse for the group away from the hotel; the Marx brothers; Jascha Heifetz; Edna Ferber; Dorothy Parker (whom Frank had "raised from a couplet"); Marc Connelly; poet John Wheeler; actress Margalo Gillmore; journalist Frank Sullivan; Peggy Leech, recent Vassar graduate, who collaborated with Broun in a comprehensive biography of Anthony Comstock and who later married one of the Pulitzers; writer Corey Ford; Kate Sproehnle; Harold Ross and his wife,

Jane Grant; Ruth Gordon; George S. Kaufman; journalist and poet Alice Duer Miller; Robert Sherwood; Robert Benchley; journalist Ruth Hale; actress Peggy Wood and her husband, poet John V. A. Weaver. Others were welcome occasionally, but the regulars formed the group's backbone. Although they rarely attended lunch, Edna St. Vincent Millay, Herbert Bayard Swope, and Ring Lardner were greatly admired by the rest and so were honorary members.

Saturday noon at the Round Table quickly became the precursor to the main event for the men, a lively all-night poker game upstairs in one of the hotel's large rooms. The *Stars and Stripes* had produced more than friendship. In its Paris offices, a regular game had started, and after the war, it floated across the ocean into various rooms and apartments, finally landing in digs provided gratis by ever-alert Frank Case. Charter members of the game included Adams, Ross, Rice, Woollcott, and Broun from France, and recent additions Kaufman, Connelly, Toohey, and Swope in the United States. Others came and went at the whim of the others. It was an exclusive group, and venom was considerable when a guest was found to be unfamiliar with the game's house rules, or boring. The latter was a greater drawback, of course, but even bores were countenanced when their ability to bring pretty actresses to lunch had been demonstrated.

With his orderly mind, excellent memory, and stone face, Frank should have been a good poker player, but he wasn't. Often armed only with a pair, he raised the bet round after round, then threw in his cards for fear somebody would call and he'd be humiliated. His ruses were transparent, but he couldn't learn not to bluff. The inability was characteristic of his stubborn game, a weakness everybody except him knew about. But if his card playing was predictable, his wit remained inspired. One night a game was running into dawn, and the players were tired and hungry. The room-service waiter arrived when the group was in the middle of a hot hand. Broun was trying to raise the limit, somebody else wanted to call, and suddenly, in an attempt to be inconspicuous, the waiter lost his balance, and a tray laden with plates, sandwiches, potato salad, pickles, and cole slaw skidded and banged upside down across the table, with ghastly results. The players were horrified. "Well," said Harpo Marx finally, "the waiter drops." Frank shrugged and began sorting through the mess. "He only had a tray," he said, topping a Marx brother.

The name of the game became the Thanatopsis Poker Playing and Inside Straight Club. Frank christened it, borrowing the name from Dr. Will Kennicott's friendly Gopher Prairie gathering in Sinclair Lewis'

Main Street, which everybody was reading. With rare exceptions, women weren't allowed to play. Ruth Fleischmann (Mrs. Raoul) and Neysa McMein were tolerated, separately, on two occasions each. Treasured female Algonks like Dorothy Parker, Beatrice Kaufman, Peggy Wood, and Alice Duer Miller were permitted to watch if they remained silent. Robert Benchley often joined the group at lunch but never played poker, which he hated, as he did all parlor games. Once in a rousing session of The Game (a refinement of charades), Benchley, an unwilling participant, had to act out the name of Hungarian playwright Ladislaus Busfekete. The others watches him expectantly as he glanced at the slip of paper, snorted, got down on all fours, circled the room, crawled out the French doors, stood up, brushed himself off, hailed a cab, and went home. Other favorites like Ring Lardner, who rarely lunched downstairs at the Round Table, were often part of the poker game. Ruth Hale boycotted the hotel entirely after manager Case told her that women weren't allowed to smoke in the lobby, but nobody joined her, not even the other women.

It was a curious time for professional women like Hale, Parker, Jane Grant, and Alice Miller. Reputedly they were treated as equals, but the men unquestionably called the shots, no matter how it looked to outsiders. The person with the authority to decide who is equal holds the power, especially when there is no appeal. Supplicants are always inferior.

A phenomenon of the newspaperman's life was the traditional banding together of the "boys" at a local saloon once the paper had been put to bed. A measure of manhood was the amount of liquor consumed before the onset of incoherence. When Prohibition forced the saloons underground, this aspect of newspaper life continued, strengthened, in particular locations that quite frequently forbade women. Bleeck's, later Artists and Writers, which adjoined the *New York Tribune* building, held to a strictly men-only policy, and its patrons bent elbows and argued about baseball strategy and heavyweight contenders without interruption by anyone but their bookies. So, too, Moriarty's on East Fifty-eighth Street. There were no like establishments restricted to women. And occasions when women drank in coed speakeasies without male escorts were infrequent.

Women's wages rarely equaled men's, and their careers were often devastatingly interrupted by the exigencies of family life. This was something that rarely happened to men, who were expected to work harder and produce more with the advent of a child to support. Men had careers that supported the household, and women raised the children and ran the house. If they were writers, mothers most often crammed their work into the hours not taken up by their families.

Dorothy Parker was in the same boat as her female colleagues, even though she remained childless. Her male friends paid her way whenever she needed money. Although men took loans from one another, frequent borrowing led to loss of face and deadbeat status. It wasn't manly to owe money habitually, but the dependency that led to the condition was countenanced if you were a woman, destined to be supported by a man sooner or later. Chivalry dictated that women didn't have to make good on loans from their men friends. Always having somebody at your elbow willing to pay your share was a mixed blessing, as dependency inevitably is.

Ruth Hale's promising career was never the same after the birth of Heywood Hale Broun, although its decline was something she never admitted. Her husband said so later, in his touching 1934 obituary of her. She and Jane Grant founded the Lucy Stone League, whose feminist membership also included Janet Flanner, Fola La Follette (daughter of Wisconsin's Sen. Robert La Follette), and Freda Kirchwey. Their creed was "My name is the symbol of my identity and must not be lost." (Kaufman is supposed to have quipped that "A Lucy Stone gathers no boss.") Few of the other women Algonks joined. Parker said she'd gotten married in order to *change* her name—she'd been born a Rothschild of an unrich American branch. Edna Ferber never married, and Alice Miller and Beatrice Kaufman took their husband's names long before the league was founded. Other female Round Tablers like Peggy Wood and Helen Hayes were actresses who kept their names in an unpolitical desire not to confuse their audiences. Nevertheless, Hale remained adamant and refused to go abroad as long as the U.S. State Department would issue a passport that identified her, even after a battle, only as "Mrs. Heywood Broun (known also as Ruth Hale)."

As feminists, Miller, Hale, and Grant said they didn't expect men to open doors for them or hold their chairs, so the men made a point of not rising whenever any of that outspoken group approached the Round Table. However, the men made a great fuss whenever a good-looking young woman appeared as somebody's guest. But the women members were good sports about the teasing. The clan was tightly knit, and an overly vehement defiance of its unusually relaxed rules made one an outsider. Nobody wanted that. It was all so very special.

Despite the fact that drinking wasn't allowed in the Algonquin dining rooms, much occurred elsewhere, both upstairs in the room Frank Case provided for the poker sessions and in speakeasies that proliferated in every neighborhood. Idealism dressed in the garb of character improvement produced Prohibition, but countrywide abstention was an impossible objective. The Eighteenth Amendment backfired hugely, resulting in a terrifying and enlarged new underworld and in widespread drinking. Everybody knew a bootlegger, nobody was without a drink, and alcoholism became a national disease.

Nor were members of the Round Table immune.

When straight-arrow Robert Benchley fell off the wagon, he was never able to recapture his sobriety. His friends had considered his abstention a challenge to their ingenuity, and they continually tried to tempt him into taking a drink. At last he did. His first drink was supposed to have been at the instigation of Donald Ogden Stewart. A few years later when the finally sober Scott Fitzgerald tried to discourage him from drinking by telling him alcohol was "slow poison," Benchley replied gently, "Who's in a hurry?"

Of the Algonquin set, Dorothy Parker, Robert Benchley, Herman Mankiewicz, Ring Lardner, and Heywood Broun were alcoholics. Although a precise definition of alcoholism is difficult to encapsulate, basic to the condition is its ability to interfere with work, family life, and health. There was no denying that dependence on alcohol deeply affected the lives of this group. It did increasing harm to their relationships, their work, and their health as the years passed. Lardner died at forty-eight, Benchley and Mankiewicz in their fifties, as direct consequences of alcoholism.

Why they drank is difficult to establish from this distance. They were gifted, intelligent, and admired. All of them were charming, first on everybody's list of favorite companions. Mankiewicz, Benchley, and Lardner had children and loving, erudite wives. Though Broun maintained an unusual arrangement with his wife during their dozen years of marriage—separate bedrooms and mostly separate lives—he thought the world of both Ruth and their son, as they did him. When Ruth died, Heywood said he'd lost his best friend. Dorothy Parker married twice—three times if you count her repeat marriage to the same man—and although she had no children, she always had friends. Yet, with Mankiewicz's screen masterpiece *Citizen Kane* as tantalizing evidence, not one of this group left the important body of works others expected and of which each was capable. The poignant, funny stories Lardner wrote serve mostly to make the reader long for more. Witty and perceptive, Dorothy Parker described herself as "a short-distance writer" to explain why she never wrote a novel, but even her output of short fiction was paltry, especially considering she lived into her seventies; although she and her husband collaborated on several screen-plays, including the Fredric March and Janet Gaynor version of *A Star Is Born*, her talent never developed to the extent of its promise. And, of course, Benchley, bumbling, lovable, and exquisitely gifted as he was, never came close to fulfilling his. Each of them was deeply socially conscious, but except for Broun, very little of their work reflects this.

It wasn't a jolly thing to be drunk all the time.

While alcoholism itself may have sprung from a genetic peculiarity, its most obvious symptom, habitual drunkenness, required intention. It was easy to confuse the symptom with the disease. Separating one from the other was a major breakthrough in its treatment, but it was difficult for alcoholics and their families to accept that they were victims of disease. The admission was isolating and somehow demeaning. Besides, separating the condition from the symptom meant something could be done about the symptom, and alcoholics couldn't tolerate the idea of suddenly ending their drinking. That was why they claimed they could stop whenever they wanted. Life without a drink, forever, was a ter-rifying prospect to people who secretly believed they couldn't live with-out one.

Before people understood that alcoholism was a chronic disease, there was little hope for achieving sobriety.

There was little hope of recovery for the alcoholic members of the Round Table. Alcoholics Anonymous, with its quiet network of support and understanding—"one day at a time"—came later, in 1935. If one was drinking excessively in the 1920s, there was nothing to do but go on the water wagon. But this was an unworkable solution because of the relentless nature of the disease. When you started drinking again, you went quickly back where you'd been. An alcoholic couldn't have only *one* drink. He couldn't have *any* drinks.

When drinking in the 1920s became dehabilitating, drinkers were sent away to dry out for a few weeks. Iron willpower was supposed to be inherent to the national character. Heroes were unflawed, rugged individualists like Lindbergh and Babe Ruth (whose drinking was care-fully hidden from "the kids," who weren't supposed to guess he had a problem). They were examplars of the revered American frontiersman: determined, indefatigable, independent, and optimistic. Giving in to temptation was despicable. Americans set their jaws and never gave in. Habitual drunkenness signaled un-American weakness and shameful lack of character. In a world where perfection was possible and free-will choices achieved it, people became successes—or failures—on pur-pose. Of course, alcoholics denied their dependence. So they drank more to ease the sharp edges of their failure, and the cycle continued.

After several years of active alcoholism, alcoholics feel awful most of the time. Their hands shake. Even lighting a cigarette or holding a cup steady is difficult. They have trouble remembering things, or concentrating, and they can't think much beyond the next drink. The keen attention to the organization and selection of words required by writing is nearly impossible, especially when, typically, alcoholics think their work is worthless anyhow. There's no reason that people, especially writers, would select the life of an alcoholic unless they couldn't help it. And in the 1920s, they couldn't.

Occasionally Frank drank enough to get drunk, but his drinking never interfered with his work or social life. On the surface his strong personality didn't hold within it secret agonies of inferiority and dependency. He didn't suffer from insomnia or self-doubt. If he knew he wasn't greatly gifted, as were many of his friends, he seemed to accept the knowledge. He accommodated his limitations and pleased himself. His self-assurance appeared genuine. He'd turned his competence into a good living and a good life. Often he worried about his friends when their alcoholism made them lose control, anathema to him. Losing power over his speech, emotions, or mental agility was a fearsome state, so he rarely permitted himself to drink too much.

But he had an addiction, and it was as potentially damaging as alcoholism. He gambled, increasingly often and for increasingly large sums of money. For a long time, he managed to control the amounts he bet and the number of times a week he played. Later in the decade, however, his losses became troublesome, then frightening. Several members dropped out of the Thanatopsis as the stakes grew prodigiously. One night John Weaver lost all the royalties from his popular book of poetry, so he quit the club, demonstrating enviable mental health. But few of the others enjoyed his ability to abstain.

On another occasion, Harold Ross lost $30,000 when his assets totaled no more than $10,000. Somehow he made the debt good and stayed on. Weaver and the others who fell by the wayside as the years passed were replaced by wealthy men who could easily go home to untroubled breakfasts without fear of revealing their losses to their wives. Not everybody could afford such casualness. Although Heywood Broun won his house on West Eighty-fifth Street playing poker, he lost it in another session a few years later. Periodically he quit the game, but he always came back.

F.P.A., a wage earner, didn't belong at a poker table in company that might include a Harriman, a Swope, a department store or food-chain heir, a wealthy stockbroker, or a millionaire playwright. Frank's erstwhile protege George S. Kaufman, who was a brilliant card player, became rich by writing and directing plays. As the years went by, his annual income surpassed Frank's by hundreds of thousands of dollars. Yet Frank remained with him at the table. Kaufman was the game's cashier and treasurer, keeping the records straight and making sure debts were honorably paid. His comments ("I will now fold my tens and silently steal away") became famous, thanks to F.P.A., and he won so often it behooved him to volunteer for the position.

Frank continued to gamble, even when the stakes grew dramatically beyond his means, even when he played badly and lost far more frequently than he won. His compulsive participation under these circumstances indicated a trait stronger than eccentricity. The game he picked, year after year, ostensibly for pleasure, revealed much about his personality.

One of the primary characteristics of the Round Table was its exclusivity. There were stringent, if unwritten, requirements for inclusion. No small part of the fun was the ability to exclude other people and to be upheld in doing so by other members, no matter how capricious the exclusion. Like Frank, most of the participants were liberal in abstract political and social outlook but needed the ego-bolstering that accompanied the role of insider. Despite his apparent self-confidence, Frank's continual placing of himself within the most exclusive group he could find and his preoccupation with recording names, activities, bright remarks, and beliefs indicated a strong sense of personal insecurity. The underlying message of the name-dropper is always, "See how important I am; all these important people are my friends." Reflected glory warms their self-defined empty grate. "The Conning Tower" was more than a list of names, of course. But the name-dropping element, tip-off of a fragile sense of worth, was distinctly present in every column Frank wrote.

Poker was the appropriate game of choice for Frank. With its necessity for a thorough knowledge of complicated etiquette, rules, rankings, and prescribed at-table behavior, it was a game in which neophytes were unwelcome. Like the lunch table, the Thanatopsis closed itself off from people who "didn't belong." Frank, tough and cigar-smoking, never countenanced an ignoramus at poker, even with the tantalizing prospect of many pots to be won. Yet, ironically, bad playing was acceptable to him and everybody else as long as it was accompanied with appropriately sophisticated conversation and knowledge of the rules of the game. In addition, familiarity with the group's various peculiarities was expected before the first hand was dealt. There were no patient teachers in the membership, no matter how they behaved elsewhere. Thanatopsis "purists" were conservatives who ridiculed upstart versions of poker, allowing wild cards or unusual betting, but within this framework the game itself was curiously democratic. In poker the suits aren't ranked, as they are in bridge, and although hands are ranked, what's best differs with every deal. And with a bluff it's possible for a deuce or a six to be as good as a queen. At the Thanatopsis, as in all poker games, there was room for a clever player to perform successfully and with considerable leeway even while adhering to the stringent rules. It was a place where craftiness or a dashing attack could win, where brilliant strategy was sometimes, unpredictably, more successful than substance. Playing was an individualistic adventure, and a dangerous one because the stakes were high.

Frank's compulsive bluffing demonstrated his feelings about himself. He was smart enough to win in more conventional ways, but he didn't have the confidence to wait for the right cards. The insecurity he felt among these talented people forced him to conclude that the only way he could win among them was to pretend he was better than he thought he was, and so he bluffed. And failed. His losses justified his opinion of himself.

Poker wasn't a team sport, so for once it was true that winning wasn't as important as how the game was played. Manly virtues were celebrated. Stakes were sometimes enormously threatening, but besting one's fellows or gallant behavior in the face of loss were more important than the safety of the individual wallet. The need to prove oneself brave among one's peers was paramount. Manhood and value to the group was expressed not through victory—though winning was important—but by consistent display of the Thanatopsian versions of sportsmanship and fearlessness. Exemplary game deportment was what Hemingway called "grace under pressure."

And with continual reshuffling and dealing of new hands came fresh opportunities for conquest. It was possible to become powerful and important, no matter how lacking in gifts one felt one was in the outside world. A chance for a new start was always present.

For a group that supposedly revered conversation, possibilities for discussion of any topic were meager at the poker table. Wisecracks were encouraged, of course, as were put-downs and insults, but serious or ongoing dialogue among players fell ultimately to somebody's command, "Deal, for Chrissake," or, "Get off the soapbox and bet!" The Thanatopsis was the perfect place for one-liners, and Frank shone there.

But gags don't make conversation, and conversation is one of the major ways people make connections with one another. In fact, poker habitues are noted for their curiously cold attitude toward one another. Part of the unspoken rules of the game includes the imperative never to admit sympathy for the plight of the other guy. Nobody stood up and said it was preposterous and unacceptable when the turn of a card lost Broun his family's home, nor did he expect or want such a reaction. He paid his debt like a man, and Ruth and Woody had to pack up and move. It was all part of the game.

Poker players like to think themselves tough and ruthless, and they work at maintaining the image. Resentment of financial and family obligations often impels a player, and requirements for emotional involvement on the "outside" also factor into his playing. Nobody gets close to anybody else at the poker table—that's one of the game's basic characteristics. It attracts people who have difficulty with emotional attachments. When Broun died, everybody loved him, but each of his friends felt that somebody else knew him better than he did. Harold Ross married three times and saw to it that people didn't get too close by operating behind an enigmatic, unpredictable persona, full of contradictions—pronouncements, judgments, simultaneous evidence of tenderness, compassion, and prejudice. Woollcott's surprise-attack cruelties prevented closeness, even with people he seemed to care for. Frank's personality was carefully constructed, even "well-defended." Nobody knew his deep feelings and, in fact, he often denied having any. At Thanatopsis he could spend hours with people who wouldn't disturb his privacy.

IV

Game playing of all kinds—not just poker—occupied the Algonks much of the time. Fierce competition appealed to them, and most were masters of parlor games like murder, categories, twenty questions, anagrams, scenes from famous plays, famous persons, the word game, and The Game. In the word game, each participant used a multisyllabic word as a pun within ten seconds. Nobody could top Dorothy Parker. Once, assigned "horticulture," she snapped: "You can take a *horticulture,* but you can't make her think." And, in a musical mutation of the game, "Do you know the celery song?" she asked. " 'Celery gather at the river?' Or the Irish song, 'Irish I Was in Dixie?' " She went on, unstoppable.

"How about the French one—'Je suis have no bananas,' and the Spanish national anthem, 'Jose Can You See'?"

Woollcott was remembered for his twist on the name of a famous Greek: "*Demosthenes* can do is bend and hold the legs together." George Kaufman, inveterate playwright, preferred to set a scene: "A man has two daughters, Lizzie and Tillie; Lizzie is okay, but you have no idea how *punctilious*." Frank told of "*Theophilus* show" he'd ever seen, and wished everyone "a *meretricious* and a happy new year." And Gummo Marx reported that when their mother told his brothers to go out and play, they asked, "Which one?" and she said, "*Euphoria*."

One night Frank was at the Swopes' playing cribbage at the card table in a corner of the vast living room. Swope sat nearby, arrogantly interrogating a visitor about German poetry. (Swope acted as if he knew everything and came close to being right.) When he demanded "Who was Kleist?" (rhymes with "sliced"), Frank answered, unbidden, "The Chinese messiah," and took a pull from his cigar.

Frank played all kinds of games and didn't care if his opponent was child, a drunken adult, or an important visitor from a foreign country. He was a formidable, relentless, and unforgiving foe. For him it was never "all in fun." It was crucial for him to prove his superiority over and over again. No one bested him at word games, and his tennis was good enough once to qualify him for the Veterans' Tournament at Forest Hills. (Veteran meant over thirty-five.) Tennis was a lifelong obsession. Characteristically, he believed his game would improve if he kept working on it, so he played feverishly every day when the weather was good, sometimes five or six hours at a stretch. He worried endlessly over his mistakes: He'd placed a lob too high; he should have crowded the net or relied on his baseline game, or ignored it; he should have served harder, or softer, with more spin; he should have told his partner where to stand and what to do. He was often rude to his partners; frequently he had difficulty finding one thick-skinned enough to play with him. A friend of many years, Eva Levy, married to contributor Newman Levy and a tournament player herself, became fed up with Frank's rudeness. She didn't speak to him for months because of his boorish behavior at a tennis match. Frank didn't know that she and Newman weren't speaking to him until they appeared at his office one afternoon to discuss the situation. As soon as he learned of his rudeness, he apologized. For nearly a year, he hadn't been aware that two of his best friends weren't speaking to him!

Besides his own skill—or lack of it—tennis and poker were dependent on intrusions like luck and the competence of his partners and opponents. He couldn't control these factors, so no matter how much he enjoyed playing, he was never entirely satisfied. In word games he was in magnificent control. And language was the ultimate puzzle. He was happiest when he could use his vocabulary in tandem with his powers of deduction and reasoning, not only because of his huge vocabulary and knowledge of Latin but also because of an excellent ability to reject and select words, to organize, hone, polish, and manipulate them. He was a great editor, even as his avocation.

In 1913 Arthur Wynne, editor of the Fun Page in the Sunday *New York World*, had created the crossword puzzle, basing his idea on a children's reading game. His brilliant innovation was to add numbers and sprinkle black squares among the blanks. Of course, Frank was delighted with the invention, and he attacked the paper with new relish after breakfast every Sunday. By the time Wynne left the *World*, F.P.A. was working there himself. John O'Hara Cosgrave, the Sunday editor, had a bright young secretary, Margaret Petherbridge, a 1919 graduate of Smith, whose duties rapidly evolved to include less stenography and more puzzle editing. When Wynne left, Petherbridge was promoted to official crossword editor. She and Frank often had their heads together in order to come up with the perfect combinations. She called him her "counselor."

By 1927 Margaret Petherbridge was the wife of John Farrar, a *World* reporter who later founded the distinguished publishing house of Farrar, Straus and Giroux. Frank introduced her to two other young men who were starting out in the publishing business. They were Richard L. Simon and M. Lincoln Schuster. Frank's idea was that their first book should be a collection of crossword puzzles. It was. They published it on April 9, 1924. F.P.A. announced it that morning in the Tower:

BOOK REVIEW

Hooray! Hooray! Hooray! Hooray!
'The Cross Word Puzzle Book' is out today

It was the first such book, and Margaret Petherbridge Farrar was its editor and chief constructor. The little book was a bombshell, selling an astonishing 350,000 copies and assuring success to the fledgling firm. Ultimately, before her death in 1984, Mrs. Farrar was responsible for 133 puzzle books and for helping to develop the unique talents of *New York Times* crossword editors Will Weng, Eugene T. Maleska, and Harriet Wilson. Of all the different word games, crossword puzzles became Frank's favorites. He was glad to have been instrumental in their development.

Parties for the Algonks and their friends were constant, hilarious, and never-ending. On the weekends, celebrants visited the Swopes' estate on Long Island (next door to the Lardners) for daytime croquet—"polo for pedestrians"—and nighttime revelry, or journeyed to Woollcott's island on Lake Bomoseen in Vermont for more croquet and swimming, for fishing and canoeing and, of course, for more games. The objectives at these gatherings were the winning of whatever game was being played and the invention of wisecracks that would be repeated in "The Conning Tower."

When Raoul Fleischmann told George Kaufman, "I didn't know I was Jewish until I was eighteen," late-bloomer Kaufman replied thoughtfully, "That's nothing. I didn't know I was a boy until I was twenty." F.P.A. was there to record it.

Another time, Marc Connelly arrived early for lunch at the Round Table. He sat quietly, looking over the menu as an acquaintance, not a regular, spotted him and came over. "My, my," said the interloper, grasping for a bon mot as one did when confronted with one of Them, "your head is as soft and smooth as my wife's behind." Marc rubbed his hand reflectively across his bald head, smiling pleasantly. "And so it is," he said. The outsider never attempted to intrude again, especially because everybody in town soon knew of the put-down.

At a party given by music critic Samuel Chotzinoff, Frank and actress Pauline Lord, who was starring with Louis Wolheim in *The Hairy Ape*, acted out a vigorous pantomime in a lively session of The Game. Next George Gershwin played the piano, all his own compositions, with the loose-wristed, oh-so-smooth Gershwin treatment unmistakably demonstrating his ownership of the piano and, in fact, most of popular music. He sang to the guests in what he described, in an unusual moment of self-deprecation, as his "small but disagreeable" voice. (Once, talking about his mother, Gershwin said, "And the extraordinary thing about her—she's so modest about me.") Irving Berlin bounced around in his elevator shoes and played and sang his songs in his inimitable squeaky tenor. The culmination of the unforgettable evening came with an uproarious endurance contest. Classical violinists Joseph Fuchs, Jascha Heifetz, Paul Kochanski, Albert Spaulding, and Efrem Zimbalist had all brought their violins, expecting to be asked to play. It seemed more fun to ask them to compete with each other to see who could play and replay Paganini's "Perpetual Motion" the most times without pausing. Whoever remained on his feet still playing after the others had quit would win. Of course, the violinists each knew the piece by heart. Marc Connelly started the frenetic performance with a blast from a stage pistol. The guests shouted encouragement and threw money on the floor, betting on their favorites. The virtuosos played furiously, swooping, flailing, and producing excruciating cacaphony. At one point, Heifetz, still standing but close to surrender, rested his bowing arm on the top of the upright piano and continued madly sawing away. One by one, the fiddlers collapsed and fell into the arms of the shrieking on-lookers. Finally Joseph Fuchs prevailed. He'd played the number at breakneck speed for twenty-one consecutive minutes. Everybody cheered.

Collaboration between Algonks Marc Connelly and George Kaufman produced their first successful stage comedy in 1921. They called their play *Dulcy*. The young woman of the title, the first in the tradition of Gracie Allen–Judy Holliday–Carol Channing types on Broadway, was played by Lynn Fontanne, an English actress who'd been discovered and encouraged in America by Laurette Taylor. The character was based on "Dulcinea," an enchanting, impulsive, and guileless female whom F.P.A. had created in "The Conning Tower." He named her for Don Quixote's romantic ideal. From time to time, he'd quote one of her just off-the-mark observations: "Dulcinea has a new hat. 'What could be sweeter?' she asked us yesterday. 'Was it costly?' we inquired. 'You don't know the half of it,' she thrilled." And, "After a long motor ride Dulcinea sighed, 'I don't believe I had as good a time as I think I had.' "

Connelly and Kaufman acknowledged Frank's contribution to their show by making note of it on the playbill and ceding him 10 percent of the profits. They were honorable men. Although Kaufman remained drama editor at the *New York Times* for several years after he'd become a successful playwright, he scrupulously avoided mentioning any of his own plays editorially. When Toohey asked him how client Helen Hayes was supposed to get attention in the good gray *Times*—she was starring in Connelly and Kaufman's own *To the Ladies*—Kaufman smiled. "Shoot her," he said.

Nearly all of the Algonks were stagestruck. Once they were on the way to becoming more or less successful separately, it was inevitable that they'd decide to amuse themselves by writing and performing in their own show. In 1922 a Russian import called *Chauve Souris* romped nightly at the Forty-ninth Street Theater, produced by David Belasco's son-in-law. One of the Algonks suggested that their group take over the theater on a Sunday evening when the Russians were off, when the decidedly amateur actor cast of Algonks could be augmented with friends who were professional performers, also off for the night. They'd invite all the theater people they could think of, pay $1.50 for each seat to defray production costs. They'd call the one-night replacement for the Russian review *No Sirree!*, an approximate rhyme, and in it they would parody popular playwrights and actors.

Since many of the Round Tablers were theater critics and writers, they assumed they could demonstrate it wasn't so hard to devise a quality show. You just had to know what you were doing, they told each other. Extravagantly abetted with illegal hooch from the various neighborhood speakeasies, they set to work. On April 30, 1922, the show opened and closed, as planned. It announced itself "An Anonymous Entertainment by the Vicious Circle of the Hotel Algonquin," and the cast included just about all the insiders.

In one of the sketches, Toohey, dressed in a long ragged skirt and a ratty wig, played Elizabeth Inchcape, "known as Coal-Barge Bessie, a retired waterfront prostitute." The scene, derivative of the work of Toohey's finally known playwright-client Eugene O'Neill, took place either in the backroom of Billy the Bishop's saloon or on the firemen's forecastle on a freighter bound east from Rio. The audience was asked to vote for one or the other, and since the scenery was nonexistent, either location was credible. Jascha Heifetz played offstage music but wasn't allowed to come forward for a curtain call. ("To keep him in his place," according to Marc Connelly.) He also accompanied the action from the wings for "Zowie, or the Curse of an Akin Heart," in which Harold Ross was listed as Lemuel Pip, an old taxi driver. Ross, with his bad posture and shuffling walk, wasn't allowed onstage either. To protect Ross' feelings, several of the other actors were instructed to refer to him repeatedly.

The pit orchestra was conducted by Deems Taylor and consisted of Irving Berlin, Arthur Samuels, Neysa McMein—who hurried onstage whenever required—and Nate Salsbury. In the show's bombastic opening, Heywood Broun was interlocutor, impersonating the Russian revue's master of ceremonies, Nikita Balieff, in a rousing introduction entitled "Spirit of the American Drama." Given to realistic appraisal of her worth as a performer, Ruth Hale wisely declined to participate but had coached Heywood and the others. She sat in the front row and laughed and applauded Broun's impersonation so enthusiastically that somebody cracked that in the future she might allow herself to be dubbed Mrs. Heywood Broun.

As shouts and applause followed Broun's departure, the chorus boys hurried out, arms akimbo, in various stages of grotesquely overdone makeup. They were Woollcott, Toohey, Benchley, Kaufman, Connelly, and Adams, who locked arms and clomped to the footlights, warning they'd kill anybody who tried to leave early. Later Frank appeared in a skit he'd written with two Conning Tower contributors, Nate Salsbury ("Baron Ireland") and Emil Breitenfeld ("Sam Hill"). It was called "The Filmless Movies." His piece de resistance came in a three-act playlet called "Big Casino Is Little Casino." In it he stomped around as O'Brien, a detective whose lines were unintelligible because of a gruffly inaccurate brogue. The strong smelling smoke from the cigar he held to ward off the demons of stage fright surrounded and obscured his face. Woollcott appeared with him in the potboiler as a butler named Dregs. George Kaufman, as Mortimer Van Loon ("A decayed gentleman"), stood stage right and devoured a prop sandwich without contributing further to the action.

Chorus girls so individualistic they had to be seated on the floor to keep in line included Helen Hayes, appearing on other nights in Connelly and Kaufman's *To the Ladies*; Leonore Ulrich, star of *Kiki*; Tallulah Bankhead; Dorothy Parker; Mary Kennedy, soon to marry Deems Taylor; Jane Grant; Beatrice Kaufman; Alice Duer Miller; Ruth Gillmore; and Mary Brandon, in a few weeks to become Mrs. Robert Sherwood.

"The Greasy Hag," another takeoff on O'Neill, whose *The Hairy Ape* was shocking audiences a couple of blocks away, contained a line so full of swear words that nobody would quote it in mixed company.

In "Mr. Whim Passes By," a parody of a play by A. A. Milne, a scene between Helen Hayes and Sidney Blackmer as Cynthia and Nigel took place in the morning room at the Acacias, in Wipney-cum-Chiselickwick, England.

Benchley had promised to prepare a monologue, but in his customary easygoing manner, failed to come up with a title for it by the time the playbill was printed and so his solo turn came as a surprise to the audience. At the last minute, he decided to perform "The Treasurer's Report," a spinoff from his "History of the Watch Industry," given to the Contribunion dinner a dozen years before. The performance was hilarious, and Irving Berlin decided on the spot to ask him to perform it in the upcoming *Music Box Revue*. Benchley agreed that $500 a week couldn't be refused and thus began his career as a popular performer.

At the curtain call, somebody brought forward a huge horseshoe of radishes, carrots, onions, and tomatoes, which Dorothy Parker, looking like Betty Boop, coyly accepted.

Since many of the city's dramatic critics were in the cast, it seemed unlikely that any of the papers would carry a review. With this in mind, Woollcott invited Laurette Taylor to write her response to the extravaganza in his space in the *New York Times*, since she, as a leading actress, was often criticized by him and other cast members. While he may have thought her friendship would kindly affect her reaction to their efforts, she rolled up her sleeves to turn the tables. Venerable actor Wilton Lackaye, appearing every night but Sunday in *The Goldfish*, covered the production for the *New York World*. No other Manhattan papers took notice.

The audience was a who's who of theater folk and important New Yorkers. Invitations were fiercely coveted. David Belasco sat up front, where he enjoyed himself as the actresses cum chorus-line flappers flirted and winked at him in their number "He Who Gets Flapped." (The Theatre Guild's *He Who Gets Slapped*, starring Margalo Gillmore, was a current Broadway offering.) Also present were Bernard M. Baruch, Lee Shubert, John Golden, Florenz Ziegfeld, Walter Damrosch, Ruth Draper, Sam Harris, Channing Pollack, Minnie Maddern Fiske (who perched on the top of her seat in the last row of the gallery brandishing a spyglass), William Rhinelander Stewart, Frank Crowninshield (editor of *Vanity Fair*), Constance and Norma Talmadge, Gene Buck, Ernest Truex, DeWolf Hopper, Frank Craven, Mrs. William K. Vanderbilt II, and Learned Hand, famous jurist and First Amendment expert. Most trooped uptown afterward to a splendid party at the Swopes' twenty-eight room duplex at 135 West Fifty-eighth Street.

Both Lackaye and Taylor were firm but not zealous with their criticism, although it must have been difficult to resist savaging the undertaking. Each enjoyed the opportunity to at last remark upon the bad manners of professional aisle sitters. Lackaye was a respected alumnus of forty years of professional acting, a member of the Lambs Club and noted for his wit. His definition of a gentleman was "the one who opens the door of a bathroom, sees a lady in the tub, backs out closing the door and saying 'Excuse me, sir.' " Of the evening's performance he said, "I was instructed, as a tyro, to follow the critical habit, to come late and leave before the performance was over. [So] the best numbers on the programme were those I didn't see." He added that "the names of the authors were not given, a thing to be regretted, because the burlesques were admirably written—the acting, well, however." He assumed that most of the sketches had been written by George Kaufman, and ended his gentle essay by asking, "If I may be allowed to quote from a little thing I once did at the Lambs:

> *The moral of this playlet is the*
> *trite but trenchant fact:*
> *That the actor shouldn't author*
> *and the author shouldn't act."*

Taylor wrote breezily, saying she'd "lost my program in the dark and I couldn't stay for the finish and I was late arriving. I realize this conduct would not be tolerated on this particular paper but I have seen it done on others." She brought a keener, more ascerbic approach than Lackaye's to the assignment, but hardly waxed unfair, suggesting a "new vest and pants that meet" for the notoriously sloppy dresser Heywood Broun and elocution lessons for Woollcott. "I advise them all to leave the stage before they take it up. A pen in their hands is mightier than God's most majestic word in their mouths," she said.

"The audience was not awfully exclusive, except in brains, so we had no trouble with behavior there," she added. "The first beautiful sight I had was of the chorus boys in dishabille, and believe me, Mabel, it was terrible." She quoted the "one gorgeous line in the play," from "Zowie": "My darling, you are like the long-lost laughter of an unfrocked priest." She admitted her bias, an unwillingness to make fun of talent or to tolerate it when misused: "Jascha Heifetz played off-stage music off-key, and that's how the evening went—making fun of a fine writer, hitting the movie industry right in its middle, Heifetz playing off-key. A night that rather makes you wish some people didn't have any sense of humor."

She reacted against an overbearing egotism: "It was also an evening of the perpendicular pronoun, and I think the two who will come out of it the best known will be the ones who would have no nonsense but came downstage and sang 'I'm Kaufman and that's Connelly.' O Marc, Marc, that you should have been born again a Connelly, with a Kaufman instead of a Cleopatra!"

Both she and Lackaye seemed confused as to exactly what Benchley had been talking about. Lackaye cited an "exceedingly funny" presentation having to do with an explanation of the reason for the publication of *Life* magazine. Taylor wasn't enthusiastic: "Robert Benchley came out and read, as far as I could understand it, the multiplication table, or perhaps it was a time table. It put me in mind of my check book, the time I accused the bank of being short some $1,900, and after many arguments the President, whom I knew personally, went over my account and pointed out that I had added in the date. Ever since then I have hated figures. So, being a critic for the moment, I suppose it is all right for me to say I don't like figures so Benchley's monologue did not interest me. That's what one said about jazz and I suppose you can say it about figures.''

She summed up by admitting it was a "most amusing evening, but it didn't amuse me because I was all dressed up not to be amused.''

After the performance there was a general Broadway buzz that the Algonks were getting too big for their britches. Burton Rascoe, literary editor of the *New York Tribune* who wrote a biography of Theodore Dreiser in 1925, described the evening as having been "unduly exhibitionistic and quite as vulgar as if they had consented to demonstrate fountain pens in drugstore windows free of charge, for the chance it gave them to be seen.'' Such carping didn't bother the insiders. A few days later, Deems Taylor, Woollcott, Donald Stewart, Jane Grant, and Neysa McMein whooped overseas where they met Edna Ferber in Paris. She'd missed the show, something she insisted she didn't regret. (Anita Loos gives their trip short shrift, writing in *Gentlemen Marry Brunettes*, "And they had a marvelous time, because everywhere they went, they would sit in the hotel, and play cute games and tell reminiscences about the Algonquin. And I think it is wonderful to have so many internal resources that you never have to bother to go outside yourself to see anything. . . . And I really do not know why the geniuses at the Algonquin should bother to learn about Europe any more than Europe bothers to learn about them. So they came back, because they like the Algonquin best after all. And I think it is remarkable, because the old Proverb tells about the Profit who was without honor in his own home. But with them, it is just the reverse.'')

Upon their return they learned that Kaufman and Connelly were deep into plans for another Vicious Circle presentation, this one intended to be respectable and professional and expected to turn a profit.

Kaufman and Connelly asked their friends to help by writing sketches for the revue, to be presented at the tiny Punch and Judy Theater, on Forty-ninth Street. The production was called *The Forty-Niners* in honor of the location of the theater as well as the one in which *No, Sirree!* had been housed. The new show was produced by veteran Broadway producer George Tyler, and it opened with a professional cast on November 6, 1922. Ring Lardner's contribution was entitled "The Tridget of Greva.'' Irish actor Joe Kerrigan (sole remnant of the *No, Sirree!* cast and 1921 winner of the Contribunion watch for his poem "Frankie and Johnny in the Style of Synge''), Roland Young, and Sidney Toler played lackadaisical fishermen whose rambling conversation sounded both obscure and whimsical, predating by three decades the existential theater of the absurd. Unfortunately, in 1922, few people understood or appreciated the avant-garde nature of the exercise. "Is it all supposed to take place in an insane asylum?" asked a baffled Frank Case afterward.

Benchley and Parker collaborated on a "historical" sketch called "Nero," not remembered by them or anybody else with affection. It appeared to have been written in an evening of casual alcoholic merriment, and nobody had the good sense to demand they rewrite it. Benchley, eager as always to accommodate his friends, also wrote a script for a monologue but wasn't able to perform it himself—he was by this time appearing in the Berlin revue downtown. Denman Maley delivered it, "tolerably well," according to Woollcott, once again at his critic's desk at the *New York Times*. Woollcott wasn't involved in the production, and his harsh treatment of it the morning after the opening was thought by some to be a jealous reaction to having been left out. While there may have been some truth in the accusation, the fact remained the show wasn't good. Woollcott was responsible enough to notice and say so, despite the fact that his best friends were involved.

Frank took young reporter Marian Spitzer to opening night. Although he didn't confide to his readers what he thought of the revue, presumably because he'd been involved in it, next to the Tower in "It Seems to Me," a few days later Broun described it as "an amusing show. It seemed pretty bad to us the first night, but at a second visit [when the miscast master of ceremonies had been replaced by Marc Connelly] we found it much improved." With an affectionate nod to his neighbor, Broun added, "There is a lot of fun in 'The Love Girl,' the burlesque musical written by Franklin Pierce Adams."

Woollcott described F.P.A.'s sketch as "fair to middling." In an effort to assuage the feelings of his old friend, he added that it hadn't had a fair chance, coming as it had late in the evening, too light and frothy to wake the sleeping audience. In fact, Woollcott said, the whole production was "rather like a dinner consisting of five courses of perfectly splendid lemon meringue pie."

He concluded his critique by admitting that when the curtain came down, he'd "slunk away disconsolate into the drizzling November rain," that "it wasn't fun. Not at all."

The show closed after two weeks. Nobody regretted its failure, except, perhaps, Frank, who, as usual, kept his feelings secret.

A year later Herman Mankiewicz and S. Jay Kaufman tried again with a mix of Algonk and professional talent. Their musical review, *'Round the Town*, opened at the Century Roof. There were sketches and songs by themselves as well as by George S. Kaufman, Marc Connelly, and Dorothy Parker. Broun appeared in a dinner jacket and discussed critics, audiences, actors, actresses, and censors. But Julius (Groucho) Marx had had it with amateurs pretending to be professionals, no matter who they were. He wrote to Broun: "At the present time," he said, "show business is in none too healthy a condition, what with the Equity trouble, George M. Cohan writing books, the feud between Mr. [Louis E.] Shipman and Percy Hammond and your entering the profession as an active performer, monologist and general all around ham sandwich actor.

"Mr. [Robert] Benchley really started all the trouble. After he saw *Abie's Irish Rose*, he reasoned, 'Well, if that show can make a million dollars I certainly ought to be able to make a little money as an actor.' Then I suppose you saw Mr. Benchley, and you figured, 'Well, if he can do a monologue, I might as well take a crack at it.' And so it goes, in an endless and vicious chain.

"Unless we actors get relief from Congress or the Equity, all the actors will wind up doing free performances for the radio, and all the critics will be getting fat salaries from the Broadway revue managers. So please go back to your farm and column and don't take the bread out of our mouths."

Groucho Marx had nothing to worry about. On its own the gang decided to end the lark and return to what they did best. *'Round the Town* was the last collective attempt by the Algonks to harness their special talents for Broadway.

V

Frank's friend Herbert Bayard Swope was a dynamo. Born in St. Louis in 1882, Swope strode into prewar New York City with the unerring instinct and shameless curiosity of a born reporter. His gigantic ego swelled and dazzled, alternately seducing and devouring lesser lights and earning a unique reputation in a city where inhabitants exalted in their arrogance and ambition. He never forgot anything or anybody. The telephone was an appendage as useful as his hand or nose, and his apartment contained twelve of them. With his deep voice and relentless charm, he used the instrument with consummate skill. People couldn't resist telling him whatever he wanted to know. As more and more sources equipped their homes and offices with telephones, his newspaper career bolted upward, as if in direct ratio. And he didn't have to leave his desk, so he could talk to many times more people than would otherwise have been possible. A scant year or so after he'd arrived in town, he knew everybody—cops on the beat and their bosses, politicians, lawyers, actors, socialites, musicians, judges, even financiers Otto Kahn and Bernard M. Baruch. Baruch became Swope's mentor and the primary reason for his youthful millionaire status. While nobody could get rich on a newspaperman's wages, tidbits from the Street a la Baruch made the difference. And Swope was a fast learner.

His bailiwick was Joseph Pulitzer's sons' *New York World*. The heirs weren't the journalists their father had been, nor could they hold a candle in that department to Swope. After his speedy rise through the ranks, it was his creativity, not theirs, that unmistakably stamped every page. A reporter who worked for him during the *World*'s glory days described Swope as "a Conqueror—an Alexander, Caesar, Genghis Khan, Napoleon." Nobody talked about his compassion, tenderness, or subtlety, but these characteristics weren't requirements for a topnotch editor, or even desirable. Often he and his paper took the part of the underdog and raised hell with whoever was in charge, substituting his authority for theirs. Swope's crusades were politically liberal and usually popular, or they became popular as a result of his advocacy. During the Spanish-American War, the senior Pulitzer, competing with Hearst, published dispatches from Cuba by Stephen Crane; Swope took on the rejuvenated Ku Klux Klan in 1921.

The *World* was an early subscriber to the services of the Associated Press, unlike Hearst's *New York Journal*. A joke went the rounds of city rooms describing how, when the *World*'s first edition reached the offices of the *Journal*, the staff cheered:

> *Sound the cymbals, beat the drum!*
> *The* World *is here, the news has come!*

Reporters liked working for Swope because he recognized and rewarded talent. He paid huge salaries to a few giants, competitive rates to the rest, demanding commitment to match his own. And he got it.

The men and women he gathered around him became legendary, their work and many of their names standing out sixty years after the paper's last issue. He enticed dapper intellectual Walter Lippmann from the *New Republic* with an offer to write and edit the editorial page, with emphasis on foreign affairs. Frank Cobb, James M. Cain (who later wrote *The Postman Always Rings Twice*), Allan Nevins, Maxwell Anderson, and Arthur Krock wrote editorials. Famous prewar reporters included Albert Payson Terhune, a reporter until he left for New Jersey to raise collies and write about them, and O. Henry, who wrote headlines and leads to augment his undependable income. Gene Fowler was Swope's city editor for some years. Once Swope assigned cub reporter John Farrar an interview with Baruch. Farrar had never heard of the financier, and practical jokers in the city room sent him on a wild goose chase to Queens to interview somebody they found in the phone book with the sound-alike name of "Baroo." Swope hit the ceiling when he heard about it, but the game young man kept his job.

Swope offered George Bernard Shaw $15,000 to cover a heavy-weight championship fight, but disappointingly Shaw declined, as did Eugene O'Neill, who said he didn't know enough about boxing to do justice to the subject. The fact such unusual sportswriters had been sought for the assignments demonstrated the flair and vision Swope brought to his association with the paper.

For a while unknown shorthand whiz Billy Rose took the Swope dictation. Alison Smith was one of his prized music and drama writers (she later married Russel Crouse). Harlan Thompson, who went to Hollywood and created the Crosby/Hope/Lamour "Road" pictures, worked for Swope. Briton Hadden, co-founder of TIME Inc. with Henry Luce, took a year to learn the ropes at the *World* upon his graduation from Yale. Charles Michelson covered the Scopes "monkey trial" in Tennessee. Swope telegraphed Michelson instructions to ask creationist William Jennings Bryan if he thought the world was flat. Upon hearing the impudent question, Bryan thundered, "I am a classical scholar and will not stand for any of this impertinence!" But a *World* reporter sooner offended the three-time Democratic Party presidential candidate than neglected to ask a question from his redheaded boss.

Probably the most influential and long-lasting of Swope's innovations was the organization of the page opposite the editorials into a place with a respectable identity of its own. There dramatic, musical, and literary criticism ran, as well as cultural, political, topical ruminations of one sort or another, written by well-known journalists and critics. Ever after, the *World*'s "op-ed" page was imitated on every big city newspaper. Swope said the idea germinated from the realization that "nothing is more interesting than opinion when opinion is interesting." He added with an almost innocent arrogance—and some justification—that it "became the most important page in America." Op-ed was a place not for news, but for opinions, opinions sometimes booming in marked contrast to those expressed by facing-page editorials representing the Pulitzer position. This made for exciting reading, as controversy always does.

Swope set out to collect the best columnists from around the country for the op-ed. The breed was enjoying remarkable popularity, and Swope knew that if his page was to succeed, he'd need the best. In the *New York Tribune* F.P.A. printed a contribution indicating just how important columnists were to newspaper circulation:

THE COLUMN HABIT

Rising at an early hour
First I read the Conning Tower.
Then I don my pants and shoon
And scan the works of Heywood Broun.
Then, of course, I have to read
Benchley's literary meed,
Alex Woollcott's play review,
The rhymes of Jimmie Montague.
When my daily toil is done
I read Don Marquis in the Sun.
And what I almost like the most
Is old Kit Morley in the Post.
I do not know who won the war,
I don't read sports news anymore,
The current value of the pound,
If Nicky Arnstein has been found.
To read these things I must refuse,
I have no time to read the news.

Swope lured Woollcott from the *New York Times* and Broun, F.P.A., and Deems Taylor from the *New York Tribune*. Dramatist Laurence Stallings reviewed plays until his own, written in collaboration with Maxwell Anderson, *What Price Glory?*, thundered onto Broadway, when he left the paper to devote himself to play- and screenwriting.

Benchley wrote a book column for a time, but refused to branch out to drama criticism. "I don't think that I could do regular newspaper theater reviews because I don't know enough about the theater or about what the public likes," he told Swope modestly, then left the *New York World* and, ironically, became one of the country's most widely read and admired drama critics, first at *Life*, then at *The New Yorker*. But Benchley's defection was a rarity. Samuel Chotzinoff was a classical pianist who'd traveled with and accompanied Jascha Heifetz, Alma Gluck, and her husband Efrem Zimbalist. While still a young man,

Chotzinoff sought feverishly to replace Deems Taylor when Taylor left the *World* to compose. Chotzinoff's pal Arthur Samuels was a friend of Swope's, who pasted an essay Chotzinoff had written on a mammoth piece of posterboard and delivered it to Swope's bed, where the executive editor was momentarily incapacitated, suffering from a cold. According to Swope's biographer, E. J. Kahn, Jr., "Swope agreed to hire Chotzinoff if only somebody would move the weight off his chest."

Frank had worked for the *New York Tribune* several years when Swope beckoned him. It was a tough decision to leave the *Trib*, for he was comfortable there. Swope had to use all his considerable charm, as well as promises of more money, to persuade F.P.A. to change venue. Frank had written that "in eight years of columning on the *New York Tribune* nobody in authority ever has suggested that we conform to any policy or hinted that such and such a theme would better not be treated." He valued such independence and had to be convinced the *New York World* would recognize his rights with equal sensitivity. Still, the opportunity to significantly increase his income was a persuasive factor. As it was, Broun fled to the *World* several months before Frank, and exalted that there he was "as free as a bird." The *Tribune* city room seemed empty, even with its noise and jumble, without Broun. Frank sorely missed him.

The owner of the *New York Tribune*, Ogden Mills Reid, while not a friend, had been a good boss. He was the only son of Whitelaw Reid, from Cincinnati, who'd attracted the attention of Horace Greeley when serving as war correspondent with the Union Army during the Civil War. As managing editor of the *Tribune*, Whitelaw continued the Greeley tradition and provided leadership that saw the paper enhance its reputation and influence. Reid was appointed minister to France in the 1890s, then became U.S. ambassador to Great Britain from 1905 to 1912. He named his son to replace him as editor in 1913. Wife of the ambassador and Ogden's mother, Elizabeth, was a distinguished executive who had headed the nursing division of the American Red Cross during the Spanish-American War, then chaired it in London for the duration of World War I. Their son, F.P.A.'s employer, was a curious combination of insecurity and bravado, as is often the case with children of dynamic parents. He was a sound editor and an intelligent man, but was also a heavy drinker, hypersensitive and difficult to get along with. His wife, Helen, the paper's business manager and a charming, intelligent woman, was Frank's friend. It was often necessary for her to smooth the way between the two. When Frank left the *Trib* on New Year's Day, 1922, Reid was badly hurt. F.P.A.'s abandonment was something he wouldn't forget.

Frank found the environment at the *World* even more congenial than it was at the *Trib*. For example, one of his most consistent crusades was the ridiculing of grammatical errors and ludicrous overstatements in advertisements, even when they appeared in his own paper. The *World*'s advertising manager, Florence White, became so exasperated by his making fun of good advertising customers that she finally wrote a biting memo to Swope. "Why not order F.P.A. to ignore advertising copy in his criticisms?" she demanded. "He has the whole book world to shoot at. . . . No other newspaper in this country would stand for his deviltry. Why do we?" No record exists of Swope's reply, if any. But F.P.A. went right on making fun wherever his fancy took him, even when his target was a department store that annually spent thousands of dollars advertising in the *World*. Once he wrote that Swope's "leaving me alone [is] almost ostentatious."

Of all the distinguished *World* journalists, Frank was the only one who had an office. There was room in it for his cluttered rolltop desk, a bookcase, a filing cabinet, and a straight chair for visitors. And the office had a door, with a pebbly opaque window that said "F.P.A." Even Walter Lippmann didn't have an office. Everybody else worked in the giant city room with typewriters clacking, telephones ringing, people talking or shouting. Frank's cubicle, and the precious privacy that went with it, was an important measure of his prestige, as was the placement of "The Conning Tower": first column on the left of the op-ed every morning. When he went back to the *Tribune* after the failure of the *World*, his cronies secretly removed the door and had it installed at his new office as a surprise.

It was a wonderful time. And it lasted the decade.

But by the end of the 1920s, the *World* was in big trouble. Circulation had dwindled alarmingly, especially after the Pulitzers decided to raise the newsstand price from 2 to 3 cents, against Swope's vehement opposition. Although the objective of the price hike was to increase revenues, the price change caused the opposite to occur as readers left in droves. When the business managers saw they'd have to cut ad rates because of the drop in circulation, they put the price back to 2 cents, but only about half of the lost readership was recaptured. It was a costly miscalculation, with repercussions that the shaky *World* couldn't withstand.

In addition to the decline in the paper's popularity, during the late 1920s the Pulitzer brothers increasingly interfered with Swope's authority. When Heywood Broun aggressively criticized Harvard president A. L. Lowell's handling of the Sacco-Vanzetti case, Ralph Pulitzer, a

Harvard alumnus—as was Broun—fired him, and took a box on the front page to do it. The episode rankled and disillusioned Swope. Punishing a journalist for writing what he thought wasn't one of his guiding principles.

Moreover, penny-pinching grew to blind foolishness. The production manager was ordered to buy the cheapest newsprint paper, and it was so flimsy one could see through pages to the inky stories on the other side. Photographs reproduced on it became blotchy and unclear. And Swope wasn't permitted to buy spot radio advertisements to promote op-ed pages. He rightly felt that the page was the paper's strongest reader inducement, but was overridden. Circulation continued to plummet.

When the youngest Pulitzer brother, Herbert, joined his brothers, Swope had had enough. Saying he was through being "a hired man," he left the paper on October 16, 1929. The *World* didn't last long without him. It lost $1,677,000 in 1930, and competitors started sniffing around to see if the Pulitzers could be bought out. After a frantic few weeks when Swope, William Randolph Hearst, the *Toledo Blade*'s Paul Block, and a consortium of *World* employees and their colleagues all tried separately to purchase the newspaper, the *World* was bought by Scripps-Howard and became the *New York World-Telegram*. Everybody was fired.

A week after the paper's collapse, E. B. White wrote in *The New Yorker*: "The *World* had collected a handful of writers and turned them loose. They wrote almost continuously about themselves. That particular brand of autobiography would have frightened or bored most publishers, and it drew a sharp line between the *World* and such magnificently solvent organs as the *Times*. Imagine the *Times* chronicling the fact that one of its reporters had won twenty dollars yesterday playing kelly pool with a friend! Maybe that's why the *Times* is where it is today, and the *World* where *it* is; but the fact is, we miss the *World*."

In his last Conning Tower for the *World*, F.P.A. wrote, "Nobody ever ordered anything to be printed or omitted. . . . Not infrequently one would find Mr. Broun, on page 13, briskly knocking the props out from under something that an editorial writer, over on page 12, had diligently built up. . . . The *World* had more than merely a liberal and uncensored staff, though. It gave to life, in some inexplicable way, a continuity—a subtle feeling of progression. . . . Lovers, despairing of a more private expression of adoration, used to pour out their hearts in a Conning Tower poem, safe in the knowledge that it would not be published if it were bad, confident that it would be carefully proofread, and pretty sure that it would be seen by the right party next morning. Friends who seldom saw or wrote to each other kept in touch, now and then, through their contributions to the *World*. . . . No paper was more articulate, editorially.''

He closed the column with a melancholy farewell: "And so to all concerned the Conning Tower, trying to stave off the final word like a child asking for another drink of water before the light is turned off, says 'Good-by.' ''

Later that night he and Broun called at Swope's apartment to commiserate. Thinking of once wealthy stock speculators selling pencils and apples on street corners, Frank pointed to a bowl of fruit and asked, "Mr. Swope, where have you been buying your apples?" Nobody laughed.

This time, although F.P.A. was still a desirable newspaper commodity, finding a new spot wasn't easy. Newspapers, like the rest of American business, were cutting back. When the handwriting on the wall signaled the necessity for his departure from the *World*, Frank sounded out various friends on other journals. After a few weeks he determined that the most desirable new location for "The Conning Tower" was where he'd been until Swope had lured him away. Reid had merged the *Tribune* with Muncey's collapsed *Herald*, so since 1922 the paper's name had been the *New York Herald Tribune*. Frank negotiated his return. "The Conning Tower" didn't miss a beat and appeared the day after the death of the *World*, on March 2, 1931. But there wasn't much joy in the return and reunion with old friends. Frank took a salary cut, to less than $22,000. Eating crow wasn't his specialty, and he resented it. Now there were bad feelings on his part, too, and they would never go away. But he quietly moved his desk back to the *Herald Tribune* and set about the final years of writing his column.

With the collapse of the *World*, something vital and young went out of Frank's life. For him and for the other Algonks, the gaiety and optimism of the 1920s ended with the *World*.

CHAPTER FIVE

Minna
Esther
The New Yorker

Oh, Life is a glorious cycle of song,
A medley of extemporanea;
And love is a thing that can never go wrong;
And I am Marie of Roumania.

—DOROTHY PARKER

Will you love me in December as you do in May,
Will you love me in the good old-fashioned way?
When my hair has all turned gray,
Will you kiss me then and say,
That you love me in December as you did in May?

—NEW YORK CITY MAYOR JAMES J. WALKER

Captain Mitty stood up and strapped on his huge Webley-Vickers automatic. "It's forty kilometers through hell, sir," said the sergeant. Mitty finished one last brandy. "After all," he said softly, "what isn't?"

—JAMES THURBER, The Secret Life of Walter Mitty

I In 1923 Minna and Frank had been married nineteen years. Once skinny and shambling, Frank had thickened slightly but still shambled, his head thrust forward as if magnetized by something nose high and just out of reach. He commented that the loss of his boyish waistline only added to his irresistible appeal. His reputation as a man about town persisted despite an increasingly unprepossessing appearance. His mouth was wide, his lips juicy and thick. His chin disappeared into his collar without a trace. The once abundant hair, still dark, was thin. Haphazard wiry strands stuck up or bent across his forehead. He had the balding man's reluctance to permit the barber to trim the previous remnants on top, as if their meager presence somehow held at bay the fearsome prospect of hairlessness and old age. And his large ears seemed more prominent than ever. He couldn't decide whether to grow a mustache and experimented, thinking, incorrectly, that whiskers under his nose would disguise its prominence. (Once humorist Irvin S. Cobb entered a musty room dominated by a moose head hanging above the mantel. "My God, they've shot Frank Adams!" he said and asked for a drink to help him recover from the shock.) Even so, Frank Sullivan remarked that Frank Adams possessed "a certain electric dash and affected a kind of leer which seemed to madden women." He continued to dress carelessly, once suggesting that a gold service stripe sewn to the sleeve of a cherished suit for every year of its wear would find his closet aglitter with admirals' uniforms. On the rare occasion when he purchased a new suit, hat, or tie, he told of it in the Tower and invariably complained about the price, the difficulty of locating a courteous salesman or a competent tailor, the impossibility of selecting a durable fabric in a pleasing color. He was set in his ways, cranky; he was the kind of man who was rude to servants, said Heywood Hale Broun sixty years later.

But like Henry Higgins, the question wasn't whether Frank treated servants badly but whether he treated anyone differently. He was grumpy with everyone. Once he was seated next to a flirtatious actress at a dinner party. "I think, Frank," she pouted, "all you care about is my body."

"You're damned right," he said, glancing appreciatively at her decollete, "and a beautiful body it is. And let me tell you, young woman, you'd better take care of it. Because when it's gone, you won't have a damned thing left."

Yet he was unexpectedly gallant and congenial, flashing a boyish grin that disarmed and even melted hearts.

He was famous and relished the fact of his fame, if not the intrusions strangers made into his life. He didn't enjoy it when people came up to him on the street or in restaurants to ask him for his autograph; it was more than the vanity of a middle-aged man that prevented him from printing his photograph with the column. He didn't want his face widely known. Although he occasionally sat for photographic portraits, he rarely smiled in them, instead he looked sternly at the camera, as if warning off interlopers and busybodies. He appeared formidable, which was exactly what he wanted. He was F.P.A., premier columnist for the *New York World*, and he liked his life. He didn't want just anybody to share in it, no matter how friendly his Diary sounded.

One morning he received a request from D. M. Atkinson, of the MacFadden Publications, who wrote, "You have given happiness to so many people that I am sure you won't mind adding to their debt to you by telling them what was the happiest moment in your life, and why you consider it so. What you have to say . . . will be used in a symposium in one of our magazines and perhaps it will be published later in a book form." Frank's response was typically prickly. "Well, Mr. Atkinson," he replied for all to see, "if we could give the secret for happiness we should have to print it in the *World*, as our [fifty-year] contract has a clause to the effect that that publication shall have the utmost of our energy, ability and a lot of other things that until we read the contract we hadn't suspected we owned. But we don't mind saying that one of our happiest moments will come when symposium assemblers don't say to themselves, 'I won't ask him to write without offering to pay him.' "

It was an understandable attitude for a professional writer, but since Frank owed much to his contributors—who'd *never* been paid—his publicizing the request, and his bad-tempered (if justified) response in the Tower added to his reputation for arrogance. He didn't seem to mind. Arrogant or not, contributions still came to him, though familiar nom de plumes were less frequent. Old contributors occasionally remarked upon the evolving situation. One spring morning in 1923, "Sam Hill" (Emil Breitenfeld) submitted the following poem, which F.P.A. printed at the top of the column:

> *There was a time when GSK*
> *Contribbed to beat the band,*
> *Just sent his stuff to FPA*
> > *To see it land;*
>
> *When Baron Ireland's name was signed*
> *To lilt and roundelay,*
> *And Smeed and Flaccus you could find*
> > *Most any day.*
>
> *But nowadays the Satevepost*
> *Has lured some faithless wights*

And others, too, gets paid for most
Of what they writes.

Thank heaven for those still firm enough
To scorn such greedihood.
Think you that I would sell my *stuff?*
(Last line furnished on request.)

Minna's health, at almost fifty, was no longer robust. She'd been in the hospital several times for minor surgery, suffered every winter from prolonged chest colds and lingering coughs. Still handsome, she nonetheless looked her age. Her eyes had softened, the dazzling blue-whites of youth turning slightly pink and milky. She wore spectacles to read and sew. As often happened with childless couples, their life together was routinized and self-centered. Minna spent every summer in the country with friends, and Frank joined her in August on his vacation. Their white Angora cat, Mistah, received their doting attention.

Broun often wrote of his son in "It Seems to Me." Next door in the Tower, Frank bragged about Mistah, how alert and playful he was, far smarter than other cats. Frank sounded like a parent, telling how he and Minna had to spell words in front of the cat lest he become conceited: "See how H-A-N-D-S-O-M-E he is." Harold Ross and Jane Grant named their kitten "Missus" and planned to marry her to Mistah when she was old enough to fancy him. Ross spent hours teaching her tricks. Unfortunately Missus turned out to be a roving-eye Tom who vanished forever one romantic spring evening, much to Ross's disillusionment.

Sometimes Frank wrote about Woody Broun, born in 1918, with nearly as much affection as his adoring parent Heywood. One Sunday afternoon at the Swopes' in Great Neck, Long Island, there was the usual glittering gathering including Woollcott, Ross, Dorothy Parker, the Lardners, and several Marx brothers. Instead of joining the adults, Frank played with Woody. "He was for telling me tayles," wrote F.P.A. afterward, "albeit I told him I had heard all the stories there were. But he said I had never heard about the man who came into the restaurant, and ordered some soup, and the waiter brought it, and the man said, You have your thumb in it, and the waiter said, I don't mind, it isn't hot."

F.P.A. vociferously scorned the contributions of children and was supposedly as bored with the little tykes as the next tough guy. But his friends and their children knew he was a soft touch. Ten-year-old John Lardner prepared a weekly newspaper in Great Neck with his brothers.

One weekend he showed a copy of it to Frank, who admired the work of the obviously talented youngster and promptly published "the piece I liked best" in the Diary. It read:

> *Babe Ruth and Old Jack Dempsey,*
> *Both Sultans of the Swat,*
> *One hits where other people are—*
> *The other where they're not.*

This side of the cantankerous F.P.A. suggested a wistfulness he didn't often reveal. If he and Minna had wanted children, no one but them knew of it. Yet he had a gentle attitude about them that coexisted in his personality alongside the grouch. And it was Woollcott and other of his friends who complained about noisy youngsters or joked of the endless carrying-on of new parents. Rarely did Frank join the grousing if that were the subject. But he never spoke of missing the experience of parenthood, and nobody supposed he did.

On their 18th wedding anniversary in 1922—also Frank's forty-first birthday—he came home from a late night and found Minna asleep. She'd carefully wrapped a pair of slippers for him and hidden the present under his pillow, then secreted a fine new hairbrush under the covers at the bed's foot. Upon discovering it he woke her, laughing, and presented her with "a costly pair of stockings," calling her "a lucky little rogue," to be married to him. The next morning he found a bottle of lilac shaving lotion, from Mistah, at his place at breakfast.

Their life together was friendly and easygoing if not passionate, like most marriages of many years. Surprises were for newlyweds. Minna and Frank knew what to expect from each other. Often when they went to parties, they went home at different times, with different people. Sara Mankiewicz told how he'd "discard her at the door" as soon as they arrived, and journalist Marian Spitzer described Minna as "just a wife, a shadowy person hovering in the background, somebody he had to report home to every once in a while, but not a person of great importance to the way he lived his life." Spitzer was certain there were "other women."

Sixty-three years later, neither Mankiewicz nor Spitzer could remember what Minna looked like; Mankiewicz couldn't remember her name. Their memory of the Adams marriage probably was modified by subsequent knowledge, for in 1922 the couple was as comfortably married as most other long-standing duos. Minna and Frank understood one another and could make each other angry, even after so long a time. This was an indication they still cared about each other.

And each could still make the other one laugh. On a hot July afternoon, Minna and Frank drove back to the city from Hartsdale, New York, and Frank told of "my wife composing songs all the way in, very adroit and comickall," and a few days later he bought her a bottle of perfume for no particular occasion. And he reported their going to the movies one night, secretly, to avoid their ever-present friends. They sat in the last row, giggled, nudged each other, and made fun of the titles. "A seven-year-old child could read them several times over in the time they linger on the screen," he complained. They hissed and cavorted in their seats until the people in front of them ostentatiously moved.

Most Sundays they solved the *New York World* crossword puzzle together. One day he reported himself "very merry with my wife this morning, calling out to her one joke after another, all worthless. But we had a game of making sentences using prescribed words and we came to 'disdain' and I said 'I think John Barrymore in Hamlet acts dis Dane excellently.' " Frank starred himself in the recapitulation, but his tone was unmistakably affectionate.

II For those long-ago evenings, farsighted radio pioneers were discussing the huge problems of financing regular broadcasts. Cross-country reception in living rooms seemed a ridiculous fantasy to all but a few. Electronic at-home entertainment didn't exist. And most movies were primitively photographed, clumsily written and acted. Their main attraction was the novel fact that they existed. Even though the decade seems recent because during it people talked about subjects that concern contemporary Americans, in some ways—certainly in the ways people amused themselves—the era more closely resembled the hundred years preceding the decade than those years that came immediately after. Social life was entirely dependent on visiting with friends, sitting together for meals and drinks, playing games, making parlor music and conversation, going to the theater. People went out in the evenings or friends dropped in. Except for the Victrola, home was silent unless people talked or made music themselves. There were no elaborate sound systems, no blaring radios or televisions. It was a time when the middle class had domestic help and frequently dressed for dinner. Newspaper ads for clothing stores featured dinner dresses of dark velvet or spangled silk. In that more formal era, maids were trained to serve from the right and clear from the left, one of those things everybody knew then and few know, or care about, now. Hostesses seated guests carefully with an eye to talkativeness or taciturnity, mutual interests, sex appeal, or open-mindedness. Discussion of politics and religion were forbidden at conservative gatherings, but they were embraced along with every other conceivable topic at the Hale/Broun household, at the Swopes, Grant/Rosses, and Adamses. Women spent afternoons arranging the table and making out seating cards. Some of Dorothy Parker's most caustic stories focused on careless men and women who were obsessively concerned with small talk and dinner partners.

During the fall-to-spring season, the theater was a several-times-a-week diversion. It was a remarkable time for indigenous theater, when unknown playwrights became famous overnight and disappeared just as quickly, when the cigar-chewing entrepreneur could afford to bet on an unknown to make a bundle or go broke, when the pioneering spirit strolled along Broadway with his hands in his pockets and his hat on the back of his head, whistling a popular tune and dreaming of the riches he'd make in show business.

Frank and his critic friends were given free tickets to every show. He and Minna went together, often split up after an early dinner, and she'd go with a friend to one show, he'd take somebody else to another. Sometimes he'd go afterward for a "beaker of buttermilk" and a couple of games of pool at his club, the Players, on Gramercy Park. Bedtime came at midnight or twelve-thirty, usually with a book. Often he'd read to Minna before they turned out the light. They both enjoyed it, especially Frank, whose physical vanity focused on his deep, mellifluous voice and ability with it to give expressive and dramatic interpretations.

Both Minna and Frank were often in the company of other men and women, but that was an ordinary circumstance in those nights of trading tickets and escorts and escortees. Their world consisted of a large group of friends, but it was surprisingly parochial. Everyone knew everybody else, and even when important visitors from overseas like Rebecca West, D. H. Lawrence, or George Bernard Shaw visited, the same people entertained them and showed up at the various honorary fetes. At the theater, the friends all sat within a few seats of each other and remarked the next morning in print on the general decorum and on any responses that were particularly memorable.

Frank's enviable position as escort to beautiful and talented women was marked and admired by other men, giving him a sense of power among them. Being Frank's guest was an honor coveted by many women, although Minna, housewife and coinhabitant of many years, no longer shared the excitement. She saw to it that fresh shirts were stacked in his drawer every week and stood between him and the cook when he threw a tantrum about the incidence of nutmeg in his morning baked apple; but she had long grown beyond the possibility of a quickened heartbeat at the sound of his step on the stair. If Frank dallied on occasion, and he probably did, given the extraordinary opportunities available to him, and the new sexual freedoms, he always came home afterward.

Divorce was something not yet respectable in those self-conscious, barely post-Victorian times. Sophisticated people talked about the changing sexual mores, the rising divorce rate and its new social acceptability, but in the 1920s, as usual, it was the actors, painters, and musicians who acted out new social attitudes. The reporters who commented on these phenomena weren't on the cutting edge of change themselves, being, at their core, middle class in the ways of the heart. They gave lip service to accepting dissolution of marriage as an appropriate solution to incompatability. But the law lagged behind, reflecting the way the middle class really felt on the subject. In New York only adultery was sufficient reason to end a marriage, and arranging for divorce proved distasteful enough to deter most but the strongly determined. Gertrude Benchley never divorced Robert, although he lived large chunks of his life as if he were unmarried, and they couldn't have been happy years for her; Dorothy Parker didn't unload first husband Eddie Parker for years, even though he was the butt of her bitterest jokes, and they weren't content together for several years after his return from the war. She went her way and he his, but she delayed the divorce long past the time they separated. "Open marriage" was a way of life for newspaper people in the 1920s. It was much easier and far less painful than going through a divorce.

Broun and Frank talked about the subject frequently in their columns. In February 1923, Broun commented that ". . . we feel there's a certain naivete in the notion that prevalence of divorce means unhappiness and that a curtailment indicates contentment." And a month or so later, F.P.A. quoted a Justice Morschauser: "Divorce is a cancer in the vitals of American life sorely needing the knife. . . . The only way to cure the evils of divorce is to completely abolish divorce." F.P.A., the realist, added, "One way to cure the evils of cancer would be to abolish cancer."

But liberal attitudes toward divorce continued to exist at variance with establishment mores. Morality, not only as it pertained to marriage and sexuality but to twentieth-century life in general, was discussed as if it were possible to pass laws to induce it—that's how Prohibition happened. There were continual efforts to raise the standards of behavior through inspirational propaganda and the publicizing of heroic achievement. In 1923 the coveted Pulitzer Prize was awarded to Willa Cather for her novel *One of Ours*, not because it was an honest or moving work, but because it "best presented the wholesome atmosphere of American life and the highest standard of American manners and manhood." The winning play O. Davis' *Icebound* represented "the educational value and power of the stage in raising the standards of good morals, good taste and good manners." Idealism and life as it should be were celebrated as if attainable. Realism was pessimism, and nobody wanted that. Sprites and elves dancing under mushrooms were preferable.

In "The Conning Tower," F.P.A. was blissful because his friend Edna St. Vincent Millay had won the award for poetry, the first woman to win a Pulitzer Prize.

F.P.A. easily tired of phonies and blowhards. One evening at dinner when Ellis Lardner asked him the kind of person he preferred, he answered, "People without pretense." He took every opportunity to ridicule the self-righteous or those who pretended to know right from wrong in murky matters of the heart. "What has taken all our waking time," he wrote, "is the compilation of a list of Ten Lists of 'Ten Books I Enjoyed Most' I enjoyed most. Thus far our favorite list is that of Professor Stuart P. Sherman. He says he enjoys Boswell's *Life of Johnson* and Milton's *Samson Agonistes*. Now, it takes all kinds of readers to make a world, and among them may be those who 'enjoy' Boswell; but it seems to us that anybody who says he 'enjoys' *Samson Agonistes* would rather do calisthenics in the bathroom mornings than play golf or tennis.

"To our unbigoted notion any list of Enjoyable Books that fails to include *Davy and the Goblin* is just ridiculous. . . . Reading of most of these lists leads to the conviction that they should be entitled 'Ten Books I Want People to Think I Enjoyed Most.' "

Frank and his friends were children of Victorians, so while they enjoyed bravely taking on the world's hypocrites in matters of abstract principle, rebellion against the ghosts of their parents proved not so easy. None of their parents had divorced. So the Algonks tended to be more straight-laced in their feelings about personal relationships than onlookers might have supposed. Even when they were breaking ground in other ways, it was inevitably difficult for them to live or react intimately without residual and unguessed parental interference. It took more than a generation to displace ancient taboos. Supposedly outmoded emotional attitudes dictated behavior in unpredictable subconscious ways. When people behaved differently from their parents, it was only after intense, often painful exertion.

Of course, everybody knew about Freud, the Oedipus complex, and the mysteries of the subconscious. F.P.A. laughed at fads and thumbed his nose, even at the most fashionable of totems:

> *Don't tell me what you dreamt last night, I must not hear you*
> *speak!*
> *For it might bring a crimson blush unto my maiden cheek.*
> *If I were you, that subject is a thing that I'd avoid—*
> *Don't tell me what you dreamt last night, for I've been reading*
> *Freud.*

Frank remembered that his parents had lived together in a state of truce until his mother's death. With temperaments vastly differing, each of them had been keenly unhappy from time to time. But the idea of separating or dissolving their marriage would have horrified both of them. They'd felt that marriage was for life. So no matter how progressive Frank's public views were, when his friends split up, he was saddened and frightened in a deeply secret place. Such emotional profligacy introduced disorder into his neat life, and threatened chaos. He wanted people to live within the tidy strictures society imposed. For him, the institution of marriage was an important civilizing influence. He felt more comfortable observing men like Broun and Benchley who had love affairs but stayed married. That was his intention, too.

Until he met Esther Sayles Root.

III   Esther Sayles Root graduated in 1915 from Smith College, hotbed of future Algonquin wives. Gertrude Darling (Benchley) was a classmate who had graduated a year earlier, as had Ellis Abbott (Lardner), a few years before that. (It was a small world. Ring Lardner attended Frank's alma mater, Chicago's Armour Institute, for a few misguided weeks at the turn of the century. He studied mechanical engineering. "I can't think of no walk in life for which I had more of a natural bent unless it would be hostess at a roller rink," he said.) During World War I, Esther did volunteer work in Europe, first in Paris with the Red Cross, then later with the Quakers helping to find homes for Belgian refugees. She played concert-level piano, having studied in Italy, Spain, and England. After her return to New York in 1921, she became music editor of the *New York Morning Telegraph*, a paper with a plaid-suit reputation based on its boisterous coverage at the track. Esther called her music column "Over Periscope Pond." She was tall, beautiful, intelligent, and sprang from an impeccably credentialed old and wealthy WASP family.

The Roots traced their ancestry back to John Roote, of Badby, Northamptonshire, England, a Puritan who immigrated to America in 1640 in order to avoid conscription into Cromwell's army. His (four-greats) grandson was Esther's grandfather, fervent abolitionist and song-writer George Frederick Root. He wrote the words and music to more than a hundred popular songs and hymns, among them "Tramp, Tramp, Tramp, the Boys are Marching," "The Battle Cry of Freedom," "Just Before the Battle, Mother," and "The Hazel Dell." He lived in Chi-cago, where he headed a firm that sold musical instruments and pub-lished songs and a magazine called "The Song Messenger." Root and Cady rented offices in the Crosby Opera House, which was destroyed in 1871 by the fire. His fortune was only momentarily discommoded by the disaster, and he lived to see it multiply. His wife was Mary Olive Woodman, and their third child was Charles Towner Root, born in 1849, who moved to Short Hills, New Jersey, and became president of the Textile Publishing Company (later the Union Publishing Company) in New York City, which produced several trade publications, among them "The Dry Goods Economist," "The Dry Goods Reporter," and "Iron Age."

Besides the family home in New Jersey, Charles and his wife, Elizabeth Sayles Root, who died in 1922, maintained a sprawling brown-shingled summer residence on Bailey Island, Maine, and an apartment at 2 West Sixty-seventh Street in Manhattan. His career prospered as did his family; there were seven children. The second youngest, born in 1894, was Esther Sayles Root. Her financial position, and that of her siblings, was made secure by their parents. When she and each of them reached the age of twenty-one, they were presented with their share of the family fortune—$100,000 each—and told to say no more about it, to use the sum to achieve independence. It was a particularly Yankee method of sending one's children into the world. They didn't have to wait for the death of the patriarch, with the ensuing squabbling and unseemly avarice. They were equipped, turned out, then left alone. Parents were expected not to hover, nag, or attach strings to the arrangement. Once they'd reached their majority, children were to move along on their own, not to whine or cling, to take care of their own affairs without inviting advice or seeking any but the most impersonal assistance. Brothers and sisters helped one another, but more often folded their arms and looked the other way. They didn't invite closeness. Such a hands-off policy often produced aloofness and an accompanying fear of intimacy, which could become dependency. And loneliness. When Frank met Esther, she was nearly thirty years old and unmarried.

She'd met Edna St. Vincent Millay, who'd been traveling in Spain with her mother, after the war. The Millays called Esther "Tess," as did her college friends. Esther had come back to New York in 1921, and upon the poet's return from Europe in 1923, she moved back into an apartment on Waverly Place in Greenwich Village. Esther lived upstairs. It was there that Edna, consciously matchmaking, introduced Esther to her good friend Frank Adams.

The year 1922 ended well for Frank. His mood was hopeful and upbeat. A few days before Christmas, his physician, Dr. Edmond Devol, came for dinner, and Frank regaled him with tales of the various ailments that had plagued Samuel Pepys. Besides copying the style and language of the diarist, Frank was his student. Minna had given him a two-volume copy of the *Diary*, and over the years Frank filled it with annotations. He liked to conjecture on the life of the famous scribe, compare seventeenth-century urban life to his own. Pepys had suffered from gallstones, for which he underwent surgery. He was also afflicted with a slightly hypochondriacal concern with the various aches and infirmities of aging; his vision deteriorated as he grew older.

At the dinner table Minna laughed, teasing that the worst of Pepys' plagues had been his wife Elizabeth, who nagged and bossed him unrelentingly. Ah! said Frank, but Pepys was lucky in that respect; she'd had the good sense to die by the time she was twenty-nine. "I meant the remark in a merry way," explained Frank who was never too shy to repeat his own bon mots, "and so I think it was taken."

On Christmas Eve he printed his Christmas wishes in the Tower:

A merry Christmas this December
To a lot of folks I don't remember.

He returned home early Christmas Eve morning from a poker game at Harold Ross' and found on his bed "a fine Christmas gift from my wife, three nightgownes of linen with my initials worked on them, which

I shall try to remember to tell her is a great convenience, since when there are dozens of us in a bed it will be easy to distinguish me by the embroidered initials." He couldn't resist being funny, even at the expense of tenderness. "Yet I hope to forget to tell her," he said, more softly, "forasmuch as the initials are very featly made, and doubtless she was at great pains to make them." He wasn't an uncaring husband, though affectionate demonstrations were rare, and he chose to appear blase before the world. Yet his audience could read between the lines, whether or not he intended them to.

On New Year's Eve he reported his "huge good humour" because "this year was the best ever I had, in health, in happiness, in my adventures with money, . . . for which I thank heaven."

He and Minna stopped at Ruth and Raoul Fleishmann's early in the evening, where the two little boys "rolled me over and walked upon my face, and to judge by their noisy laughter, had a merry time of it."

These year-end journal entries were written by a satisfied man. At forty-two he was on top of the world. Or so he would have it appear.

Later that night at a boisterous party welcoming in the New Year at the Hale/Broun house, he spoke at length to glamorous singer Grace Moore and later described admiringly what she'd been wearing, and that she sang in "as clear and sweet a voice as ever I heard anywhere." He didn't mention meeting Esther Root at the party. When he and Minna returned home early the next morning, Frank wished Mistah a happy new year, then went sleepily to bed.

For the next few weeks he frequently mentioned Grace Moore. The singer was beautiful and delightful. In a "survey" conducted by a movie magazine a few years later she was asked by the gushing interviewer what she collected. She responded "emeralds." (In Hollywood upwardly mobile Joan Crawford answered "symphonic records" to the same question.) Moore pouted that "poorly laid tables" was what she disliked most. Her ironic wit and ability to make fun of herself attracted Frank as much as did her beauty. But it was all in fun. There was nothing serious about their friendship.

On January 30, a damp bleak day, Frank received a postcard from Grantland Rice, Ring Lardner, and George Ade, vacationing together in Florida. He yearned to leave the city himself, and on the way to his office he picked up a travel folder extolling the languid pleasures of Bermuda. "If I had been weaker, or stronger—" he said, "I cannot tell which—I would have got aboard a boat at that moment." Instead he went to work, preoccupied all day with thoughts of that island's clear turquoise water and sunny beaches. Later in the evening he greeted

Edna Millay, just returned from her two years in Europe. He took her
to her place on Waverly Place, where a large welcome home party was
in progress. Two of the guests were Dudley Field Malone, a lawyer
who was Clarence Darrow's associate at the Scopes trial, and his wife,
distinguished feminist Doris Stevens. There was much heated talk of
religion and politics. Frank enjoyed himself. The party's hostess was
Esther Root. When she showed him around her apartment upstairs, he
is supposed to have told her, "It's nice here. I'd like to move in." He
didn't report the statement in the Diary, but people said they'd overheard
him. The comment wasn't exactly romantic, but still it was a sexual
approach, unique, brusque, unmistakably F.P.A. Nobody bothered to
record Esther Root's response. As yet there wasn't any reason to note
her reaction. She was just another pretty face.

Nevertheless, her name began cropping up in the Diary, along with
flames of earlier duration like Hilda Gaige, Dorothy Parker, and, of
course, Grace Moore. At first, when Frank saw her, Esther seemed
usually to be accompanied by Edna Millay, but there were subtle in-
dications he quickly began taking notice of her, separately. One Saturday
in February he played two sets of tennis, lunched with Moore, and took
her to an artist's studio for a look at some examples of his work, then
ate dinner with Woollcott and accompanied him to *Icebound*, which he
praised, but not excessively. (The wife was "too sweet for my taste,"
he said. "In a day or two she would have bored her husband so that
he would have left the farm.") He and Woollcott dropped in at the
home of Lawrence Langner and Armina Marshall—founders of the
Theatre Guild—and he reported having "a pleasant time with Edna
Millay's mother and with Miss E. Root." Two days later he stopped
by the house on Waverly Place on the way home from work (which
required getting on and off the rush-hour subway and a walk of several
blocks in the cold, not exactly a stop "on the way" for the ever-impatient
F.P.A.). There he had a "gay time of it." Later he and Minna went
to see Ethel Barrymore in *The Laughing Lady*, a drama about marital
infidelity. He conjectured that the play ended unsatisfactorily because
"the lovers decided to return to their spouses, and the certainty was that
at least four persons would be achingly unhappy instead of possibly
two."

A few nights later he dreamed of a "warm, sweet spring," then
awoke to find fresh snow and dreariness, leaving him inconsolable. He
was too depressed even to play tennis at the armory. Usually he bounded
off to play, no matter what the weather. Clearly his lack of energy and
the conspicuous despair from which it sprang were unique. But his

mood changes were rapid, almost laughable. The next afternoon, a Sunday, old friends Marjorie and Walter Trumbell came to the Adamses for dinner, along with Esther, this time without Millay. Esther played the piano. Afterward Frank and Minna journeyed downtown to hear a string quartet, an unusual classical excursion for them. Later they went to the Hale/Brouns. Before he went to bed that night, Frank read Sherwood Anderson's *Many Marriages*, which described a man's state of mind when he was about to tell his wife and daughter he was going to leave them. Adultery and the abandonment of hearth and home were untypically painful themes for him to concern himself with, but in the next few weeks the same subjects cropped up in the column repeatedly: the breakup of longtime marriages, the relative merits of remaining in an unhappy relationship, the difficulty of breaking the news that you no longer loved or wanted to stay married to a wife you didn't dislike. Together with these unconsciously relevant ruminations were energetic, delighted reports on the imminence of spring. "Spring is but a month away!" he exalted one February morning, but his mood may have reflected happy anticipation of seeing Esther that afternoon as much as the long awaited change of season. By this time she was dropping in often at the Adamses, frequently escorted by one or another of Frank's friends, who were used to playing "beard" for each other. Edna Millay rarely visited at the Adams home, which may have meant that Minna preferred not to entertain her; possibly Frank's longstanding and vocal attraction to her had something to do with Minna's turning a cold face to the poet. This coldness may have produced Edna's enthusiasm, uncluttered with scruples, about introducing her dear friend Frank to her dear friend Tess. In any case, Frank invariably saw Millay elsewhere, never at home, and rarely when he was with Minna. One Saturday night Marc Connelly brought Esther over, and the four of them played the piano and sang, and Connelly recited his hilarious versions of "That Old Sweetheart of Mine," "Barbara Frietchie," and "Clear in the Cool September Morn," with requisite gestures and grimaces. Minna played some songs from *The Pirates of Penzance*, and everybody went late, contentedly and separately, to bed. Minna and Frank used twin beds, as did most of their modern friends.

Frank admitted, as March became April, then May, to daydreaming more often than usual, to attention that fluttered and bolted inexplicably. One evening when Joe Wise came over for a game of casino with Minna, Frank stood silently gazing out the window for nearly half an hour. "They both made game of me," he said, "and said I was mooning over a youthful love . . . which may be true or may be not."

In the Tower he reported that Peggy Hopkins Joyce was posing for a painting at Neysa McMein's, then the next day corrected himself, the model was Alice Duer Miller instead. Within the week his car ran out of gas—his mind was on "other matters." He had to undergo the ignominy of accepting a tow to a Staten Island blacksmith's. Carless and depressed, he took the ferry alone back to Manhattan. A few days later he was short-tempered with Minna, snapping "some harsh words for her being verbose at the telephone." He apologized later, but his jittery turns of mood and continual preoccupation bore all the symptoms of a man who was falling in love.

One morning he drove Minna to City Hall, where she called on the mayor to complain about the proliferating garbage being dumped near their home in a lot at the end of West Seventy-ninth Street. But Frank spent the afternoon gazing from his office window, reflecting on the beauty of the city, feeling glad to be alive "for this brief span," curiously inert, detached, indifferent to the garbage situation, for once passively letting Minna attend to it. A few days later when his sister Amy visited from Chicago, it was Esther, not Minna, who accompanied the brother and sister when they saw Don Marquis' *The Old Soak*. Undoubtedly Frank proudly wanted his favorite relative to meet Esther. And he wanted Esther to meet this representative of his family, an indicator to both of them of his seriousness of purpose.

In May he visited with his old friend Edna Ferber. Over lunch in her apartment, and then all afternoon, they discussed his relationship with women, his attitudes toward them. He may have sought Ferber's advice, although his obtuseness exasperated her. Finally she told him he knew so little of women that he wouldn't be able to pass the entrance exams at the "Moron Kindergarten." She accused him of insensitivity, blindness. They were talking about Minna and Esther. But Edna couldn't wave a magic wand to fix anything, so he left her apartment as it was getting dark outside, unhappy and preoccupied.

As the year progressed, mentions of Esther in the Diary increased as he spent more public time with her. He spoke less frequently of Minna, mentioning her only impersonally, in connection with visits to friends, or when he dropped her off or picked her up at the station. Sometimes on cook's night off she fixed him something he liked for dinner. But they went out together less frequently. When their nineteenth anniversary arrived on November 15, 1923, he didn't mention the occasion. Dorothy Parker threw a party for his birthday, and he gloated about his presents and the number of well-wishers, and afterward at another fete, this one given by Ruth and Raoul Fleischmann, they teased him that they weren't honoring him, but instead George Kaufman (for *his* birthday) and Arthur Krock (for his) and themselves because they'd been married three years. There was no mention of Minna, or their anniversary.

In the Tower the clues abounded as to his romantic state. He selected not very good but oh-so-sentimental poems for the top:

GRATITUDE

I pass through
City Hall Park
And Union Square Park
And Madison Square Park . . .
In fact, any park
That has benches.
And I see bewhiskered,
Cowed, and beaten forms
Of what surely must have been
Men,
And I whisper to God:
"I guess you never gave them
A sweetheart
Like mine."

—ARTURO

Winner of the 1923 watch was a poem called "Snowfall." It was an unusual choice. Not a classic translation, satire, or parody, or even a ballade or rondeau, it was quiet, wistful, simple:

Wires strung with diamonds,
Shanties decked in white,
Our shabby little village
Turned lovely overnight.

If I were dressed in satin,
With diamonds in my hair,
Do you think, perhaps, that someone
Would say that I was fair?

—I.V.S.W.

For the first time since its inception, there was no Contribunion award dinner. Times had changed, people's lives were jammed with other activities, the whole thing had become too cumbersome. Newman Levy and Adelaide Hahn were occupied elsewhere, and nobody came forward to make the arrangements for them. Strangely enough, no one seemed to notice the event's cessation. It was laid to rest without eulogy or apology, a relic of other times.

At year's end Frank described 1923 as a year in which he "had the joyousest content of any year," then admitted without explanation, "and the lowest times, too." The first day of 1924 found him at the opera, *Tosca*, with Esther. While he said he no longer enjoyed grand opera, the occasion was paradise compared to his experience a few nights later at the International Composers' Guild, where he "could make naught out of the music save a deal of unpleasant noise, nor did I think it was too good for me, but more likely I was too good for it. There was a piece called "Octandre," wrote by E. Varese, full of whistles and disharmonies, and it had to do with a flower having eight stamens, the program said, but Lord! quoth one in my hearing, if that be saying it with flowers, I am grateful that he did not say it in brussel sprouts. And I told D. Taylor if I had to guess at the title, I should say it was Fun in the Willys-Knight Service Station."

If Esther was attempting to improve or enlarge his musical vocabulary, it was an uphill battle.

The last time he spoke of Minna in the Diary was on January 22, 1924, when he told of escorting her to Zona Gale's play, *Mister Pitt*. He complained about the "falsely happy ending." He never mentioned Minna again.

During the Spring, gaps in the Diary began to occur. Some Saturdays he'd run the weekday Tower without explanation. There'd be no recital of his doings. Two or three weekends later, again without fanfare, the Diary would reappear. His fans began to complain.

He didn't explain, and the missing entries persisted. He was busy courting Esther and had scant inclination to maintain the Diary. In order to keep Minna in the dark, it was necessary to conceal his activities. He could safely mention dates with Esther at public events every couple of weeks. But more frequent detailing of their engagements invited suspicions that were difficult to counter because they were justified. Since much of the courtship happened before the eyes of many who were Minna's friends as well as his, Frank felt it wise simply to omit all references to what he was doing. The original Pepys, of course, hadn't bothered to conceal his extramarital affairs. But he hadn't been writing for publication in a daily newspaper.

And as the relationship evolved inexorably, it became necessary to protect Esther from implication. Adultery was the only ground for divorce in New York State, and if it came to that, Frank didn't want Esther named by Minna as corespondent. He was concerned and worried, caught in escalating emotional turmoil. One morning he admitted he was "as low as ever I felt." When Esther quit her job to go abroad, he missed her terribly and sank even lower. He wrote her long agonized letters, occasionally punctuating them playfully, stealing time from column versifying:

> *As Hunter misses the side line,*
> *As Harvard misses the crew,*
> *As Benchley misses the Scarsdale train*
> *That's how I miss you.*

His attitude was one of wonder, surprise at the depth and quality of his feeling, an almost naive belief in the one-of-a-kind nature of their relationship. The cynic had vanished: "And, Root, I never single-spaced to anybody else. And I had trouble filling one page at that. God! if my letters give you a tenth of the happiness yours do me, there must be something in it, as I was saying only a year ago last February [a month after they'd met]."

Much of the Diary and the column was given, in those early summer days, to ruminations on impersonal matters and discussions of what he was reading. The poems he published by others were long ones and often took up most of the column. One day he even published a several-hundred-word excerpt from Arnold Bennett's latest novel, *Riceyman Steps*. It was a transparent ruse. Frank had never been so lax, but for once he didn't care.

One spring morning he buried a contribution halfway down the column:

> *There are lots of things to do in Barcelona*
> *Besides writing couplets on the old Corona.*

The contributor's initials were E.S.R.

Longstanding friends were divided on the matter of Frank's treatment of Minna. Some felt that he was behaving unchivalrously and should renounce Esther. Others, caught up by the way things looked, preferred a continuation of the love affair so that the marriage could be preserved, a hypocritical but conventional solution. Had that happened, Esther's role as the other woman would have been perpetuated, something Frank didn't want, nor did she. Her background and education hadn't prepared her for backstairs status. Besides, they were crazy about each other. At forty-three he was thirteen years older than she. His position as premier New York columnist gave him extraordinary prestige and power. Yet suddenly he was behaving like a boy in love for the first time.

With a history of difficulty in establishing intimate relationships, and having recently lost her mother, Esther had been uncertain and a little scared. She hadn't known what—if anything—she wanted from her career, yet there seemed nothing else with which to become intensely involved. With Frank she found herself trusting somebody else, willing to merge her destiny with his, giving up independence she wasn't entirely comfortable with without betraying or abandoning her training and temperament. She knew that being F.P.A.'s wife would give her an opportunity to live the kind of life she wanted. And she yearned for a family, as did he.

Each of them grasped for the other as a crucial, lifesaving chance.

During the spring of 1924, Minna agreed to a divorce. On May 15 Frank topped the column with his own poem, a soft, unusually gentle and romantic verse called "Parting."

> And now the bells, from their confining tower,
> Announce our parting to a heedless world.
> Now they proclaim the irrevocable hour—
> I shall be brave. Already I have furled
> My spirit's banner, and its colors droop
> Like listless flowers when the wind is still.
> But you—you will not see my courage stoop;
> With head held high I'll leave you on the hill.
>
> You will not walk with me until the gate
> Over whose palings locusts trail their hands,
> And sunbeams weave a mesh of tenuous strands;
> Alone now I shall hear the swallows prate
> Beneath my window. But you'll never know
> How deep my wound, so bravely will I go.

On August 1, 1924, Frank stopped writing the Diary altogether. He didn't begin it again until the following January. During the interval, he and his lawyer arranged for him to be observed performing an adulterous act with a woman hired for the occasion. Witnesses also provided by his attorney were paid to sign an affidavit attesting to their rehearsed discovery. On the basis of this arrangement, Minna obtained a divorce. She and Frank divided their household. She took Mistah and most of the furniture and moved to Washington, D.C., where she'd lived and made friends during the war. She spent the rest of her life there, Frank paying alimony every month until her death nearly three decades later. Minna, the aging chorus girl, was the hapless casualty of Frank's midlife romance. Many regretted her treatment, felt sorry as she departed quietly, even missed her for a while. But ranks closed quickly around F.P.A., and everybody went to the wedding, held May 9, 1925, in the garden of the home of Esther's friend Ruth Warfield, in Greenwich, Connecticut.

New York law forbade the adulterous spouse to remarry within the state for five years. Since Frank and Esther married less than a year after the divorce, they had to tie the knot out of state. The Warfield property straddled the line separating New York and Connecticut. A white satin ribbon was tied across the lawn, designating the dividing line, and they were careful to have the rite performed on the Connecticut side. Guests included the entire Algonquin contingent, as well as the Swopes, the Lardners, Elinor Wylie and her husband William Benet, Edna Millay and her husband Eugen Boissevain. Millay described the wedding in a glowing letter to her mother: "Tess looked perfectly beautiful, in the sweetest white dress, and carrying an enormous bouquet of lillies of the valley. I never saw her look so pretty. And I never saw Frank look so well, either, very serious and quite pale." There were "rafts of caviar and oceans of champagne."

Afterward the couple drove back to the city. They stopped at the Fleischmanns', where the regular meeting of the Thanatopsis was to take place, undeterred as always by interruption of weddings, parades, cyclones, or other acts of God. Woollcott, Ross, Broun, Swope, Kaufman, and Fleischmann took off their jackets, eased their belts a couple of notches, and sat down to the real business of the evening. Frank decided to sit in for what he promised would be a few hands. Esther and Ruth Fleischmann scrambled eggs, and Esther ate them from a platter while perched on a stool behind Frank's chair. Stakes were high, and she watched in mounting alarm as he lost the money earmarked for their honeymoon. Fortunately he was able to borrow it back from Treasurer Kaufman, who was too softhearted to see the bride cry, or break a plate over his head. A few days later the happy couple cast off for Europe on the ocean liner *Mauretania*.

Esther, ostensibly a Lucy Stoner, applied for a passport in her own name. Miraculously she received it and became the first married American woman to travel abroad under the name she'd been born with. She became a feminist heroine, and her picture appeared on the cover of *Equal Rights*, a magazine published in Baltimore. Frank was proud of her and called her his cover girl. But her commitment to feminism depended on the issue. Her marriage license listed her occupation as "housewife," indicating even before the wedding her rejection of the independent identity she'd made as pianist and journalist. And nobody ever called her Esther Root again.

For the honeymoon departure, uncharacteristically dapper Frank sported gray kid spats, a new suit, black gloves with a button at each wrist, and a homburg. It was the first and last time he was so elegantly outfitted, and it bespoke his commitment, which lasted longer than his outfit. Upon their return from Europe, he sank comfortably back into his usual state, with rumpled suits and unbuckled galoshes. He wasn't one for appearance.

The Adamses' honeymoon lasted over two months. They traveled from Rome to Perugia, Florence, Venice, and to London. Along the way they picked up Woollcott, an eager friend who always seemed to be around for other people's honeymoons. (When Grant and Ross got married, Woollcott, wildly enthusiastic because he'd introduced them to each other, arranged all the festivities. These included a gala dinner for the three of them at the Waldorf and the honeymoon trip to the Bellevue-Stratford Hotel in romantic downtown Philadelphia. Upon the return of the newlyweds Woollcott presented them with a carefully itemized bill for all of his expenses, including the $20 fee to the preacher—often paid by the best man, which he claimed to have been—and an astonishing extra $100 for his "personal wear and tear." Jane Grant said that this particular ungraciousness provided the basis for bad feelings that lasted for years.)

In Florence Esther and Frank spent time with actor Roland Young and his wife, and, with Margalo's sister Ruth Gillmore, saw the sights—including the Casa Guidi, where the Brownings had lived.

They visited art critic Bernard Berenson and attended a gigantic costume party at the villa of artist Ben Ali Habbin. There was an "endless garden with hundreds of lemon trees with electric lights hidden in them," said Frank, adding, "Over all was a smell of honeysuckle, and I walked there for a long time with my wife and confided to her that I was far from apathetick to her."

He spent an afternoon at the Biblioteca Laurenziana, which housed the huge Medici collection of Greek and Latin manuscripts, including the pandects of Justinian, the fourth-century Medicean virgin, and Boccaccio's autograph manuscript of Dante's eclogues and epistles. Even some poems by Horace transcribed in the fifth century. He was overwhelmed, delighted with the opportunity to look at the treasures. But they were leaving for Venice that afternoon, so he couldn't stay. He swore to return to Florence someday so that he might spend at least a week in the library. Of course, he never did.

He loved the gondolas in Venice, the most romantic of cities, and the fact that there were no streets, that the gondoliers moved "in a mysterious way and with adroitness [kept] from colliding." He speculated that "nobody hath wrote about this city." Esther chided him. "Have you never read John Ruskin?" she asked. " 'No,' said I. 'Neither have I,' she said."

They hated to leave Italy, but did, finally, when Frank received a telegram that read, "Come Home Stuff Rotten Regards Swope." They traveled by train through Paris to London, where they saw several shows. While at Cambridge University, they visited Magdalene College, where Samuel Pepys had studied. The diarist had bequeathed the college his collection of books, arranged not by subject or author, but, curiously, by size. Frank was shown the original diary and was suitably impressed.

Upon their return to the States, the Adamses settled into their new place on West Thirteenth Street, dubbed "Villa d'Esther," by Frank. Greenwich Village was in its heyday as the center of artistic and political activity. The marriage and this new location gave Frank fresh vitality. He even gave up the Thanatopsis for a while. If their relationship had started as just another fling, its unexpected outcome had changed his outlook; he enjoyed new confidence, new serenity, new interest in the world around him. And within the decade, he found himself with a great big new family.

IV The newlyweds rented two floors in a little house on West Thirteenth Street between Sixth and Seventh avenues. The red brick house, bright with windowboxes and shutters to close against the insistent noise, nestled among a low line of attached buildings on the crooked cobbled street, shaded by a pair of scrawny city trees. But young newcomers yearning for space in the Manhattan limelight knew well enough who lived behind the shutters. E. B. White, fresh from Cornell University, rented an apartment farther east on Thirteenth Street, in the same building with lanky Ohioan James Thurber. Years later White described how he "used to walk quickly past the house . . . where F.P.A. lived, and the block seemed to tremble under my feet—the way Park Avenue trembles when a train leaves Grand Central."

But the cozy house didn't suit the Adamses for long. A few months after their first anniversary, four days after Frank's forty-fifth birthday, Esther gave birth to a baby boy. Frank was overjoyed, unprepared for the deep feelings the baby's birth engendered. "On the night our hero was born," he reported in the *Ladies' Home Journal*, "a solitary straggler might have been seen wending his way along . . . ejected from the hospital one hour and twenty minutes after this remarkably beautiful child had come into the world . . . sensing that sleep was not for him, yearning for companionship. By midnight, so self-engrossed are New Yorkers, he had exhausted the list of his acquaintances." He continued, "I gave up trying—that night—to interest the denizens of a self-centered city. I went home."

Irving Berlin and his wife, Ellin, produced a baby the same week, in the same popular maternity hospital. The Berlin offspring was a little girl, Mary Ellin. Berlin and Adams spent the two weeks of their wives' confinement (after visiting hours) at the Players Club and various speakeasies, toasting each other and their remarkable progeny. When it was time to go home, Frank borrowed the songwriter's Mercer automobile to transport his wife and their new baby to Thirteenth Street.

Fifteen months later, on April 18, 1928, another son, Timothy, was added to the Adams family group. As soon as the toddler learned to talk, he called his big brother "Tat." Soon everybody else did too.

The following year Frank and Esther moved their burgeoning family to larger quarters, an entire house at number 26 West Tenth Street. There, in July 1931, their daughter was born. Somewhat fancifully they named her Persephone Fortune, in honor of the goddess whose release from the underworld every year brings spring. She was nicknamed "Puff." Completing the family sixteen months later, Jonathan was born on December 3, 1932.

During the 1920s Greenwich Village was turbulent with the talk and work of painters, writers, political activists, poets, outspoken people who seemed endlessly hanging out in each other's cluttered living rooms. The adult Adamses participated enthusiastically. Frank would often take Tat and Tim for Sunday morning walks, drop in on neighbors expecting hospitality and getting it, walking his children as if they were puppies. The little boys sat obediently on his lap or leaned against him, silent and too warm in their snowsuits, longing to be gone, while the grownups talked and sipped coffee.

Frank enjoyed his new role as father, although there were surprises. For a man used to locating his possessions where he'd left them, parenthood held unexpected life-style modifications. When he absent-mindedly left his expensive automatic wristwatch on the bureau, four-year-old Tat, curious because there was no stem with which to wind it, took the watch up to the sandbox on the roof to examine it further. With the help of a hammer, he found out about the watch's inner workings but not much about putting it back together. As punishment, Frank whacked Tat on the back of his hand. In a few days a tiny dark birthmark appeared on the back of the little boy's hand, exactly where Frank had struck him. It was known in the family thereafter as "Look-What-Papa-Did."

Frank was twenty-five years older than most fathers of young children, a fact that delighted and perplexed him. Except for infrequent cases when he lost his temper, he didn't spank his children, believing instead in the rule of logic, firmness, and distance. The public person and the private one were the same. He seldom spoke of personal matters at home—or anywhere else, for that matter. His children learned his opinions as they grew older because he spoke them at the table and wrote them in his column. "If you read the Tower, you knew him as well as we did," remembers one of the children, wistfully, many years later.

His friends continued to serve as his life's major focus. Sinclair Lewis and Dorothy Thompson lived catty-corner from Frank and Esther, at 37 West Tenth Street. Thompson used the second floor as her studio and had to deal at all hours with the unexpected guests of her husband. He didn't like to go out, so invited his friends over, often without informing the cook or his wife. Lewis' biographer, Vincent Sheean, described his hospitality as "incorrigible. He always asked everybody to come and never wanted anybody to go. If he felt the need of solitude, or even of sleep, he would abandon the company and retire for an hour, almost always with the solemn injunction that nobody was to go away . . . Dorothy was also extremely hospitable but she did have the habits of civilization; she could tell lunch from dinner; if she asked you for cocktails she did not expect you to stay all night; and furthermore she always recognized that other people had other things to do, which Red treated as a chimerical notion."

A block away lived poet Elinor Wylie and her husband William Rose Benet, at that time editor of the *Literary Review* (forerunner of the *Saturday Review*). Elinor and Bill were both longtime contributors to "The Conning Tower" and friends of Frank's. She wrote at a big unvarnished table, typing on blue paper with a turquoise typewriter ribbon. Louis Untermeyer, smitten, claimed that Elinor resembled Nefertiti: "the same imperious brows; the high cheekbones and the scooped-out cheeks; the proud and narrow nose; the small taut mouth; the carved and resolute chin; the long smooth column of the throat."

Edmund Wilson and his wife, Mary Blair, lived with their baby at One University Place. John Dos Passos, another Villager, remembers his first meeting with Wilson: "There appeared a slight sandyheaded young man with a handsome clear profile. He wore a formal dark business suit. The moment we had been introduced, while we were waiting for the elevator, Bunny [Wilson's nickname] gave an accent to the occasion by turning, with a perfectly straight face, a neat somersault."

In the midst of the Village hubbub was the Adamses' brownstone, five stories tall, a wrought-iron railing protecting the three-step stoop. On summer evenings its carved mahogany front doors stood ajar, welcoming conversation, friends and laughter. There was a nurse for the babies, Delia Mullen, servants to keep the place tidy and prepare meals (with Thursday evenings and Sundays off). Despite the growing family, Esther and Frank's social life tumbled on without appreciable interruption. The children ate supper early, in the basement kitchen, well before the grown-ups upstairs. The house was big, comfortable, with a second-floor living room containing dramatic floor-to-ceiling front windows and two grand pianos, which stood with their sweeping backs fitting gracefully side by side, back to back.

Many years later Tim was asked who among his parents' many famous friends was his favorite. He answered instantly: "Burgess Meredith, because he taught us to tap dance on the roof of the house at West Tenth Street."

By the time he was fifty, when many men were settling into sideline grandfatherhood, Frank was dealing with two o'clock feedings, colic, teething, bedtime stories, and baby carriages in the front hall. It was harrowing for the man-about-town to slow his pace for the toddler at his side, but so he did, and reported it.

Five years after Tat was born, Frank published "For a Birthday Boy" in the Tower, sentimental without embarrassment, clearly identifying himself as a doting father:

> *My son, when something in your eye*
> *Yesterday morning chanced to fly,*

Doctor Levine stuck in a stick
And made your eye no longer sick.

And though the cinder (known as "crumb")
Hurt you, you told him, more than some,
You said, with candor in your eye,
"I didn't cry, I didn't cry."

I'm glad the gods—or some one—gave
You such a smiling heart and brave,
But yours may be less brave and bold
The day your son is five years old.

One evening Esther was playing an obscure Brahms quintet arranged for two pianos when she heard the other part being played on the other side of the wall, at her neighbors'. Dr. and Mrs. Henry Spencer lived at 24 West Tenth Street and their piano-playing boarder was Eurena Clark, an accomplished pianist who taught at the Mannes School of Music on the Upper West Side. Esther and Eurena, a woman who'd "come through the wall" as Frank always referred to the circumstances of the meeting, became auction-hunting, piano-playing friends. Eurena soon moved in with the Adamses, and when it was time, taught piano to the children. It was Eurena, beloved of the little boys, who took Tat and Tim in her 1929 Ford roadster to their first baseball game, between the Yankees and the Tigers at Yankee Stadium, when Tat was nine and Tim eight.

Eurena was one of the few people who could hold her own with Frank at anagrams. His expertise was legendary; nobody at home and none of his friends could beat him. He never allowed himself to be beaten by any of his children, even when they were little and just learning. He believed they had to learn about "earning it," and that lesson became a primary value for them.

Soon after Tat's birth, Frank and Esther decided they and their children needed, in addition to city quarters, a place in the country. Summer fresh air, sunshine, and grassy meadows were thought to balance winters spent with slush, subways, and grimy airshafts. They wanted a place, like Ruth Hale's country cottage, where they could get away and listen to crickets at night. After a careful search, they bought a two-hundred-year old house in Weston, Connecticut. Esther set about remodeling it and making it habitable, adding plumbing, electricity, and insulation; the rambling clapboard house had a floor and a roof and not much else except charm. Starting in 1928, the family spent summers in Weston and rented or loaned the house during the winters (Lewis and Thompson stayed there one dreary February toward the end of their marriage). They hadn't intended to move there permanently when they purchased it, but, as it turned out, Depression unemployment belatedly hit Frank.

V

When Private Harold Ross had lugged Captain Franklin Adams' suitcase through the crowded streets of Paris during World War I to the office of the *Stars and Stripes*, a resonant affection began that lasted until Ross' death in 1951. Ross was as unprepossessing as Adams and seemed to care even less about the way he looked. Yet he was the only Pfc. in the A.E.F. who carried his own calling card, still another of the inane jokes to which he was addicted. Ungainly, slumped, feverishly active, with wild hair abetted by compulsive fingering, he had a space between his front teeth that could have been set with a ball bearing. Jane Grant said he was among the ugliest men she'd ever seen, but married him anyway. Certainly he was one of the most eccentric people ever to make a mark on American literature.

His peripetetic youth took him all over the country, where he worked on innumerable newspapers—twenty-three of them in two prewar years—and soaked up American culture. He wasn't a scholar, said he'd read only two books in his life. (But he never named them and friends had their doubts. He was once heard asking if Moby Dick were the whale or the man.) Fowler's *A Dictionary of English Usage* and the dictionary represented bedrock in his constant search for an honest sentence. His speech was dotted with "Jesus," "Goddam," and colorful racetrack profanity, but he was strangely innocent, didn't approve of dirty jokes even when he understood them, was often funny but invariably inarticulate around women. He cut a strange figure for a visionary, but visionary he was. And he may have been the best magazine editor who ever lived.

After World War I Ross returned to New York and began work on the *Home Sector*, the civilian version of the *Stars and Stripes*. Frank helped him out by contributing a poem, "I'm Out of the Army Now," to lend a little class and respectability to its first issue in September 1919. When *Home Sector* merged with the *American Legion* magazine in 1920, Ross continued as editor. But unsolvable differences sent him to *Judge*, a faltering humor magazine. Flitting from job to job mirrored the compulsive wanderlust of his youth, but there was a difference. He was zeroing in on his life's ambition and recognized he'd found his destination in the great New York City of readers and writers, but he had yet to figure out exactly where he fit. He was impatient working for others, publishing material under the aegis of somebody else's taste and priority. He wanted a publication of his own. He longed for editor-in-chief status so he could set style and tone, reject pretension and its glitzy offspring. His fantasy publication held within it his interests, his boundless curiosity, his energy and values. It was a tall order.

As Ross saw it in 1924, there were four possible directions for his ambition. He thought he'd like to publish a sophisticated tabloid news-paper, an idea he rejected finally because of its inherent contradiction. He also thought of putting out a detective magazine, one of the genre he most enjoyed; but there were already many good ones. The idea of a shipping newspaper appealed to him. Such a publication—wistfully named in advance of its birth *The Marine Gazette*—would chronicle arrivals and departures of ships, and other amiable waterfront gossip. It represented a fascinating prospect for Ross, but his friends assured him his preoccupation was definitely in the minority.

The vision he clung to with the most tenacity was that of an urban humor magazine. It was a strange choice given his unsophisticated approach to twentieth-century life, the fact that he disapproved of "racy" novels, blushed in mixed company at off-color stories, differ-entiated himself from the swarms of dudes he found himself among by tramping around in black boots that laced like ice skates. In any case, he didn't think *Vanity Fair* or *Life* had it right. There was room for a publication to fit nicely between the two, he believed, one that would incorporate the class of *Vanity Fair* with the unpretentiousness of *Life*. Even his most skeptical friends couldn't help believing with him that he could make it happen.

Vanity Fair, sister to the prosperous *Vogue*, was an elegant monthly owned by Condé Nast and edited by Frank Crowninshield. Robert Ben-chley, Robert Sherwood, and Dorothy Parker were, early in 1924, still on the staff, and the magazine was in its heyday. It ran over a hundred pages every month, many of them crammed with ads for automobiles, hotels and shops, tires, automobile accessories, department stores, agents for ocean voyages, and once, in January 1924, a full-page an-nouncement paid for by a New York City real estate firm: "Mr. Condé Nast has purchased a large apartment in 1040 Park Avenue. 'GO AND DO THOU LIKEWISE.' "

That year Colette had a story featured every month; other regular contributors included Aldous Huxley, Gilbert Seldes, Alexander Woollcott, John Peale Bishop. Pages were elaborately laid out, often displaying elegant photographs, many by Edward Steichen. The magazine presented sophisticated humor, cartoons, and essays. One series entitled "Artists Write Their Own Epitaphs" was actually a collective submission by Round Tablers. F.P.A.'s verse for his own tombstone was, "Beneath this green and tear-spent sod/The bones of F.P.Adams lie./He had a rotten time, but God! How he did hate to die!" Other self-invented epitaphs included:

HERE LIES MARC CONNELLY.

WHO?

HERE LIES JOHN V. A. WEAVER WHO MARRIED PEGGY WOOD

BUT JOINED THE LUCY STONE LEAGUE AND KEPT HIS OWN NAME.

HERE LIES THE BODY OF RING LARDNER.

WHAT OF IT?

HERE LIES ALEXANDER WOOLLCOTT WHO DIED AT THE AGE OF 92.

HE NEVER HAD IMITATION FRUIT IN HIS DINING ROOM.

HERE LIES THE BODY OF DOROTHY PARKER

THANK GOD!

[A later contribution had Parker saying "Excuse My Dust!"]

Regular columns talked about leisure-time activities and games like bridge and golf, cars, and fashions. *Vanity Fair* took men's clothes as seriously as women's; every season reverently presented "Our London Letter on Men's Fashions." The Stateside columnist worried continually about American slapdash tendencies, begged his readers to pay proper attention to details differentiating the immaculately attired from the merely conventional. One month, shoes were featured: "A Deauville sandal for beach and country wear" and "The brown buckskin shoe so popular with the Prince of Wales."

There was much in *Vanity Fair* that the irreverent Harold Ross snorted at.

On the other hand, he felt that the popular *Life*—at its peak, in 1921, with circulation of 250,000—wasn't on the mark either.

In 1924 Charles Dana Gibson was president of the weekly. Its pages were crammed with jokes, cartoons, and bright, punchy pieces. One of its regular features was a column by Baird Leonard, "Mrs. Pep's

Diary.'' It was a hilariously accurate parody of F.P.A.'s Diary. A July entry ran:

> Awoke betimes, distraught to my wits' end by a foreign particle under my eyelid. I tried to bethink of the Spartan lad with the fox in his jacket, and grew all a-twitter because I could not recall where and why he was in such a predicament.

> A heavy post this morning, and in it a request for aid from a home missions society, which I should give gladly did I not think they would spend it on remote Indians and mountaineers instead of looking into such vital evils as the defective tops on talcum powder bottled in glass and the salad dressing served in dining cars.

As a matter of fact, the pages of *Life* sparkled with material written by erstwhile Conning Tower contributors. Baron Ireland (Nate Salsbury continued to use his nom de plume), Montague Glass, Arthur Guiterman, and Carolyn Wells were often represented. And after Robert Sherwood and Robert Benchley were fired from *Vanity Fair*, Sherwood wrote *Life*'s movie reviews—he was the first critic who treated films seriously—and Benchley its dramatic criticism.

Ross made plans for a magazine that would offer the best of *Vanity Fair* and *Life*. He bent the ears of his friends until his obsession became one of their most persistent insider jokes. But he didn't care. He wrote his *Prospectus* and carried it around, showing it to anybody who displayed the slightest interest.

Frank introduced his friend Raoul Fleischmann to Ross at a Thanatopsis game. Fleischmann's uncles were in the yeast business, and Raoul's branch of the prosperous family owned bakeries. He was manager of the General Baking Company plant on East End Avenue. (His father had invented the institution of the breadline when, many years earlier, instead of selling unsold loaves at half price, he'd handed them out from the back door of his cafe on West Tenth Street.) When Ross showed him the dog-eared *Prospectus*, Fleischmann took serious note. School rings from Lawrenceville, Princeton, and Williams, and a gentlemanly demeanor showed him to be a bluestocking. Yet he had the flamboyant secret soul of an entrepreneur. He was thrilled at the idea. Ross believed his publication could be launched for under $100,000. (''We were babes in the woods,'' Fleischmann admitted later.) The two men shook hands and agreed to make a run for it. Ross put up their entire savings of $20,000, his and Jane Grant's money, and Fleischmann contributed an initial $25,000. John Peter Toohey casually christened the fledgling weekly.

Within two months of its first issue on February 21, 1925, *The New Yorker* had devoured all of the $45,000 and desperately needed more. Fleischmann quit his job and frantically raced around raising additional money while equally frantic Ross tried to improve the quality of the decidedly unpromising new magazine. He may not have been exactly sure what he wanted, but he knew what he didn't want. Frank's former employee from the *Tribune* Sunday magazine, Rea Irvin, became Ross' art editor. His distinctive taste manifested itself quickly on the publication; cartoons became a huge reader draw. ''Advisory editors'' were listed for the first issue under the Irvin drawing of Eustace Tilley (named by Corey Ford) going over his correspondence. They included Marc Connelly, George S. Kaufman, Alice Duer Miller, Ralph Barton, Dorothy Parker, and Alexander Woollcott. Later, when the magazine was standing on wobbly legs of its own, Ross removed the names; he said presenting his friends as if they were part of his staff was the most dishonest thing he'd ever done.

In the first issue Ross' love for gags and well-turned sentences was already apparent. The first ''Profile'' was a short piece about Giulio Gatti-Casazza, flamboyant manager of the Metropolitan Opera Company. Brief and forced as it was, it foretold the distinctive *New Yorker* flair for capturing a personality with telling detail. The essay concluded, ''[He] sits apart, on some old trunk behind the scenes, or in the moody elegance of his own sanctum; sits apart, shivering a little . . . for he is in a cold country . . . and silently fondles his fine, memorable nose.''

A cartoon showed a portly middle-aged couple in their dinner clothes. She stands in front of an open steamer trunk, he watches her disconsolately from the bed, saying, ''I don't know what I shall do, Amelia, when I think of you alone in Paris.''

A gossip column, ''In Our Midst,'' was obviously cribbed from F.P.A. and expressed Ross' intention to present a breezy view of city life as if it were a small town:

Jerome (''Jerry'') D. Kern was in town one day buying some second hand books.

Mrs. Harry Payne Whitney's memorial at St. Nazaire will be a statue of an eagle carrying a doughboy carrying a crusader's sword. The idea sounds quite artistic.

In a similar column, ''Jottings Around Town,'' attributed to ''Busy Body,'' an item announced that ''one of the best known newspaper men in the city writes all his correspondence in green ink.'' You didn't have to be an initiate to know that was F.P.A., who greatly added prestige to the glossy new magazine by contributing his piece, "Short-Story Scenarios," coming through for Ross as he had for the first issue of the *Home Sector*.

The first "Talk of the Town" was painfully coy. Its writer, "A New Yorker," used "I" instead of "we," making a colossal negative impact on its tone. Rather than recording the notes of a bemused observer, "Talk" cloyed and giggled: "According to the advertisements 'celebrities' contributed all the puzzles in [the latest Simon and Schuster crossword puzzle book] and (business of blushing furiously) they tell me (oh, how my cheeks are burning) mine is the best in it. At least I think it is."

There were some ads but not nearly enough, mostly local bookstores and specialty shops, and theaters. In the "Where to Shop" classified section, listings included Beads, Antiques, Restaurants, Portraits, Beauty Culture, Ladies' Tailors, and a "Corset Hospital."

A year's subscription was $5.00. *Vanity Fair*'s was $3.50.

By May circulation had skidded to under ten thousand. Fleischmann was ready to throw in the towel. He'd raised thousands of dollars above his initial investment, but no matter how much money he poured in, the voracious magazine needed more. He and Ross met with R. Hawley Truax (roommate with Ross, Grant, and Woollcott in their big messy house in Hell's Kitchen, on West Forty-seventh Street) and magazine consultant John Hanrahan. Over lunch at the Princeton Club, Fleischmann announced the well was dry. Publication would have to stop. As the group trudged sadly back to the office, Fleischmann overheard Hanrahan say, "I can't blame Raoul for refusing to go on, but it's like killing something that's alive." Fleischmann felt the same way himself. Later that week, at Frank and Esther's wedding, buoyed by champagne and the promise of a new life for the forty-three-year-old groom and his thirty-year-old bride, Fleischmann told Ross he thought he could find the money for another six months. Ultimately, he invested $500,000. It turned out to be the soundest and most profitable expenditure he ever made. *The New Yorker* never lost money again.

E. B. White, a steady contributor to "The Conning Tower," joined Ross' staff in 1926. Where Ross was a blunderbuss, White was delicate, gentle, ironic. Yet they both sought the same crystalline prose, the same honest viewpoint. Neither was intellectual. Ross liked to read the *Encyclopaedia Britannica* in his never-ending search for facts, and White enjoyed strolling around the city looking into store windows, visiting the zoo, observing and absorbing the city's smells and colors. He was a poet, not a scholar.

In Ross' early selection of "Casuals"—short fiction, observations, "notes"—he saw that *The New Yorker* lived up to his purpose, which was to reflect contemporary life with "gaiety, wit and satire," without "bunk." Nothing was sacred, and while, in the first five years, most of the material was funny, the writers spoke for many people curiously uneasy with the Jazz Age, its leaders, values, and climate.

In "Glorious Calvin, a Critical Appreciation," Wolcott Gibbs poked fun at the president. Calvin Coolidge, he said, "is essentially a comedian. There is more than a hint of tragedy in the shy little figure staring with solemn bafflement on an inexplicable world. There is a great pathos about him as he goes awkwardly and unhappily through the gaudy antics which are so hilariously at variance with his appearance. This great sense of the comic value of paradox was never better illustrated than in the magnificent film in which, resplendent in buckskin and feathers, he was created a chieftain of the Blackfeet Indians. . . . His expression, which never varied throughout the ceremony, suggested the faintly apprehensive geniality of an elderly gentleman who has been dragooned into a game of Post Office. The effect was irresistible."

In keeping with its objective of "small-town newspaper style," the *New Yorker* writers talked about each other, inimitably, funnily. In a short story, "Pannickin," Robert Nathan imagined "an acrid debate . . . between the Rev. Hattan, of Tennessee, and Mr. Heywood Broun, on the proposition: 'Resolved, that God has always been dressed, since the beginning of time, in underwear, socks, garters, a shirt, a tie and a suit.' During the debate, in order to explain himself, Mr. Broun divested himself of most of his clothing, an act which inevitably cost him the victory."

Ring Lardner, in "Dante and ———," paid homage to Beatrice Kaufman: "It is her modest boast that she is never seen in the same costume twice and generally not even once. . . . George often says that Beatrice won his heart through his sense of humor. As they were walking up Broadway together, he spied a small eft on the curb and made as if to scrunch it. 'Don't step on him!' cried Beatrice. 'It might be Mary Pickford and her mother!' . . . The Kaufmans have a summer camp in the Adirondacks, near Lake Placid. It was formerly owned by Boss Tweed, who built it entirely of knot holes."

E. B. White pondered "How to Tell a Major Poet from a Minor Poet" and concluded that "all women poets, dead or alive, who smoke cigars, are major, and . . . all poets whose work appears in The Conning Tower are minor because it is printed on uncoated stock—which is offensive to major poets."

Benchley, who wrote dramatic criticism under the pseudonym of Guy Fawkes, produced an occasional Casual. In one, called "La Presses Perverse," he talked about French newspapers. "In reading French newspapers there is always one consolation: no matter how little of the meaning you are able to get, you aren't missing a thing. . . . The left-hand column of the front page is usually given over to a red-hot story called something like: 'Moliere During the Middle Period of His Productivity.' The right-hand column is probably a signed outburst by the owner of the paper urging the restoration of the Bourbons or calling attention to the drought in what the French persist in calling '*Tchecoslovaquie.*' . . . All summer *Le Matin* has been giving over the two right-hand columns of its front page to a series called 'My Fishing Trip in Newfoundland.' This has been illustrated copiously each day with photographs taken by the author, reproduced by means of cuts such as only French newspaper-engravers can make, presumably etched on pieces of bread. (I read the first two or three laboring under a slight misapprehension owing to the word for 'to fish' being the same as the word for 'to sin' and hoping that someone had gone to Newfoundland on a 'campaign of sinning.' You couldn't have told from the pictures whether it was sinning or fishing the author was engaged in.)"

James Thurber's first published piece in New York had appeared in "The Conning Tower." In a burst of private-joke hilarity, he signed himself "Jamie Machree." F.P.A. took the day off and devoted the entire column of September 28, 1926, to "If the Tabloids Had Covered the Famous Sport 'Love-Death' Scandal of Hero and Leander." Upon its publication Thurber decided against going back to Columbus, Ohio, a return he'd been planning despondently. Within a few months he was hired by Ross and ended up sharing a tiny office with White. Probably the genius of Thurber and White did most to create the style and tone of the magazine Ross had dreamed of. Together with Robert Benchley, Katharine Angell White, and Wolcott Gibbs, cartoonists Helen Hokinson, Peter Arno, and Rea Irvin, *The New Yorker* survived its first five years and made history.

Its story became the stuff of legends. People are still trying to figure out the peculiar chemistry that so magnificently bewitched the upstart. All who invested in it received unprecedented returns, not only financially but less tangibly, in the respect accorded them, as if they'd wisely predicted the publication's enormous prestige. During his pre-1929 salad days, Frank acquired several hundred shares in the magazine. He lost them all in poker games, something Esther didn't learn until many years later.

In the 1920s, invention was in the air, life-giving, energizing, contagious, almost an end in itself. Iconoclast Ross hadn't cared whether he made a million dollars or died broke. His dream was to parent a uniquely American publication. His friends helped, not because they thought they were empire-building, but because they believed in the idea and were caught up with the vitality and optimism of the times. They were able to use their extraordinary talents in its fulfilling. With Ross' timely creation, the tempestuous, unruly turn-of-the-century newspaper style achieved integrity without sacrificing its uniquely American sense of humor.

It remains a major irony in the history of American letters that this gauche, poorly educated Westerner created a publication known widely not only for its humor but for its taste, sophistication, and erudition. Historian Geoffrey Perrett wrote in 1983 that *"The New Yorker* stood for excellence. It was the best-written American publication of the twentieth century."

It was quite a legacy left by Ross and his friends of the Round Table.

PART
THREE

CHAPTER SIX

The Thirties

*I think the true discovery of America is before us. I think the true
fulfillment of our spirit, of our people, of our mighty and immortal
land, is yet to come. . . . And I think that all these things are as
certain as the morning, as inevitable as noon.*

— THOMAS WOLFE
You Can't Go Home Again

*You will eat, by and by
In that glorious land above the sky (way up high)
Work and pray, live on hay
You'll get pie in the sky when you die (that's no lie).*

— JOSEPH HILLSTROM, nee JOEL HAAGLAND (JOE HILL)

I ain't a Communist necessarily, but I been in the red all my life.

— WOODY GUTHRIE

I   The 1920s strutted and bragged and dressed itself in every
kind of preposterous costume, but when it came time for
the curtain call, the decade was revealed as prosperity's
flamboyant imposter, not the real thing at all. The insu-
larity, the insubstantiality, the boosterism and acquisitiveness that people
had been calling American know-how were shabbily revealed through
the mirror of the Great Depression. The farmers hadn't shared in "prosperity"; by 1929 they were fearfully debt-ridden. The failure of the
banks coming hand-in-hand with the drought that extended for endless
miles across the Southwest expelled thousands of ruined families forever
from their land. They took up lives for which they were totally unprepared, as did workers in towns where factories were boarded up. Pros-

perity had never touched millions of Americans, including blacks and minorities who'd always scraped along on its edges, their contribution to the culture ignored or misrepresented. Paul Whiteman's celebrated orchestra never employed a black musician even though the most inventive and indigenous American music was played, not by him—the publicist-proclaimed "king of jazz" who once conducted from atop a white horse—but by people like Louis Armstrong, Blind Lemon Jefferson, Leadbelly, Lester Young, Robert Johnson, and others who made music on harmonicas, banjos, guitars, and upright pianos in the front rooms of whorehouses.

The division between the haves and have-nots was chasmlike in the 1920s, but few noticed it until the 1930s, when, democratically, everybody scrambled for a seat in the same lifeboat and found it was full of holes.

Writers came to the disastrous new decade with fresh purpose. Many of them joined the Communist party, and instead of writing stories about birth, life, and death, ponderously wrote about economics. These books were dubbed "proletarian literature" by critics. Most of them have been justifiably forgotten. They "were shallow, contentious, polluted with jargon," says Malcolm Cowley, "and devoted to questions of the day presented in terms of liberal or Marxian or Freudian orthodoxies." But the American writer's preoccupation with social ideals provoked sound writing, too. John Steinbeck, Erskine Caldwell, James Agee, Ernest Hemingway, Thomas Wolfe, and others produced memorable work during this period, which reflected the despair and anger of the times. Recognizing the power of many speaking as one was a preoccupation of American writers, the good ones as well as the second-raters.

For the first time the government jumped into funding the literary process. Under the auspices of the Works Progress Administration (WPA), the Federal Writers' Project was created. When Martin Dies, head of the House Un-American Activities Committee and a loud-mouth enemy of the New Deal, criticized the Writers' Project, WPA's first administrator—one merely had to mention his name to guarantee sending Dies into fits of apoplexy—Harry Hopkins, responded: "Hell, [writers] have to eat too."

As in other WPA projects, writers had to qualify as paupers in order to receive assignments. Many were too proud to participate, preferring to starve genteelly, but hundreds of others set to work and turned out, in the first four years, 320 publications: one hundred full-size books, the American Guide Series—state, city, town, and highway guides—ethnic studies, oral histories, and works on folklore, geology, economics, and zoology. By 1939 six hundred additional books were in the works. In 1936 nearly seven thousand people were on the Writers' Project rolls. There were offices in all the states and in several big cities. *Pathfinder* magazine called it "The biggest, fastest, most original research job in the history of the world," and historian Charles Beard called some of the oral histories "more powerful than anything I have read in fiction."

And when, in 1939 Federal One (the shorthand name covering all the federal arts projects) was struggling to continue life, Alistair Cooke wrote an awkward but sincere tribute for the *London Times*: "The Federal Writers Project is doomed to die. . . . They have left in print several million words of penetrating and humane documentation, possessing which some future American generation may well marvel at the civilization recorded by a small library of government-sponsored volumes in those turbulent years between 1935 and 1939." Later Cooke wrote Writers' Project director Henry Alsberg, who'd just been fired, and enclosed his article. "I hope if you see any spare copies lying around of further State guides," Cooke wrote, "you will not lose sleep wondering where to send them. I hope to buy, beg, steal, annex or 'protest' a complete library of the guides before I die."

The list of writers who worked on the projects is formidable, and includes Conrad Aiken, Nelson Algren, Saul Bellow, Maxwell Bodenheim, John Cheever, Ralph Ellison, William Gibson, Zora Neale Hurston, Bert James Loewenberg, Henry Lee Moon, Philip Rahv, Studs Terkel, and Richard Wright, who quit a post office job to sign up.

In 1939, when Federal One was reeling from Congressional body blows, Heywood Broun was asked to lead a march to Washington to demonstrate for appropriations. He was unwilling to do so, not for lack of enthusiasm but because he felt his name would do more harm than good. He felt he'd been associated with left-wing causes too long. He suggested they ask Woollcott. Jerre Mangione, National Coordinating Editor of the Federal Writers' Project, met with Broun at his residence. Mangione, who describes the incident in his book, *The Dream and the Deal*, remembers that it was raining when he and his companions left Broun's apartment, and Mildred Holtzhauer, assistant to the director of the arts project, was dressed in a thin summer dress. Broun removed his jacket and tucked it around her, then escorted her to her car in the downpour. "It was the instinctive gesture of an innately considerate man," said Mangione, "and it was the first image of him that came to me when I read of his death a month later."

Woollcott wasn't nearly so accommodating or committed to saving the Writers' Project as was Broun. "He resembled a turkey as he strutted and performed, mainly for the entertainment of the young homosexuals who formed his entourage," sniped Mangione. Woollcott denied that Broun had telephoned him with Mangione's request, and when introduced to Hallie Flanagan's assistant at the Federal Theater Project, he snapped, "I remember you. You were the perpetrator of a dreadful play I once had to review."

Woollcott was at his most preposterous. He sneered at their request, saying he was indifferent to the arts project. He didn't like the "so-called liberals" who were running things and insulted the ex-playwright by quoting passages from his grossly unflattering review. The writer, undismayed, told of a generous review of a Woollcott book Mangione had written. Immediately Woollcott became unctuous, cloying, fairly rubbing his hands together. "He said he remembered the review very well," said Mangione. "He shook my hand, apologized for his 'foul mood' which he attributed to some dentistry committed on him earlier in the day, and promised within a few months, when he would have more time, to help the arts projects in any way we wished. That would be too late, I told him, and quickly led my companions out of the place."

Time had laid its hand on the Algonks. Not only had Woollcott forged a separate persona, but by the end of the 1930s, each of the Round Tablers lived and worked at a greater emotional distance from their former stamping ground, each of them intently heeding different drummers. Dorothy Parker, whose hands shook as she put on her almost black lipstick, acted as if she were ashamed of her former associations. From Hollywood she bad-mouthed other Round Tablers as inconsequential smart alecks. Ring Lardner died in 1933. Broun and Hale divorced, as did Harold Ross and Jane Grant. Frank and Esther pulled up city stakes and moved to Connecticut. Ross talked only of his magazine with people who wrote for him or helped him get it out; he never had time for elaborate non-*New Yorker* conversation although he still had time for all-night poker sessions. Word games were passe. F.P.A. left journalism and became a radio personality, and Benchley spent so much time making movies in California that *The New Yorker* had to replace him as dramatic critic; characteristically, the gentle humorist spent the entire lunch at which he was fired consoling Ross' heartbroken emissary. Ross' notorious cowardice prevented him from firing his old friend himself.

Edna Ferber told how she returned from Europe in the third or fourth year of the decade and rushed into the Algonquin dining room, plumped herself down at the accustomed table, only to find herself sitting among strangers, a dumbfounded family from out of town. The Algonquin set had moved on. Frank Case no longer reserved for them the big round table in the center of the room. But they were so preoccupied, the Algonks hardly noticed that something once precious had vanished.

II With the stock market crash in 1929, Frank's comfortably enlarging fortune was obliterated. For several years he'd been investing in stocks with the aid of tips from his friends, mostly from Swope. During that time, he was prey, like everybody else, to the foolish presumption that the ever-multiplying profits sprang from his own remarkable timing and canniness. While the crash and subsequent Depression wiped out his savings, the calamity reintroduced realism to his basically skeptical nature. It put him back at his desk, dependent again on a weekly wage, and he never forgot the comeuppance. Esther's money had been safely and conservatively invested, so the collapse of American business hadn't ruined the family's finances. Yet from his erstwhile position of power and influence, Frank felt himself become the scrambling husband of a well-off wife, and he didn't like it.

Because he was a steadily employed person with a regular paycheck, the Depression was outside Frank's experience. Breadlines, unemployment, frantic searches for shelter and food, crushing losses of family income and status, and incalculable anguish and despair were sad topics for the dailies, and he read about what was happening with sympathy. But he was no more gut-aware of the devastating effect the economy's collapse was having on other people than were his children, safe and well-fed in their nursery on the fourth floor of 26 West Tenth Street. Frank went about his business of reporting the Broadway and literary scenes with scarcely a reference in the column to the staggering hardships other people encountered. When President Franklin D. Roosevelt abruptly closed the nation's banks in 1933, Frank was mildly nonplussed: "I wish I had withdrawn a few dollars yesterday, forasmuch as I have but $4 to dure me and my wife and my young quartette and my retinue until the banks reopen." His intellectual sympathies were all for the New Deal and with the jobless and displaced, yet his humanism never became all-consuming, never produced an agitating or revolutionary fervor. He lived, worked, and carried on exactly as before, industriously, calmly, and isolated from the swirl and wrench of change; as always, he left the passion to others.

One morning in March 1933, the *New York Herald Tribune* published a boxed column, "Job Problems," to take up some of the slack on the nearly empty want-ads page. That day the feature included a poignant query from an unnamed job seeker: "How can I get in touch with a number of firms not large enough to have a bookkeeper but who might require a bookkeeper's services a few hours a week or a month? I am a middle-aged man with thirty years experience." The *Trib*, reacting with a sensibility honed in the go-getter 1920s, brightly suggested the writer send out a mailing, get stationery and business cards printed, and make sales calls. On the same morning, on page 9, F.P.A. devoted most of "The Conning Tower" to a discussion of parody and the inclusion of a lengthy comic verse imitation of Calverley by Sir Arthur Quiller-Couch. It wasn't that Frank was insensitive or uncaring, but he simply couldn't imagine a different tone than the one his readers expected. Other columnists, like Broun, waxed darker and heavier as the Depression plodded on. F.P.A.'s offerings were precisely what they'd always been. The world was changing faster than sanity could follow, but the Tower was a rock of stability. People continued to read it, if they could afford to buy the paper.

World news was disturbing, too. In April 1933, shortly after the Nazis captured control of the Reichstag, a short piece, datelined Berlin, appeared next to the Tower: "American jazz music, especially that brand produced by Negro orchestras and singers, which Germans call "Verniggerung," has been banned from the Berlin broadcasting station under the new government radio restrictions. . . . The ban was placed in accordance with Chancellor Adolf Hitler's cultural ideas, it was said."

A week later, on page 1, a story from Berlin ominously presaged Nazi intention to purify the Nordic race by returning religion to the good old ways of heroic paganism. The Nazis planned to trash the Old Testament, to erect in its stead the sagas and fairy tales of Germany and the leading personalities from German spiritual, philosophical, and artistic life.

During this period, some of F.P.A.'s topical epigrams included:

'Four Ewes Auctioned at City Zoo'—Headline. "Ay tank," said Mester Yonson, "dis ban some vork by Hitler."

What this country needs is a bunk holiday.

'Just as though my wages weren't minimum enough already,' said the fellow who can complain, 'Roosevelt now has got to make it compulsory.'

Five thousand students marched in Berlin's bonfire parade on Wednesday, "singing Nazi songs and college melodies." Such as "Keep the Tome Fires Burning"?

And one morning he suggested that Hitler's calendar should omit the months of "Jewn" and "Jewly."

A major area of agitation in the 1930 was the broad unionization of the working class. Newspaper men and women observed the tumult as outsiders and wrote about what was happening as if it had nothing to do with them. Yet most of them vociferously upheld the right of others to organize. Among the Algonks, Heywood Broun and Dorothy Parker were outspoken proponents of a worker's right to strike. During 1933 they, with Woollcott, demonstrated with the Waldorf-Astoria employees picketing the elegant hotel. Afterward, inexplicably, they snuck into Jack and Charlie's '21' Club where they ignored a similar picket line of waiters. Benchley raced in after them. Parker tried to flirt him out of his outrage at their defection, but he'd have none of it. "Don't blink those ingenue eyes at me," he commanded, and stormed out past the pickets, who gave him a hand.

Broun was more committed to the notions of organizing workers than that episode indicated. In 1930 he was the Socialist candidate for Congress from his Manhattan district. He lost. But his position as principled leader among his friends was strengthened. When journalists in Buffalo and Cleveland began talking about organizing newspaper editorial people, he concurred enthusiastically, even though, as a columnist working under contract (and receiving $49,000 annually), his position didn't fall naturally with those who were paid by the inch.

At the time New York reporters received an average of $4000 a year. Many earned less than $1000. They worked six days a week for ten, twelve or fifteen hours a day, and were expected to see a story through until it was finished, no matter how long it took. They never seemed to go home, but instead banded together after work at inns and saloons, drinking heavily largely because their lives couldn't easily accommodate other kinds of companionship. Many reporters never married; they often had troubled marriages if they did. Family life was almost non-existent. Yet they clung to their independence with a fierceness bordering on obsession.

It was the "romance" in newspapering that offered its most effective enticement. The adventure beckoned, as did the chances to poke, pry, know everybody, to be tough and alone. Such an outlook didn't take kindly to organization because reporters knew that when people banded together, disparate voices were stilled. To individualists like them, silence—even for the good of all—was an appalling idea. But even the most outspoken loners among them knew something had to be done. Their situation was precarious.

The golden years of newspapers were ending. Between 1929 and 1933 newspaper revenues dropped almost forty percent, at the same time that radio doubled its share of national advertising. Layoffs and newspaper closings dotted the country. The number of editorial workers dropped nearly ten percent in the first three years of the decade. Publishers were hurting badly, and they wanted their employees to share in the increasing risk. But reporters had never shared substantially in the bosses' prosperity. They'd always been underpaid.

Still, it wasn't easy for reporters to join together, no matter how strong the pull to fight for their rights. Besides their temperamental intransigence, traditional rivalries between newspapers made unity difficult. Friendly as they might be at the local speakeasies, the reporters from different city rooms were unaccustomed to cooperating with one another. Probably they would never have become organized if it hadn't been for Heywood Broun, who, on August 7, 1933, headed his *New York World-Telegram* (and widely syndicated) column, "A Union of Reporters." He called for the organization of his colleagues, deplored their go-it-alone snobbishness, made fun of their prissy delight in being referred to as "gentlemen of the press." He chided his friends for being too snooty to organize themselves like blue-collar craftsmen, whose record at winning wage hikes was enviable.

Broun's essay was a bombshell. Suddenly he became the leader of a nationwide movement to organize journalists.

During the summer of 1933, fifty or so of them met regularly at Broun's cluttered West 58th Street apartment and made plans for a newspaper guild. Frank Adams was among them. Despite the fact that Frank, like Broun, was far better known and made more salary than most reporters, he was widely respected by his peers. They later elected him president of the New York chapter of the American Newspaper Guild. (Broun became national president.) Frank's sympathies were firmly on the side of the working reporter. It was appropriate that he head the New York City chapter because he was nationally known as the quintessential New York newspaper man.

All but two New York publishers opposed the group. Joseph Patterson of the *New York Daily News* was a no-nonsense conservative as tough and lucid as his paper. He believed people had to look out for themselves, that there were no handouts without strings. Even "if I were working for Patterson or any other publisher," he told Morris Ernst, Broun's and Adams' fiery liberal lawyer and the Guild's legal advisor, "I'd still join the Guild." The iconoclast publisher relished the opportunity to show up his self-righteous competitors as hypocrites. David Stern, owner of the *New York Post*, was also sympathetic to Guild objectives. But no other New York publisher, no matter how "enlightened" his editorial pages were, supported the rights of reporters to bargain collectively. They considered it a question of economics, not principle. So did the reporters.

The publishers' vigorous opposition helped doom the dreams of Guild founders in creating a union of only reporters. Newspaper owners' cries of "Communist-inspired" took public attention from the reporter's legitimate needs, which resulted from repairable flaws in the capitalist fabric, and focused them instead on the fearsome abstraction of anti-Americanism. Adding to the confusion, and in fact sabotaging the project, was the fact that some of the early Guild members *were* Communists. Their interests lay with following the party line and not with helping sister and brother journalists.

But there was no substance to the charge that the Newspaper Guild was created by Communists. For its first years, Communist members weren't in positions of major influence because liberals like Broun were in control. But Broun, who'd run for Congress under the banner of the Socialist Party, was highly suspect in the eyes of the newspaper owners. They refused to negotiate with him. The Guild became dominated by militant Communists when responsible leaders like him were thus rendered impotent. Morris Ernst observed that "From a society of journalists, the Guild was converted into a left-wing trade union by the constant opposition of the publishers. Roy Howard [of Scripps-Howard, in New York represented by the *World-Telegram*] and Helen Reid, among others, did that job without intending to."

In 1936 Broun was arrested and jailed in Milwaukee when he picketed the Hearst paper there with his Guild colleagues. He was an idealist who believed ardently in the right to free expression, even when unpopular ideas were expressed—much like earlier Americans Thomas Jefferson and Alexander Hamilton. Guild Communists wanted him discredited as much as the publishers did. When he was fired from the *New York World-Telegram*, they got what they wanted.

Broun died a few weeks after he lost his job in 1939. Unlike many of his Round Table friends, who'd become cynical and tired, he never lost his idealism and his belief in the efficacy of the American dream.

With America's entry into World War II, the Newspaper Guild returned to non-Stalinist control. It opened its ranks to all white-collar editorial employees, including clerks, typists and general office workers. Reporters, outnumbered, lost interest.

With America's entry into World War II, the Newspaper Guild returned to non-Stalinist control. It opened its ranks to all white-collar editorial employees, including clerks, typists and general office workers. Reporters, outnumbered, lost interest.

Before leaving the New York chapter office the Communists burned its files. No meeting minutes, correspondence, lists of officers and members, no record of committee discussions, arguments, or recommendations during the 1930s survive. The gift the Communist Guild members left to those who came later was to erase their story from history.

By the end of 1936, Frank's value to Ogden Reid was negligible. According to the publisher, not enough people still read "The Conning Tower" to justify keeping F.P.A. on the staff. Unlike his wife, Helen, Reid had never been an F.P.A. fan, and he'd been waiting patiently for the time when his popularity would decline. He'd never forgiven Frank's betrayal when he'd left the old *New York Tribune* for the *New York World*. It was no secret that the publisher hadn't wanted Frank back when the *World* folded, but he'd bowed to the pressure of Frank's undeniable popularity and hauled him aboard. Helen had acted as go-between, but it wasn't a happy association. In 1934, when Frank's first contract with the *New York Herald Tribune* ended, Reid sat on his hands before renewing it, apparently for no other reason than to discomfit Frank. "The Conning Tower" missed a day before it reappeared, the first time that had happened since its beginning in 1904. Pointing to the exigencies of the Depression, Reid cut Frank's salary from $25,000 to $21,852. Frank was infuriated but helpless. When time came to renegotiate in 1937, Reid wanted to cut him still further, and this time Frank refused. "They just wanted me to work for less money, whereas I wanted to work for more," he explained laconically when somebody asked why he and the *Herald Tribune* had parted company. Typically, he hid his anger. (The departure was ironic in more ways than one. That year, Frank's book, *The Melancholy Lute*, a selection of his best poetry over the years, was considered by the Pulitzer Prize Committee for the 1937 poetry award.) Esther argued that leaving the *Trib* would be a big mistake, but she didn't understand that his catbird-seat position was shaky even before he was fired. The fact that he wasn't able to find a new spot for more than a year afterward was a clear signal that the parade had moved past his viewing stand.

During the 1930s he devoted many inches of the column to stories about his children, a surprising switch for the self-defined old codger. Perhaps he remembered that Heywood Broun had talked often about the young Woody, making subtle points about his own views on politics and society when doing so. Unfortunately, Frank's views were fast growing passe, so drawing analogies between the activities of his children and what was happening to grownups wasn't particularly pertinent, although the ruminations were often charming.

Life went on in the Diary much as it had:

> So all day at the office, answering the telephone and riding in the elevators and telling a gentleman from what he called the National Broadcahsting Company that I had no desire to say a few hundred words over the wireless, especially at the price offered, which was nothing. I was what my wife would call rude to him, and what I call ineffectually ironick. Then a fellow . . . came in to ask me whether I was busy, and I said, No, I came to the office to practice penmanship, and he said that I had no reason to insult him, that he wanted only to give me a chance to invest my money in a sound company, so I apologized and said that if he would give me only five minutes to myself I could write a fortune, all of which he could have.

Simon and Schuster published *The Diary of Our Own Samuel Pepys* in 1935. The two hardcover volumes included most of the Diary entries published in the *Mail*, the *Tribune*, the *World*, and the *Herald Tribune* between 1911 and 1934. As editor, Frank omitted material he felt was repetitious or ''conspicuously trivial, such as the results of all the baseball games that I attended or of every tennis match that I played.'' He added nothing, altered nothing, though he admitted he was tempted to change his views when they turned out to be wrongheaded or no longer funny. But he was honest, admitted the temptation but didn't succumb. Reviews were favorable, and the volumes sold more copies than any of his other books. In later years, the *Diary* was of invaluable help to biographers of the Algonquin set and historians who wanted a picture of what the New York literati was up to during that period. It was too topical to be of general interest even a few years after its completion; the style was too precious, the point of view too narrow, the events and conversations described too superficial and oblivious to be of lasting interest. The *Diary* was too much of its time and obviously belonged in no other.

After being cut from his newspaper job in 1937, he was without a regular byline for the first time since 1903. He freelanced furiously, providing Harold Ross with several sprightly columns of nostalgia, entitled "I Remember, I Remember," along the lines of:

> It was on September 23, 1908, that lots of us, at the Polo Grounds, saw Johnny Evers accuse Fred Merkle of failure to touch second base, a failure which cost the Giants the 1908 pennant, and which permanently put the word "bonehead" into the American language. They still were singing "Bedelia," but Ben Burt's "Wal, I Swan," with its "Git-dap, Napoleon!," was sung by everyone who could remember the words. And vaudeville artists put rhymed advertise-ments in the *Clipper*, such as the "notice to managers" inserted by Joe, Myra, Buster, Jingles, and Baby Louise Keaton:
>
> *Did you ever go to a theatre and see a vaudeville show*
> *And watch the many different acts and see the way they go?*
> *But there is one that is the thing and it is hard to beat 'em*
> *And that's that act that's headed by the only Buster Keaton.*

The surprising popularity of the series prompted Ross to ask Frank to provide *The New Yorker* with a weekly column devoted to tennis during the 1937 and 1938 season. Frank's outstanding essays were among the sharpest, cleanest writing he'd ever done. He approached the project with the important lesson learned from classic sportswriters Ring Lardner and Grantland Rice: Let the game tell the story using its own punchy, picturesque words and get on with it. The columns were de-lightful.

Because Frank had been a student of the game since the turn of the century, he was able expertly to compare contemporary players with those preceding them. And his zest for the game was infectious:

> It is thought, almost utterly erroneously, that Grant's game is patball. His severity is unspectacular; he makes no Tilden or Budge service aces, no Tilden or Vines smashes from deep court, and few Richards short volleys at the net. But there is severity in those drives, and many of what his opponents consider aces are returned. Before the 1927 final of the National Singles, which Tilden lost to Lacoste 9–11, 3–6, 9–11, Tilden was questioned about his opponent by a man who hoped to draw Tilden's contempt of a game utterly unlike

his own. "He gets 'em back hard," said Tilden, "and makes no mistakes. That's great tennis, and enough to win any championship."

On another occasion he observed scornfully:

McGrath was handicapped in the doubles by an infected playing hand, and suffered the added liability of having the worried and obviously faltering Jack Crawford as a partner. Parenthetically, I want to apologize to Mr. Crawford, who was born in 1908, for having called him thirty-nine in *The New Yorker* of May 29th. Mr. Crawford is twenty-nine. Nobody who saw him play that weekend, however, upbraided me for my error.

After two years he concluded his last column with a typical starchy and, to those who knew him, self-chiding comment:

The men of 1938 are an ordinary lot. Reason totters at the prospect of 1939 if Budge becomes a professional. Not that it is a matter of life and death. After all, it is (laughter) only a game.

Except for payment for the tennis columns and a few freelance magazine pieces, Frank was without income. His friends who were magazine editors encouraged him and tried to buy what they could. But, except for tennis, his favorite topics seemed at last to be without an audience.

He was unemployed for over a year. It was a panicky time. The Adamses moved permanently from the house on West Tenth Street, to Weston, Connecticut, where Esther worked part time as a real estate salesperson. In the summer of 1938, to his immense relief, Frank was hired by the *New York Evening Post*, and "The Conning Tower" had a home once again, this time until 1941.

But the big news for Frank wasn't his reemployment as a columnist. Seemingly overnight he became a widely admired radio performer in one of the country's most popular programs. A whole new career opened for him at the astonishing age of fifty-seven.

III

Esther learned that old friend and distinguished foreign correspondent Dorothy Thompson was making a lot of money appearing regularly on radio. Broadcasting seemed a natural medium for a journalist: Words, cleverly selected and honed, helped to make an arresting radio personality, while looks, general tidiness or lack of it, didn't count at all. A sonorous voice and droll wit like Frank's were added advantages. Esther encouraged him to talk to Dorothy about the possibility of her helping him find work in radio, but he dragged his feet. He, who'd given so many favors, was reluctant to ask for one. Besides, his idea of radio was dolefully unenthusiastic, and he had no wish as a dyed-in-the-wool print person to participate in the vagaries of the unpredictable and not quite respectable new medium. But when Esther told him that Dorothy was making six figures in the glitzy new industry, ever-practical Frank changed his mind. He telephoned Thompson, and she generously invited him to lunch to meet her radio agent, John Moses.

According to Frank, at lunch Moses "interrupted Dorothy . . . just long enough to tell me that he too was a Chicago boy who'd attended the University of Michigan, and that if anything in my line came up he'd let me know." Frank supposed this was a polite way of telling him to go fly a kite, so he tried to forget the meeting and get on with his freelancing. However, John Moses knew a man named Dan Golenpaul, who was wrestling at that very moment with an idea for a new kind of quiz program. Frank didn't know it, but his fortunes were about to change.

Golenpaul was a bright young New Yorker, brought up in the Williamsburgh section of Brooklyn, New York, by immigrant parents. He'd been a teenaged officer of the Young People's Socialist League, where he'd selected speakers and organized discussion groups. A tall, bespectacled, cigar-chewing combination of Sammy Glick and Jay Gatsby, he'd hustled and scrambled most of his life, arriving in radio via a route that included political campaign managing and publicity management for Heywood Broun. On WBAT, the station owned by the *Jewish Daily Forward*, he produced an interview show in which Broun talked with various authors on a fifteen-minute program sponsored by Macy's. Among other pressing responsibilities, it was Golenpaul's job to keep a glass of gin in front of the columnist. (On a couple of occasions guests sputtered and choked on the air when they mistakenly sipped Broun's drink, thinking it was water.) Later Golenpaul's "Magazine of the Air" was an innovative if short-lived program in which sponsors paid for "pages" in a broadcast offering segments on current events, theater, sports, music, and literature. In 1934 sponsors wanted to be identified with the programs they paid for, and they felt that such identification wasn't achieved in Golenpaul's format. So, despite inventive programing, the program died.

Undaunted, and operating out of a single room at the Ansonia Hotel serving in the daytime as his office and at night as his bedroom, Golenpaul went on to produce "The Forum of the Air," with famous people debating current issues. Despite interesting guests like Constitutional lawyer Arthur Garfield Hays and columnist Max Lerner, the show never got a sponsor and was pulled after a few weeks. Then he almost hit pay dirt when he presented "Raising Your Parents," which provided a panel of children suggesting solutions to problems sent in by other children. The program was broadcast every Saturday morning until NBC canceled it due to "budget cutbacks."

But he wouldn't quit. He studied audience participation shows, a type of program that provided unusual dash and electricity even in those frantic days when broadcasts were live and performers learned to rescue themselves from every conceivable embarrassment while keeping their voices calm. Radio was an unprecedented entertainment medium. Step by shaky step, pioneers invented what was sent over the airwaves. They experimented with all kinds of ideas, some of them good and many of them awful. Staged shows in theaters were its ancestors, but there were uniquely intimate elements in broadcasting. Radio went into people's living rooms. They didn't have to dress up or go anywhere to listen. It was a baffling, invigorating proposition: How did you entertain the family when you and not they were the guests, when they could leave the room or turn you off at any time, when you couldn't be seen, couldn't even wave your arms to get attention, could use only the sound of your voice to create the illusion that you were among them? One way to maintain listener interest was to provide a vehicle in which they could identify with and root for the people they heard. An innovator of this technique was "Major" (Edward) Bowes, who was master of ceremonies and producer of a popular program, "The Amateur Hour." He selected ordinary people who played spoons, or "Lady of Spain" on a washtub, recited poetry by Edgar Guest, whistled birdcalls, or wobbled "Pixies on the Giant Swing" on the saxophone. The most popular acts were chosen by the studio audience to reappear the following week. Bowes recognized that first-rate entertainment wasn't nearly so important as establishing audience rapport and identification. And he was immensely successful. His program—and its descendants—lasted more than thirty years, ending with Ted Mack on television long after Bowes had died.

Another popular audience participation program in the 1930s was "Professor Quiz." The "Professor," Craig Earl, invited people in the studio audience to talk with him on the air. When he'd put them at ease, he asked them to answer questions about generally known topics. Most of the time the hapless participants were unable to answer and ended up looking foolish. Golenpaul, instinctively siding with the underdog, didn't like the format. He longed to turn the tables, to put the "expert" in the hot seat, allow the audience to obtain revenge. He thought he could build an intensely loyal following in this way, so he talked over the idea with Bill Karlin, the program director at NBC's Blue Network. Karlin gave him a green light. Golenpaul wanted something more literate and respectable than "The Amateur Hour," but with the same ability to evoke audience partisanship. He was determined to create and package it.

He decided that a panel of several experts, rather than one, would add spice and variety to his quiz show's format. In addition, he planned to have the studio audience prepare and ask questions he would screen beforehand. This turned out to be unworkable because there was no way to predict the quality of the questions, their accuracy or propriety. Who'd want to be an "expert" if there was no way to tell in advance if the questions would be fair? He decided to appoint a board to edit and okay each question, which would be mailed in by listeners. He'd pick a trustworthy group of respectable, well-educated people for the editors, and turned to a friend, Gordon Kahn, a history teacher at Thomas Jefferson High School in Brooklyn, to be editor in chief. Kahn possessed the unusual and propitious combination of an excellent education, wide-ranging interests, total recall, and a sense of humor. Together in the Kahns' backyard, he and Golenpaul met more than two dozen times to hammer out program format and questions. Golenpaul wanted them to be funny and interesting, to reflect the interests of a well-rounded, literate person. More, he wanted the amusingly phrased questions to invite even snappier answers. Kahn proved to be a master of this technique.

When time came to audition people for the panel of experts, Golenpaul had definite ideas. He wanted at least one newspaperman, since he was acquainted with several iconoclastic journalists who fit the profile of the perfect panelist: tough, succinct, smart, funny, and irreverent. Stanley Walker, city editor of the *New York World* and then the *New York Herald Tribune*, was his first choice, but Walker was out of town for the audition, and Golenpaul didn't have time to wait. He wanted a scientist, too, but not a specialist with narrow or limited interests. Somebody who knew literature, music, theater, and sports was also necessary. It was a tall order, so he decided that the panel should have only two permanent members, with different guests offering special expertise every week. The permanent panelists would afford the stability on which to drape the rest of the show.

Golenpaul had heard scuttlebutt that F.P.A., whom he knew slightly, was out of work and was in fact "up against it." He thought him a perfect choice for permanent panelist, and contacted John Moses. He described the program to Moses and asked him to sound out Adams on the possibility of auditioning for it. When Moses called back to tell him Adams had turned down the idea, Golenpaul was dumbfounded. He knew the game was right down Adams' alley and suspected that Moses had misunderstood the concept that thus botched up explaining it, so he met Frank later in the week at Moses' office on Fifty-seventh Street. "What's all this about?" asked Frank, justifying Golenpaul's suspicion. "John tried to explain it to me but I can't make any sense out of it."

Golenpaul suggested that Frank answer some test questions, like "Who was the Merchant of Venice?" When Frank responded, "Antonio," Golenpaul grinned. "Most people would say 'Shylock,' " he said. "Not in my circle," Frank said primly, and Golenpaul chortled. He asked other questions, most of which Frank was able to answer. Golenpaul liked Frank's deadpan style, the dangerous wit that lurked, ready to pounce, behind each innocent-sounding response. Frank, still baffled, said that the game was a lot of fun but when would they get down to business? Golenpaul told him this *was* the business, that the show was based precisely on this format. "You mean I'd get *paid* to play this game?" said Frank.

He was delighted, incredulous. "For years we'd played it," he said later, "at Herbert Bayard Swope's house parties—the host, Alexander Woollcott, Laurence Stallings, Arthur Krock, and I. And when Stanley Walker and I were co-slaves of the *Herald Tribune*, we had an agreement that either could call the other up at any time of day or night, and pose a question." But he'd never dreamed his quirky knowledge and love of showing it off would land him a job. Or a new spot in the limelight.

With Frank Adams, *New Yorker* book critic Clifton Fadiman was master of ceremonies, and announcer Milton Cross (who later became the voice of the Saturday afternoon Metropolitan Opera broadcasts and was replaced on I.P. by Ben Grauer, then Ed Herlihy), and three guest panelists, "Information Please" was first aired on the NBC Blue Network on Tuesday, May 17, 1938, at 9:30 P.M. It was an exhilarating, uproarious program. Golenpaul and Kahn corraled everybody they knew to come to the studio and act as ringers by asking questions prepared by Kahn and his staff. Golenpaul's friend, publicity agent Irving Mansfield, later married to Jacqueline Susann, asked on the air who was the only president born west of the Mississippi (Hoover). Golenpaul's secretary, recent Barnard graduate Edith Schick, queried why eating should have reminded George Washington of lumber (he was supposed to have been fitted with wooden false teeth). Fictitious "Mary Long of Tampa, Florida" posed a question that gave Frank the opportunity to sing "Old Folks at Home" in his silken baritone. Kahn's wife Olga—identified as Olga "Gordon"—asked the panel to identify two lines of poetry: ". . . Of one that loved not wisely, but too well" and "My own dear love/He is all my heart/And I wish somebody'd shoot him." Frank knew Dorothy Parker had written the obscure second verse, but surprisingly didn't spot the first, and better known one, from *Othello*. When the $5 prize money had been awarded to Olga Kahn, another panelist, Marcus Duffield, day news editor of the *New York Herald Tribune*, remarked belatedly that he'd almost blurted out the answer. When Fadiman suggested he should have whispered it to Adams, Frank spoke up. "I scorn such methods," he announced, and the audience roared.

At the end of the program, Milton Cross announced that Paul de Kruif, author of the best-selling *Microbe Hunters*, would be guest the following week. Golenpaul had written both de Kruif and his publisher, describing the program and issuing the invitation. He was delighted when the famous author agreed to appear. In his letter Golenpaul suggested that de Kruif listen to the first program, but when the guest showed up the following Tuesday an hour before they were scheduled to go on the air, it turned out he had no idea "Information Please" was a quiz program. "You mean I have to answer *questions*?" de Kruif sputtered. "I thought I was going to talk about my book!"

Golenpaul attempted to molify him, but he was adamant. "I can't go on," he insisted. "I'm no good at these things; I'll make a fool of myself."

Adams and Fadiman tried to persuade him that correct answers were the least important aspect of the genial half hour, but he wouldn't be persuaded. "This is awful," he kept saying, shaking his head. Finally Golenpaul appealed to his sense of honor. After all, he'd consented to appear. His name had been announced.

"Okay, okay," de Kruif said. "But I have to walk around the block and calm myself down." Off he trudged, a picture of despondency. But when he returned forty-five minutes later and only a couple of minutes before air time, it was obvious to everyone that his "walk" had taken him no farther than the nearest saloon.

Libation had enhanced his energy and self-confidence. He rushed to the stage and plopped into the designated chair behind a microphone and a printed card that said, "Mr. de Kruif." There was the sound of a rooster crowing, and Milton Cross said, "Wake up, America, it's time to stump the experts!" Fadiman and Golenpaul looked at each other; Golenpaul shrugged helplessly and the program got rolling. The change in the reticent guest was amazing. At each question he jumped up, waving his hand and Frank pulled him back into his chair. Impatiently he interrupted the other panelists, boisterously making jokes and laughing at them louder than anybody else. When the audience responded delightedly to every incautious utterance, Fadiman recognized a good thing and called on him again and again. Eleven out of the fourteen questions he answered were wrong. One of them was: "All of the following names, with the exception of one, apply to flowers. Which one doesn't? Arbutus, Coreopsis, Rubella, Phlox, Wisteria." Frank guessed that rubella was a kind of mouthwash, but de Kruif waved him aside. "No, no, no," he said. "It's a new kind of Victrola R.C.A. has built, and I've tried it out and it isn't very good."

"That's very interesting," Fadiman said, "and rubella is the word we had in mind, but my card says it's a kind of measles."

"Oh, THAT," scoffed de Kruif, and the audience howled.

Golenpaul worried that nobody would consent to be a guest after de Kruif's appearance, but he couldn't have been more wrong. Instead of making a fool of himself, de Kruif—with his enthusiasm, his eagerness to please, and his exuberant inaccuracies—had endeared himself to everyone listening. Providing correct answers to difficult questions was the least important element in the program's charm. Its appeal had to do with the wit and audacity of its participants, the breathlessly fast pace, the interplay between the panelists and the master of ceremonies, the chance the audience had to send in questions to stump these obviously literate and learned people. It proved an irresistible combination.

The following week mail poured in. Twenty-five thousand questions were received from all over the country, and Kahn and his staff set to work sorting and editing them. In the ten years the program was on the air, the rate of mail never diminished.

A large measure of the popularity of "Information Please" resulted from the compatable but individualistic brilliance of Golenpaul, Kahn, and Fadiman. Although Golenpaul was never heard, his stamp on the program was unmistakable. Before every broadcast he sat down at the table facing the panelists with Fadiman. He had twenty-five index cards on which the questions and answers were typed. Since the program rarely covered more than a dozen multipart questions, Golenpaul decided on the spot which were to be used. Areas in which guests were expected to have knowledge were identified by Kahn and his editorial staff beforehand, in a wide-ranging conversation with the guest. The strengths of regular panelists, of course, were well known, both to the producer and the audience. Guests' questions were so noted on the cards. When Golenpaul handed him the card, Fadiman could see if it was intended for the guests and could prod them into answering if they seemed reluctant. In that way attention was paid to guests without embarrassing them, even though nobody, including the regular panelists, ever knew what questions were going to be asked. It was enough that Golenpaul knew. In this way he controlled the mix and gave everybody a chance to shine. After de Kruif's memorable appearance, there was always a warm-up session in front of the studio audience to put the guests at ease and to identify and alleviate any trouble spots before the performance.

On the fourth program the second permanent panelist appeared, and he remained with Frank and Fadiman for the duration of the program. He was John Kieran, sportswriter for the *New York Times*, birdwatcher and naturalist, lover and quoter of poetry and nineteenth-century English literature. Frank had suggested Kieran to Golenpaul—he was yet another contributor to "The Conning Tower," as would be many of the guests—and he turned out to be a perfect fit. His special charm had to do with the way he revealed his broad, college-professor knowledge: out of the side of his mouth in the accents of a Tenth Avenue cab driver. Central casting couldn't have provided a better performer. The other permanent panelist, appearing every other week until he and Golenpaul had a row in 1943, was musician and Gershwin-o-phile Oscar Levant. He was also an Adams discovery. Frank had met Levant at a luncheon party in Bucks County. He talked so incessantly and brilliantly that Frank finally leaned toward a companion and whispered, "Is he *reading?*"

Fadiman was quick to pounce on an answer and twist it to hilarious advantage; he teased and deflated pomposity, encouraged a "can you top this?" repartee, manipulated the fast pace with exquisite timing, all the while employing the mellifluous tones of a matinee idol. In fact, both Fadiman and Adams had sexy, often suggestively inviting voices, an undeniable but seldom mentioned aspect of their—and the show's—tremendous appeal.

In 1939 "Information Please" was voted the best radio quiz program by the nation's newspaper editors. It garnered twice as many votes as the number two "Professor Quiz," which vanished from the airwaves the following year. In the same poll, editors chose Golenpaul's program as the fourth best show in any category, behind blockbusters Jack Benny, Edgar Bergen and Charlie McCarthy, and Bing Crosby. "Information Please" beat Fred Allen, the Lux Radio Theater, and Orson Welles. Fadiman was number three in the category "New Stars," receiving more votes than Bob Hope, Kay Kyser and H. V. Kaltenborn. Only Orson Welles and Tommy Riggs (of fleeting fame) received more votes. In 1940 the *Saturday Review of Literature* gave "Information Please" an award for distinguished service to literature; a similar prize that year from the *Hobo News* delighted Golenpaul, Adams, and the others even more.

Every Tuesday night "Information Please" careened and skidded through half an hour of uproarious, spontaneous jokes and puns, and often the guests were as funny as the regulars. When John Gunther, foreign correspondent and author of the "Inside" series (*Inside Europe, Inside U.S.A.*, and others) was asked "Who is Reza Pahlavi?", he replied, "Reza Pahlavi is the ruler of Persia." Fadiman smirked. "Are you shah?" he said. Gunther nodded. "Sultanly," he said.

Herbert Bayard Swope, master of the game and revered as dean of them all by everybody who knew him, was reluctant to accept an invitation, despite continual pleas from Frank. Swope was apprehensive lest the deck be stacked against him. He treasured his all-knowing reputation. Only once did he relent, at the behest of Helen Reid, who arranged for him to appear as a tie-in with a *Herald Tribune* charity drive. His appearance, widely anticipated, disappointed nobody, especially himself. He easily answered several difficult questions and brought down the house with one of his responses. When asked what sport called for equipment that included one leather-soled and one rubber-soled shoe, Swope said bowling, which was correct. Fadiman asked which foot wore the leather sole and which the rubber sole. Swope replied, "The left foot for the leather sole." Ever-alert Fadiman asked if he were a right-footed or left-footed bowler, and Swope said, "I am whatever makes the answer right," and retired in triumph.

Another time when Ethel Barrymore was a visitor, the answer to a question was the name of a popular song. Without warning, Fadiman commanded the panel to play it together. Levant sat down at one piano, Barrymore rushed to another with her long skirt billowing around her. A harmonica was provided for Frank, an accordion for Kieran. There followed a rousing rendition of "Let Me Call You Sweetheart," with everybody playing at varying degrees of competence. Levant, Barrymore, and Kieran sang at the top of their lungs. False dignity or reticence had no place on "Information Please." Guests delighted in the opportunity to surprise and to be themselves.

By 1945 guests had included more than four hundred celebrities. People begged to be allowed to appear on the show, but not everybody was suitable. Golenpaul was careful to weed out the merely arrogant or shudderingly incapable. Politicians who appeared included Postmaster General James Farley and Secretary of the Interior Harold Ickes, Senator Alben Barkley (later vice president under Harry S. Truman), William Fulbright, Clare Boothe Luce, Governor Harold Stassen of Minnesota, and former governor of New York, Al Smith. New York City Mayor Fiorello La Guardia showed up "ready with an answer before the question was half finished or even asked," according to John Kieran. Elliott Roosevelt appeared and muffed a question about his mother's newspaper column. Wagnerian singers Helen Traubel and Lauritz Melchior were several-time visitors, as was the handsome young Leonard Bernstein, Yehudi Menuhin and his sister, Hepzibah, pianist Alec Templeton, Deems Taylor (who lived a few blocks from the studio and was often asked to fill in when a guest couldn't come at the last minute), musician, critic, Conning Tower contributor, and Frank's tennis partner Sigmund Spaeth. Popular sports figures were often guests, and included Helen Wills, Grantland Rice, Bill Tilden, Alice Marble, Gene Tunney, and Jackie Robinson, who donated his fee to the United Negro College Fund. Writers Heywood Broun, Rebecca West, James Michener, Erskine Caldwell, Stephen Vincent Benet, Paul Gallico, John Hersey, Sinclair Lewis, and Carl Sandburg fenced with Fadiman, Adams, Kieran, and Levant, as did show business luminaries like Fredric March, Josh Logan, David Niven, Moss Hart, Fred Allen, Madeline Carroll, Alfred Hitchcock, Gracie Allen, Irene Dunne, Orson Welles, Leslie Howard, George M. Cohan, Jimmy Durante, Dorothy Parker, James Mason, Groucho and Harpo Marx, who remained silent throughout the program, answering questions by whistling. Stanley Walker guested frequently, as did all who were left of the Algonquin set.

When the war came, "Information Please" was among the first programs to go on extensive coast-to-coast tours selling war bonds. In addition, Golenpaul produced over two dozen movie shorts, shown all over the country. Suddenly they all had famous faces and were stopped on the street and asked for autographs. Strangers came up to them in restaurants and demanded answers to obscure questions. Kieran took to wearing dark glasses, and Frank slouched through crowds with his hat pulled down.

Frank's eccentricity dovetailed with the others', as if by design.

He had no built-in censor, saying exactly what was on his mind as he always had. He was funny because his comments were unexpected, quirky, irreverent. He often captured ideas nobody listening dared express, even though they agreed. His was a special kind of exhibitionism. He didn't display himself in any vulgar sense but loved to show himself as an oddity, a crochety observer and commentator. His humor was never crude; he was even something of a prude, although his manner was far from prissy. Never rude, he was direct, never aggressive, mean-spirited or malicious. He had a wonderful time.

Invitations to speak at lunches and charitable functions poured in. When Frank addressed Tat's and Tim's grammar school in Connecticut, his remarks were recorded and broadcast later in the month on the Rudy Vallee show.

After a lean six-month period without a sponsor, in October 1938, Canada Dry ginger ale signed the show, and everybody's fortunes took a leap. NBC paid Golenpaul $500 per show when the program had been "sustaining" (sponsorless). Out of this he'd paid his staff, the panel (including the guests), the listeners whose questions were used: $2 for each question broadcast, $5 when it stumped the experts. Even though reviews were laudatory, sponsors continued to be reluctant to buy in. Despite contrary evidence, they felt that it was too "high-brow". Yet "Information Please" was a smash. When the advertising manager of Canada Dry was in Syracuse, he happened to be visiting the local radio station when somebody burst into the general manager's office announcing that "all hell had broken loose" on the switchboard. "Information Please" had been preempted by the Little World Series. There were more complaint calls than the station had ever received, even though Syracuse was one of the teams in the series. The Canada Dry executive called his advertising agency in New York with instructions to buy "Information Please" the next morning, "before somebody else gets it." At the time Canada Dry was developing a franchise business. The company bought the show for $2,500 per program. Everybody got a raise.

In 1940 Lucky Strike cigarettes became the sponsor, and the program moved to Friday nights. Loyalty to the company that paid the bills dictated that everybody smoke Luckies, except Golenpaul and Adams, who preferred cigars. "Every brand of cigarettes is as bad as every other brand," they said with the smug condescension of the cigar addict. George Washington Hill was president of American Tobacco Company, manufacturer of Lucky Strikes. He was a brilliant businessman, politically right wing, a contentious, difficult person who gave Golenpaul much trouble. Hill presented him with a list of people he didn't want as guests on the program (one of the unwanteds was labor leader John L. Lewis). Golenpaul refused to be intimidated and continued to invite whomever he wanted. There was bad feeling between sponsor and producer. However, as long as the program was successful, Hill let Golenpaul alone. He knew better than to tamper with a winning formula.

Until 1942 Lucky Strikes came in green and red packages. Then the sales department suddenly decided that women, who were smoking in ever greater numbers, didn't like the color combination. The company changed it in order to appeal more strongly to them. The action happened to coincide with World War II. To push the new white package, the slogan became "Lucky Strike Green Has Gone to War," the implication being that the switch was somehow patriotic. When he found that the company wasn't giving free cigarettes to GIs, or in fact doing anything to prompt such a slogan, Golenpaul was furious. He didn't want to have to include the slogan on his show, so took American Tobacco to court, keeping, of course, a shrewd eye on the program's public image. The suit made front pages all over the country. Even with a sympathetic judge, Golenpaul lost. The ruling stated that since American Tobacco had bought the time, it could say anything on it it liked. But, as Golenpaul had hoped, the program received a large amount of favorable publicity. "Information Please" was released early from its contract with American Tobacco. Neither Hill nor Golenpaul regretted the split.

At its height, Golenpaul received $12,500 for each "Information Please" program. It made him rich. Panelists received $200 per show, Fadiman more than twice that. Gordon Kahn received less salary than any of the regulars and could never afford to leave his teaching job.

Golenpaul was cantankerous and independent. His relationships with sponsors were often dramatic and unruly, especially when the advertisers were opinionated and difficult as well. The executives at the Heinz Company, whose sponsorship followed Lucky Strikes', objected strenuously to some of the guests, especially the obvious New Dealers. "The board of directors was afraid people would stop buying their ketchup or their pickles because they didn't like our politics," Golenpaul snorted, and welcomed new sponsor Socony (Mobil) Oil, whose executives turned out to be even more rigid and conservative. They didn't like it when Secretary of the Interior, Harold Ickes, chief governmental regulator of oil and gas companies, appeared, nor did they approve of the other Democrats and liberals who seemed to predominate in the guest list, a constant source of irritation between Golenpaul and the people at Socony. When Socony dropped the show after a couple of years, NBC refused to give it another time slot. In those days NBC was the giant among the networks. Campbell Soups offered to buy Golenpaul's show, but when they discovered that NBC wouldn't give it a time, the soup company refused to sponsor it elsewhere. It looked like "Information Please" was about to go down the drain.

Summer of 1946 came. Most radio programs took summer vacations in those days, and so did "Information Please." Golenpaul went to Cape Cod and tried to come up with a solution to the dilemma that found him facing the fall without a sponsor or a network. During the bleak August in Massachusetts, Frank wrote him from Connecticut and enclosed a letter he'd just received from an old friend, Kenneth Parker, scion of the Parker Pen family. It was a brief note, a fan letter in which Parker told Frank what fun the program was and how much he enjoyed listening. Golenpaul excitedly telephoned Frank and urged him to contact Parker to see if he wanted to sponsor the show on CBS. Frank told Dan to do it himself. He did, and Parker Pen became the next, and last, sponsor of "Information Please," on CBS.

After only a few months, Golenpaul ran into a calamitous problem with the network and its president, William S. Paley. Even Kenneth Parker couldn't help him out this time. Choice of guests, always a thorny issue, was what ultimately did in "Information Please."

Governor of Georgia and ardent New Dealer Ellis Arnall had been a popular guest several times prior to 1946. In November of that year, he planned to retire from the state house since he wasn't permitted to succeed himself. Eugene Talmadge, promising to continue to restrict blacks from the elective process in Georgia, ran in the Democratic primary against the candidate Arnall supported. In a brazen boondoggle, even though Arnall's man received the most votes in the three-way contest, the pro-Talmadge legislature pulled a fast one by announcing that whoever had won the most counties had won the election. That twist unsurprisingly made Talmadge the Democratic candidate, and in those days that meant he was the next governor. Unfortunately, Talmadge complicated matters by dying. His undaunted supporters invented more mischief by naming young Herman to succeed his father as governor designate. In response, Arnall refused to vacate the office. He wanted the man who'd been elected lieutenant governor sworn in as acting governor. The donnybrook was called the New Battle of Atlanta and, depending on their political views—mostly boiling down to how they felt about FDR—people all over the country were outspokenly partisan. Probably not coincidentally, on "Information Please" Arnall was scheduled for another guest appearance. The week preceding his appearance, Fadiman was supposed to announce that Arnall was to be the following week's guest and to describe him glowingly as "the champion of democracy." Network executives were up in arms. Paley told Golenpaul that Arnall wouldn't be permitted to appear, that his appearance was too controversial, that presenting him even if he didn't mention the situation was tantamount to advocating his position. Golenpaul suspected that, rather than fearing the appearance of taking sides in a controversy, the network had taken sides or feared the appearance of siding with Arnall. Anti-Roosevelt passion was still strong among businessmen and advertisers, even after FDR died. Golenpaul's memory of what had happened at NBC was still fresh. He grudgingly volunteered to compromise by asking Talmadge to appear on another week, but Paley turned thumbs down. Golenpaul wouldn't give in, and the battle between him and Paley went on until time for the broadcast. When Paley threatened to cut him off the air if he didn't red pencil the offending phrase in the script, Golenpaul said that the network didn't need that kind of publicity and dared Paley to try it. "Everybody will be on my side," he said. "Nobody likes censorship, not after we've just won the war." He was calling Paley's bluff. Adding to the patriotic feelings of the evening, guests that week were Frank Capra and James Stewart of *It's a Wonderful Life* and *Mr. Smith Goes to Washington*. When Golenpaul told them about the impasse, Stewart said, "It's okay with me, cut me off the air, I'm scared stiff anyway. Anything to get me out of this thing."

But Paley didn't do what he threatened. The program went on. Guests Capra and Stewart comported themselves admirably, the announcement was made as written, and Arnall was the guest the following week. His performance clearly vindicated Golenpaul's decision, at least from an entertainment standpoint. Not only did he swap quips roguishly with the regulars, but he quoted Lord Byron, swiped Kieran's thunder through total recall of obscure sports memorabilia, sang both the chorus and the verse from "I Don't Want to Set the World on Fire." When asked to identify an incident from an O. Henry story, the former governor did so, then added modestly, "Of course, Mr. Adams knows more about those stories than I do."

"Not tonight," said Frank.

And when asked for a work in which pleasure was alternately compared to poppies, a snowfall, and a rainbow, Arnall unhesitatingly and flawlessly boomed a verse from Robert Burns' "Tam o'Shanter."

Toward the end of the show, Fadiman remarked, "It certainly would be pleasant to see some other hands." But it was all Arnall. And he was wonderful.

The victory was, unfortunately, a Pyrrhic one. Repercussions were immediate. Because the Parker Pen contract was up and the company was undergoing a vast new expansion program, it wanted to sign a contract with Golenpaul for thirteen weeks at a time, with options to renew at the end of each period. And it wanted to cut its payment to him to $1,000 per rating point, or around $8,000 for each program. Golenpaul refused, and Parker withdrew its offer. There were no other takers. Golenpaul's reputation as a troublesome producer had made the rounds. "Information Please" ended with the 1947–1948 season when it was broadcast over the small chain of independent Mutual Broadcasting System stations. And there was more hoopla when Golenpaul threatened to sue the American Federation of Musicians because the union demanded he hire separate studio musicians at every Mutual station. The program was sponsored locally in most cities, which made each broadcast seem autonomous. Golenpaul said he couldn't afford to hire three hundred musicians, that the cost of his pianist would escalate ridiculously from $31.88 a week to $9,564. The matter was settled amicably. Golenpaul, with his dramatic sense of publicity, hadn't really thought the union would make him toe the line. But there were other, much more damaging problems. Listeners had trouble finding "Information Please" on its new and not very well-known place on the dial. Worse, it was up against the popular "Ozzie and Harriet" on CBS and "The Sheriff," sponsored by Twenty Mule Team Borax, on NBC. (That half hour program was followed, ironically, by the slapstick quiz "It Pays to Be Ignorant" at 10:00).

A couple of years later, Golenpaul reintroduced the program as a summer replacement for Fred Waring on television, hoping that viewers would respond as radio listeners once had. They didn't. The new panel, which didn't include Adams or Levant, didn't have the old magic. The program died once and for all, but whether its influence is acknowledged or not, the sophisticated irreverence and whimsy of "Information Please" remains as groundbreaker and standard for every popular talk show since. Golenpaul recognized that intelligent people can and often do have goofy senses of humor, and that allowing them to frolic in public didn't lower their IQs or demean them in any way. The ghosts of Golenpaul, Kahn, Fadiman (the only one who is still alive in 1985), Adams, Kieran, and Levant sit behind people like Johnny Carson and David Letterman, simultaneously encouraging lunacy and demanding respect for the audience. It's an admirable legacy for a medium that too often underestimates itself and its viewers.

CHAPTER SEVEN

Later

For an idea ever to be fashionable is ominous, since it must after-wards be always old-fashioned.

—GEORGE SANTANYA

And so to bed.

—SAMUEL PEPYS

I   When Frank and Esther were married in 1925, he was at the height of his fame and power. Undeniably, a large part of his appeal to the women who fluttered around him was the unique position he held as tastemaker and literary mentor, the fact of his widely read and quoted column, his ability to attract and fascinate a stunning array of friends. With Frank, life in New York was a never-ending rush of stimulating companions and events. This remained true after they married, even with the ordinarily inhibiting intrusion of a child born at the breakneck pace of nearly one a year. But there were nannies and cooks and maids at West Tenth Street. Neither parent had to relinquish personal time or pursuit. Though occasionally inconvenienced, the Adamses were able to avoid the larger disadvantage of self-sacrifice, even in the mother and father department.

They weren't particularly good parents, although they both liked the idea of parenthood. Frank talked often and affectionately in the Diary about one or the other of the youngsters, but it was hard for him to listen to them, to consider what they were saying, to change a plan he'd made to accommodate them. Children were not as sophisticated as adults, and not nearly as interesting, if wisecracks, and parsing of sentences, clever plays on words, and grown-up games like tennis and pool were what interested you. Frank liked the appearance of doting fatherhood; he'd longed for it. But the real thing was different from what he'd imagined. Openness, and willingness to compromise were requirements in the weaving of intimacy. In addition to these essentials, relationships with children required a special patience and attentiveness. Frank respected his children, which was important, but intermittently, when he felt like it. Other times it was as if they didn't exist. And, not surprisingly, considering his uptight Victorian upbringing, it was he—the father—who decided what was important in their lives, even when it didn't involve him. There wasn't any appeal when he laid down a rule, and his rules, sometimes reasonably having to do with physical safety and health, frequently centered on irrational areas nobody was allowed to discuss. These rules were geared to prevent situations that caused Frank emotional discomfort: In his house there was no questioning of his opinions, no untoward or graceless conversation (about sex, for example), no passionate outbursts or "uncivilized" behavior. He expected much from his children but didn't devote commensurate time in teaching them just what it was he expected, or in encouraging them to level with him. This was understandable since he didn't admit to his own doubts and fears. He'd spent his life constructing walls around his most private feelings, and he didn't allow anybody to tamper with them. So, parallel to Frank's articulated standards, there were even more complicated sets of unspoken rules and doomed attempts at mind reading.

One of his strongest traits was an insistence on controlling his environment, both as an editor in what was published under his name and in personal relationships. To win Frank's affection, you did and said what he approved of. His friends had always known this. Now Tat, Tim, Puff, and Jack had to find it out. Frank was too old and well-defended to change; it was Esther and the children who learned to accommodate. Esther underwent intense Jungian analysis; the children coped by constructing their own careful defenses.

Not surprisingly, the household was more formal than easygoing. The children rarely ate with their parents, almost never intruded or made demands the servants couldn't meet as surrogates. There was a distance between parent and child, not surprising since that had always been Frank and Esther's style.

After they moved to Connecticut, many aspects of life were different. It was no longer possible for Frank to share a leisurely meal with somebody he ran into on the street since he didn't often run into anybody in Connecticut, except on the weekends. He couldn't dash off to the theater or a concert at the last minute, pop in and out of friends' homes, challenge somebody to an all-night game of pool at the Players. Because of the distance between city and country, an informal social life with city friends wasn't accessible. Frank became unhappily familiar with the relentless demands and calamities associated with commuting on the New York, New Haven and Hartford. Plans of all kinds had to be made many days in advance. Visitors were put up for several days at a time. They interfered with his orderly life far more than his children did, who had learned to keep out of his way. For Frank, guests never seemed to know when to leave. Once, when one of Esther's relatives came to make an unscheduled call, Frank spotted the car pulling up in the driveway. He grabbed Tat, and together they hid in the bedroom closet until the unwelcome in-law had departed, nearly forty-five minutes later. After that, Frank and the children called unwelcome visitors ''closet people.''

Esther tried to compensate for Frank's lack of manners, but it wasn't easy. When he was tired or had decided the evening should end, he'd go noisily and grumpily to bed, with guests still sitting in the living room, suddenly self-conscious and uneasy. Or else he'd go around peering at the clocks and sighing. He and Esther argued about this aspect of their lives, but since each believed himself or herself the wronged party, there wasn't any solution.

Because in 1938 he was no longer a city dweller, blessed (or cursed) with the sweat and scramble that that implied, Frank determinedly assumed some of the airs of a country gentleman. He didn't go so far as to buy a new car, but he took an interest, heretofore unsuspected, in gardening. He learned to tell a dahlia from a peony. On the heels of the surprise success of ''Information Please,'' the Clifton Fadimans moved into a big house not far from the Adamses. Other friends came to Connecticut with their growing families. Occasionally Frank would bring over his children and park them with a neighboring family for an afternoon, or for the day. The possibility that he was inconsiderate of them and his children never occurred to him. He assumed that was what people did, so he did it.

Weekends were spent at neighbors' tennis courts. Frank persisted in his peculiar tennis game. He cared terribly about it, worked on it for more than fifty years, but never seemed to improve. He played in a kind of haze of incomprehension. He was uncoordinated, loose-limbed, clumsy. He gallumphed. He played for hours and invariably lost, acting bewildered and perplexed after each loss, as if it were unique. He believed unwaveringly in his ability, despite decades of defeat. His enthusiasm was genuine and innocent. Whenever somebody said, ''Who's for tennis?'' he was always first at the baseline with his racket.

After dinner in Connecticut, conversations centered on boiler problems, leaks in the basement, and the desirability of paving picturesque country roads. Concerns at the Adamses became distinctly suburban.

The new persona created by the relocation was radically different from F.P.A., late of the *New York Herald Tribune* and "The Conning Tower." When the *New York Post* started publishing the column in 1938, its tone was different from the old days, and it suffered from the change. In the first place, F.P.A. had been the quintessential New Yorker, his friends the movers and shakers of Manhattan island. There'd been little languor and no rural preoccupations in the *Herald Tribune* Diary entries, which had skipped and sniffed with the vitality of a city slicker. Connecticut represented a whole new, softer way of looking at life, and it didn't translate.

The *Post*, taking advantage of Frank's new radio fame, ran his column for three years after 1938, then quietly dropped it. "The Conning Tower," which remained intellectually biased, didn't belong in the snappy liberal tabloid with columnists like gossipy Leonard Lyons and Sidney Skolsky of "Hollywood Is My Beat." And Frank's crotchety observations, once thought sophisticated and acerbic, seemed school-marmish, pedantic. In December 1938, F.P.A. commented inimitably, "By the way, it is assumed that the *Times*, by "The Night Before Christmas," means Clement C. Moore's "A Visit from St. Nicholas." Few of his readers cared whether the *New York Times* was shamed in such a minor matter. That same winter the world stood by uneasily as Hitler prepared for his march into eastern Czechoslovakia.

Contributors still mailed their cherished verses to F.P.A., but there were no wild and funny geniuses among them, no one-of-a-kind youngsters like Robert Benchley or James Thurber, Dorothy Parker, E. B. White, or Eugene O'Neill. New writers showed their fledgling efforts elsewhere, where editors weren't so concerned with sticking to conventional techniques, didn't deplore experimentation, and, in lieu of prestige, paid money for work they printed. Frank continued diligently and honorably to edit and hone his contributors' poems. He didn't compromise with form, or make it any easier to land in the Tower merely because contributions were thinner than they'd been. Fewer contributions made it to the top of the Tower, which was an indication that quality was slipping. But Frank never awarded his prize spot to work he felt didn't qualify. He maintained his standards and his self-respect.

As his decade of suburban living and national celebrity went along,

Frank fell in love with the New Deal, the Roosevelts, and, surprisingly, with politics. He began to see himself as a politician.

FDR's press secretary, Steve Early, was a hard-drinking card-playing old friend from World War I and the *Stars and Stripes*. Early arranged for Frank, who at the time still worked for the *New York Herald Tribune*, to attend an FDR press conference in February of 1936. Frank announced himself as representing "The Conning Tower," an obvious white lie okay in those loose days before the White House press corps learned to take itself with ponderous seriousness. He confessed to a longing to stand up and ask the president how he felt, but lacked the nerve to speak. Later he admitted his red badge of courage was yellow, so returned to New York without addressing FDR. Once back in New York, Frank whisked off a breezy note to Early and was rewarded, within a few weeks, with a private introduction to FDR. Being within "the presence" awed Frank, who was an admirer of Heywood Broun's social conscience. He became an ardent advocate of the New Deal.

For the first time he allowed himself to speak strongly in the column about matters he'd heretofore avoided:

> All this talk about communism and fascism in the writers' project of the W.P.A. is so much boric eyewash. How much communism or fascism can there be in a guidebook? Will there be distortion of facts? Or is there opinion in a guidebook, such as what is Worth Seeing?

And during the New York City elevator operators' strike, snappishness about the inconvenience of walking up many flights of stairs to his office became downright blue-collar advocacy:

> Among the free newspapers is the Sun which says that "a living wage should be computed on the theory that every young man operating an elevator has a wife and three children may surprise those who know that this assumption is not according to the census or the facts; but let that go." Well, we won't let it go, for one. Suppose an operator gets $28 a week, as some of them may now get. And suppose that he is unmarried, childless, and without other financial obligations. In that case, almost unprecedented, he will have $28 a week to to frivol and riot his life away on. Of course, with all that money piling up, he will probably be the prey of women fortune hunters, and some adventuress will get him.

And Frank reminded Eleanor Roosevelt, in her daily syndicated column, "My Day," to stick to journalistic rules and be specific when referring to a book or a person or an article she admired. ("Don't say 'a morning newspaper,' " he admonished. "Tell us which one.") He often referred to his sister columnist with obvious affection. One day he playfully waxed curious about the country's most famous married couple:

> When our favorite Diarist gets home from a ride on her favorite horse, Dot, she gives her . . . two lumps of sugar. For the first lump Dot has to shake hands with both forefeet, but for the second lump she has to kiss the First Lady on the cheek. How many lumps of sugar does the President have in his coffee, and does he have a second cup, and what are the proceedings?

But his curiosity was never impertinent. And his frequent sympathetic attention won him a personal relationship with the Roosevelts, who invited him and Esther to the White House on several occasions, once for a blissful two-day visit.

On "Information Please," Golenpaul invited Wendell Willkie to appear before his nomination on the Republican presidential ticket of 1940. Introducing Willkie, Fadiman described him as a "real honest-to-goodness tycoon." The dynamic Hoosier businessman answered several questions about American history and politics. He was a popular guest, but when election time came, only Kieran supported him. The Roosevelts invited the Adamses to Hyde Park to listen to the election night returns. Esther went early, for dinner, but since it was a broadcast night, Frank had to wait until after the program before his departure. Eleanor Roosevelt sent a car for him, and he was whisked from Radio City in liveried splendor for the two-hour drive to Hyde Park. Frank was in the sitting room when the president was wheeled in to greet his guests. He spotted Frank and greeted him with a breezy, "Hiya, Franklin!" F.P.A. instantly responded, "Hiya, Franklin!" which brought down the house. Later in the evening, Eleanor Roosevelt asked why her other favorite "Information Please" panelist John Kieran, supported Willkie. "Nothing personal," Frank said, protecting his friend, aware that the sportswriter was more politically conservative than most people knew. "It's the third term issue."

Frank wrote Eleanor Roosevelt several times, beginning his letters with a fond "Dear Nell," asking her to appear on "Information Please." Golenpaul wanted to have her as a guest, nagging Frank to ask her again after her first turn-down. But she was adamant. Some of her advisors felt that it would be undignified for the First Lady to appear on a quiz show, even though she endorsed products in women's magazines and had her own radio program. To Frank she confessed only stage fright.

In 1944 Frank was appointed an alternate Roosevelt delegate to the Democratic national convention in Chicago. He told Early that his mother had been born there, and also what he knew about the vagaries of the Cook County machine. He favored continuing Henry Wallace as vice president, but later relented obediently when he received instructions to support Harry Truman instead. Frank never considered supporting anybody but FDR for the top spot. He took seventeen-year-old Tat along to Chicago, and they had a good time attending caucuses and meeting the various party bigwigs. Frank bought dinner for his sisters and their families and showed his birthplace Chicago to his boy. He was proud of both.

That year Frank decided to run for political office. Inspired by knowledge that FDR's first victory (in 1910) had come in a district that hadn't supported a Democrat in the previous thirty-two years, Frank announced his candidacy for the Connecticut state senate in a district containing eleven or so registered Democrats. He promised to campaign by keeping his mouth shut, and so paid for and sent a single electioneering postcard to registered voters. Steering clear of hyperbole, the curious mailer simply announced the candidate's name in block letters, the office he sought, and his party, in the smallest letters of all. Old friend Harold Ross ran a short item in "The Talk of the Town" by E. B. White about Frank's candidacy, but otherwise the press didn't pay much attention, not even the local papers. The nation's eyes were firmly fastened on the South Pacific and on FDR, who looked awful, even in the heavily doctored newspaper photographs. Frank kept FDR apprised of his campaign activities through letters to Early. He described his speeches and reported that he always got a laugh when he told his audiences that he'd driven to whatever rally it was in his 1932 Franklin automobile, good for another four years. He admitted to speaking engagements two or three times a day, probably an inflated figure, but, once bitten by the office-seeker bug, he tried hard to win. He didn't. His opponent, Republican William E. Sheehy, did that, garnering 19,886 votes to Frank's respectable 16,900.

Frank maintained his interest in town politics and was rewarded by his party's nomination for justice of the peace in 1948. He lost again, and that was the end of his political aspirations.

II

In the summer of 1945, before the smoke of battle had settled, Golenpaul decided to take "Information Please" to Europe in conjunction with the USO. Kieran, Adams, and Fadiman were enthusiastic at the prospect. Hollywood comedian Reginald Gardiner, an old friend of Frank's who'd achieved success as a droll Britisher in sophisticated movies, and Beatrice Lillie, had guested many times and were delighted to join the show for the six-week tour.

On the trip Fadiman and Kieran noticed a change in Frank, which perplexed them. Kieran had an eye infection and had to treat it with drops several times a day. Since Frank was his roommate, he asked him to administer the medicine. Much to Kieran's (and Frank's) embarrassment, sometimes Frank's hands shook so violently he was hard put to get the drops on target. At first it was a joke, but when the condition persisted, Kieran tactfully found others to manage the delicate maneuver.

In addition to the hand tremors, at the card table Frank got quickly and uncharacteristically drunk, becoming befuddled and inappropriately irascible after only a couple of drinks. This was unusual behavior, especially when he forgot what cards had been played during a hand in one of the many late-night poker games. Occasionally he even halted play petulantly until somebody filled him in. Necessity for this special treatment baffled and maddened the others, who weren't used to such behavior, and confused Frank, who wouldn't have stood for such incompetence in anybody else. Fortunately, it didn't happen often. It became Kieran's job every morning to see that Frank was turned out properly. He had difficulty coping with his Sam Browne belt, with aligning his shirt and jacket buttons. Everything always seemed to bag, dangle, come loose, hang open.

Frank's trouble, and it was never officially diagnosed, was that he was afflicted with the early symptoms of Alzheimer's disease, an incurable and ultimately fatal brain disorder. The affliction began with uncertain memory and silly mistakes with words. As it progressed—and the changes took many years—the effects on his personality manifested themselves inexorably. He flew off the handle without warning, sometimes with outbursts directed viciously against friends and family; he couldn't remember things that had happened a few hours before, didn't remember conversations, or errands he'd promised to run.

After "Information Please" went off the air in 1947, there was little work for Frank. Loyal friends at the *New York Post* hired him to write the Diary on Saturdays for a few weeks in the winter and early spring, but his poignant reminiscences of dead friends ("I was sadly shocked to hear how Grace Moore had been killed in a plane, and I recalled when first I met her, in 1922, at Heywood Broun's, and a vital girl she was'') and descriptions of days spent watching the rain roll down his Connecticut windowpanes didn't thrill his readers. The *Post*, with up-to-the-minute columnists like Marquis Childs, Elsa Maxwell, Sylvia Porter, Earl Wilson, Dorothy Thompson, Harold Ickes (''Man to Man''), and Victor Riesel was definitely not the place for Frank's gentle ruminations on how an old fellow whiled away his days. He wasn't asked to continue the column into the summer. And so ''The Conning Tower,'' which had been discontinued in 1941, and the once indestructable ''Diary of Our Own Samuel Pepys'' finally and irrevocably died. There were few mourners.

III

Esther and Frank's had been a celebrated romance, fascinating with its intrigue and their commitment to one another against heavy odds. But by 1949 the honeymoon had long since petered out. It wasn't only their dramatically variant temperaments—in the first few years, when they'd been crazy about each other, their differences added ginger. But after more than twenty years of marriage they were at loggerheads more often than not.

Of course, Esther had no idea that Frank's infuriating personality changes were the result of a certifiable disease. She may have reflected that he was almost seventy, that his sometimes bizarre behavior was a result of what his doctor called ''hardening of the arteries,'' in those days the catchall category for a variety of disparate old people's ailments. Alzheimer's was often misdiagnosed as arteriosclerosis before its own difficult-to-differentiate symptoms were categorized and named. But arteriosclerosis, though progressive, usually attacks old people, and significant memory lapses don't occur at the onset of the disease. When Frank started losing his memory and exhibiting personality changes, he was in his fifties. People around him didn't pay any attention. He'd always been impatient, grumpy. And his phenomenal ability to remember obscure song lyrics and romantic poetry so dazzled his family and friends that they didn't notice he couldn't remember once simple errands or where he was supposed to be at an agreed upon hour. Besides, it wasn't easy watching him fall apart. Family denial is typical in these circumstances. However, the age difference between Esther and Frank, once romantic, became ominous. She was still in her fifties, a vigorous, handsome, take-charge woman. ''She was a very attractive dark-haired

Brunnehilde type,'' remembers an old friend. ''She was about 5'11''
and built to scale.'' There were rumors about her roving eye, but even
if she had extracurricular relief, living with Frank in the 1940s was a
nightmare. He repeated himself maddeningly, couldn't remember what
he'd said fifteen minutes afterward, nagged and criticized and made
demands, then forgot what he'd asked for.

When Golenpaul tried out ''Information Please'' on television, he
asked Frank to be a member of the panel. Up until then Frank's dete-
rioration had been a well-kept secret, but he had to be helped on and
off the stage. And a member of the audience remembers him ''looking
like a death's head. It was touch and go; you held your breath.'' His
mind went blank during the program. ''The others tried to cover up for
him,'' recalls another observer, ''but he simply wasn't functioning. He
was fine and then suddenly he wasn't, almost as if he didn't know where
he was. It was terribly sad.'' Although the program finished the summer,
Frank didn't reappear.

The writing was on the wall. Not only couldn't Frank work any
more, but his deteriorating condition signaled the probability of heavy
medical expenses. By 1950 Tim had graduated from Bowdoin, Tat from
Yale. Tim moved to San Francisco. His parents had been reluctant to
give him the $59 for the train fare, but when he said he'd borrow the
money from somebody else, they relented. Frank was extraordinarily
proud of Tim, who'd married, worked for the *San Francisco Examiner*,
and never again asked him for money. Before he'd left for the Coast,
he and Frank sat together at the kitchen table silently eating cornflakes
together. Suddenly Frank blurted, ''When you go to San Francisco,
don't carry on with women, and if you do, use one of *those things*.''
He bobbed his head and continued eating without looking at Tim. That
was the extent of the father-son talk. Tim confessed that it was Esther
who had filled him in on delicate matters of the birds and bees, when
he was about ten. After she had finished the explanation, the little boy
patted her stomach. ''Is there anyone in there now?'' he asked.

Puff and Jack were only just finishing boarding school, Jack in
Putney, Vermont, and Puff at Butkins, in Williamstown, Massachusetts.
They'd need college money. Esther didn't know where it would come
from. In addition, she'd never been faced before with the necessity of
taking care of herself; she couldn't cook a meal or iron a blouse. Her
personal funds were shrinking terrifyingly fast. She may have panicked
and decided to cut her losses while she still had assets. Whatever her
thinking, one Saturday she sat down to lunch with Frank and Tat when
the two younger children were home on vacation. ''Your father and I

are getting a divorce,'' she announced. Frank appeared to be as astonished at the announcement as were the children.

Esther's sudden announcement, her apparently unilateral decision to end the marriage after twenty-five years was, she felt, the only thing to do, even if it appeared cowardly and mean-spirited to others. It hit Frank hard.

Shortly after dropping the bombshell, Esther went south to obtain a "quickie" divorce. Frank moved into the top-floor apartment at the Players Club, headquartered in Edwin Booth's house facing Gramercy Park in New York City. Puff and Jack went to live with Esther's brother and sister-in-law in Westchester, New York, then moved their belongings and themselves in with Esther's Connecticut friends, the Carrs. Esther went to live in an efficiency apartment in what had been her father's apartment house at 2 West Sixty-seventh Street. She sold the house in Weston. The divorce settlement enabled her to keep the proceeds; unfortunately, the housing market was depressed, and the house and surrounding acreage didn't bring anything near what they were worth.

Frank had belonged to the Players for decades. Most of his male friends belonged, too. The club was a refuge for its members, where no women were allowed except occasionally in the dining room and at an annual open house on Shakespeare's birthday. Footsteps were unhurried on the burgundy-carpeted curved staircase. The clubhouse was an elegantly furnished, dark-paneled monument to gentler days. There a man retired after dinner to an easy chair in front of the window in the second-floor sitting room, happy with his port, a cigar, and the newspaper. Or he went downstairs for a game of poker or billiards in the dim room where Mark Twain's portrait and pool cue hung above the mantel. Twain had been a member of the Players, as were many storied stage actors, dramatists, and writers since the turn of the century. The Players enjoyed an elite reputation; it was notable for erudite conversation and its excellent library, which contained many musty first editions. Its pride in an intellectual membership given to humor without intrusions of locker-room heehaws made it singular among other theatrical clubs, like the more flamboyant Lambs and Friars. The revered John Drew was its president when Frank became a member.

On F.P.A.'s seventieth birthday in 1951, Newman Levy arranged for the club to honor him with a Pipe Night. Many of his oldest friends and contributors attended. Speakers included Russel Crouse, Marc Connelly, Howard Lindsay, as well as Levy. A several-page facsimile of "The Conning Tower" was distributed, a "sporting extra, put together

without the knowledge or touch of The Master.'' E. B. White mailed
his contribution from his farm in Maine, and it was printed prominently:

> *When Frank was one and Forty*
> > *And Smeed was in his Tower*
> *The morns were fair and lusty—*
> > *This was our finest hour.*
> *We wrote with endless patience*
> > *And seldom paid with rue,*
> *And I was two and twenty,*
> > *And, Baby, so were you.*
> *Now I am two and fifty*
> > *And Frank is God knows what;*
> *The morns are dark and empty,*
> > *The press has gone to pot.*
> *So let us toast the Master*
> > *And build again the Tower*
> *Where Frank was in his heaven*
> > *And Muse was in her bower.*

Frank Sullivan, who'd substituted for F.P.A. at the *New York
World* when Frank and Esther were honeymooning, saluted his mentor
with the following:

> *Through thick and thin we two have went*
> *Since first, on the World, we were acquent.*
> *I like your style, I like your grin,*
> *I like you when I'm foxed with gin.*
> *I like your shirts, I like your vest,*
> *I like you facing East or West,*
> *And I lift this foaming glass of grog*
> *To toast you on your natal Tag.*

A woman spoke not only to Frank but to the club's no-woman
policy. Levy, who was rigidly old-fashioned when it came to the sanctity
of men's clubs, though it best to identify her only as ''Squidge:''

> *Dear FPA, your natal day*
> *Fills us with feelings tender,*
> *Though we deplore, as oft of yore*

Our inconvenient gender.
Do gals not smoke, enjoy a joke,
And hold their own as bibbers?
Why segregate on this glad date
His feminine contribbers?
Fain would we raise a glass in praise
Of one whose rare acumen
Welcomed to print a virtual mint
Of verse from man and woman.
We'd planned to bake a gala cake
Of 70 lucious layers
Had we been bid to join you Kid—
And heaven help the Players!
Included out, not ours to pout,
But whether miss or missus,
We join to send to you, old friend,
Our birthday love and kisses.

From Hollywood, Morrie Ryskind sent his regards:

When I was one and twenty,
*   I wrote for FPA—*
And neither crowns nor guineas
*   Can take that thrill away!*
I got no gold nor rubies—
*   Joy simple was my fee:*
And when I'd top the Tower,
*   You couldn't talk to me.*

When I was four and forty
*   And writing on my own,*
I'd found the crowns and guineas
*   But lost the joy I'd known.*
I said, "I'd trade some rubies
*   To have Frank back anew."*

And I am five and fifty,
*   And oh! 'tis true, 'tis true!*

Edna Ferber's contribution came after she'd decided not to write anything, then changed her mind because of Levy's pleading and her own deep loyalty. She and Frank had been friends for forty years:

His mood was not pretentious,
      His strength was rhymes, not reams.
He shunned the lads momentous,
      For Flaccus, Woollcott, Deems.

The colyum was a showcase
      For Kaufman, Marc and Bob,
And definitely no place
      For fool or heel or snob.

Finally, from Corey Ford:

When I was a lad—a distant day—
I sent a pome to FPA;
My young ambition reached its flower
When it landed in the Conning Tower.
Today with half of life behind,
I'm still submitting pomes, I find
And joining with my fellow Players
And all alumni FPA-ers
To give three cheers, and one cheer more,
For happy birthday, Fran, From Core.

Deems Taylor, presiding, presented Frank with several gifts: a red flannel nightshirt "for breakfast wear"; an enormous house number sign reading "FPA/15 Gramercy Park/Fasten Seat Belt" in luminous characters; a sandglass for timing boiled eggs and after-dinner speeches; a mop to forestall "dry-sweeping" in front of the Players, at least. The evening was rowdy and nostalgic. Anthony came in from Connecticut to sit next to Frank and help him open the presents.

Despite his friends' brave attempts at pretending otherwise, Frank was in a bad way, though he continued to shoot pool and play cards. Fellow Players understood his condition and gallantly protected him from knowledge of it. At an all-night poker session, Frank lost all his money and was trying to win it back in a single hand by bluffing on a pair of threes. Everyone knew what he held; they'd looked. Finally, George Kaufman—taught, encouraged, applauded, first published by F.P.A. more than forty years before—threw in his cards. His eyes directed everyone else to do the same. When they did, he gathered the large pot and redistributed it in equal portions. "We were only playing for fun, Frank," he said. It was a heartbreaking admission of how things stood. Poker players aren't noted for their compassion.

Sometimes there was an echo of the wicked wit Frank had wielded effortlessly. One evening a raucous crowd at the bar interfered with his concentration at a game of pool. "Remember, this is a gentleman's club," he admonished, looking over the tops of his spectacles at the boisterous group. "And he's apt to walk in here any minute."

Another time, Russel Crouse found Frank in the men's room, bent double. "Help me, Crouse," Frank said. "I can't stand up. I think I've had a stroke." Crouse helped him into the light and discovered that Frank had buttoned his fly to his vest. Frank's laughter was loud and unselfconscious when the mistake was discovered.

In 1959 fellow Players member, writer Paul Hollister, arranged with the University of Michigan for an exhibition of Frank's work. The university library displayed editions of all his books and many of the articles he'd written for magazines over the years. The exhibit also included a handsome pen-and-ink drawing of Frank by another Player, Gordon Stephenson, whose oil portraits of Mark Twain and Howard Lindsay hung in the clubhouse, and the 1951 Pipe Night program. Hollister told Frank about the honor accorded him by his alma mater and reported him "highly pleased."

With the innate generosity he found it necessary always to deny, Harold Ross asked Frank to cull the *Congressional Record* for newsbreaks. This stipend from *The New Yorker* was Frank's only income. He asked friends to mention his name if their work was accepted by the magazine: "I'm a talent scout for that publication," he said. Frank himself submitted little of use to the editors, although he sat for long periods in the Players library, carefully turning the pages of the *Record*. When Ross died, his successor, William Shawn, continued the kindness. James Thurber reported with unbecoming petulance—and accuracy—in a 1958 letter to a friend, "*The New Yorker* supports Frank Adams, but it will never support me." Perhaps in his fear of old age and incompetence, he forgot that when F.P.A. had published the work of the penniless young James Thurber, the fledgling writer was released forever from having to return to Columbus.

Frank's health sank rapidly. Often he forgot to get dressed and shuffled around all afternoon in his ancient Indian patterned bathrobe. Sometimes he frightened visitors by confronting them disapprovingly on the stairs. "Who are you?" he'd say. Club members became apprehensive about him, uncertain of their ability to control him or his capacity to control himself.

Finally it was clear to everyone that Frank couldn't remain in the club on his own. In 1955 Dr. George Bahr, a fellow member, telephoned

Esther. "We don't know what to do with him," he said. And then, apologetically, "We don't think he can live here any longer."

Esther flew into action. She had her own doctor examine him, and she listened carefully when he described the hopeless prognosis. She spent several afternoons in quiet conversation with Frank, helped him pack his things into trunks that eventually found their way to her house on Bailey Island, off the coast of Maine. She arranged for his transfer to the Lynwood nursing home on West 102nd Street, a medium-sized facility occupying a couple of five-story attached brownstones. His room was located at the head of the stairs on the second floor, the best spot in the place. There were fluffy curtains at the window, a desk piled high with books he intended to read, and framed pictures on the wall that had once hung in his office. One showed the *Lusitania*, sunk by a German U-boat prior to World War I. His doctor liked to ask him playfully on every visit who'd gone down on the *Lusitania*. Frank, no matter how badly disoriented, no matter what else he couldn't remember, always named half a dozen *Lusitania* passengers. His doctor thought it quite remarkable.

Years before, when Frank's friend Joe Wise, brother of famous Zionist Rabbi Stephen Wise, contracted a fatal degenerative disease, Frank couldn't bring himself to visit him while he lay sick and dying. "It would break my heart," he said. Now his friends felt that way about him. Most of them couldn't make the trip uptown, and those who did got drunk afterward and never returned. Dan Golenpaul sent him a bottle of scotch every week, but never came himself. Only Esther did, two or three times a month, and sometimes one or another of their children, until he died, on March 23, 1960. He called Esther "Mommy" till the end of his days and barely hinted they weren't still married. Years after the divorce had forced his move to the Players, his cronies there were uncertain about the status of the marriage.

The afternoon of his death, twenty-three plays were running on Broadway. Top tickets for *My Fair Lady*, by that time starring people named Pamela Charles and Michael Allinson, were $8.05. At twenty-seven, Philip Roth was the youngest prize winner of the eleven-year-old National Book Awards for his novella and short story collection, *Goodbye, Columbus* ($3.75 in hardcover). Elvis Presley's twenty-fifth gold record, "Stuck on You," swaggered and bounced from the country's juke boxes, and his manager, "Colonel" Tom Parker announced that the fee for a single television appearance by Elvis was being increased to $150,000. That month American factory workers averaged a weekly wage of $81.10.

On March 23, Earl Wilson reported in his column that "Leggy" Angie Dickinson had been named Miss April by *Argosy* magazine. Wilt Chamberlain announced he'd played his last game in the NBA. Howard Taubman was named to succeed Brooks Atkinson as drama critic for the *New York Times*, which also reported that the U.S. Court of Appeals had ruled that D. H. Lawrence's *Lady Chatterley's Lover* wasn't an obscene book and could be sent through the mails. Later in the week notice ran of the death of John Lardner, thirty years younger than F.P.A., whose poem about Babe Ruth and Jack Dempsey had been printed in "The Conning Tower" when its author was barely ten. Ironically, Lardner died suddenly at his typewriter as he was banging out Frank's obituary for *Newsweek*.

The *Times* ran a photograph with F.P.A.'s front-page obituary. It was an old photo, taken in 1945, and not flattering, though Frank's look was characteristically direct. There was no photograph accompanying the notice in the *New York Herald Tribune*, though he'd worked longest there.

Many people were surprised to discover that Frank had only just then died. They'd thought him dead long before. Yet over two hundred people showed up at his funeral on Friday afternoon. It was a bright, chilly day, the temperature hovering around thirty degrees, with a biting wind out of the northeast. They packed into Frank E. Campbell's funeral parlor on the corner of Eighty-first Street and Madison Avenue, many of them first standing around on the sidewalk outside, the women tugging at the collars of their coats, men in hats and mufflers arriving in taxis, in pairs or clumps or coming along alone, eyeing the crowd to see who else was there. People greeted each other, talked, admitted they hadn't seen Frank in years, thought he'd still lived upstairs at the Players. Hushed conversation skirted the unspeakable, then faltered. How did you make conversation about the sordidness of a nursing home, all those helpless old people sitting around, staring at the wall. Could Frank have been one of *them*? The older mourners, the ones who'd known him best, shuddered and tried to think of other things. Not of F.P.A., stuck in a nursing home with a cranky practical nurse feeding him and wiping his chin with a paper napkin. Not Frank.

Algonk ranks were thin. Alexander Woollcott had died seventeen years before, in 1943, during a radio broadcast. Heywood Broun, Alice Duer Miller, Harold Ross, Charles MacArthur, Herman Mankiewicz, Ring Lardner, Edna St. Vincent Millay, and Robert Benchley were dead. Dorothy Parker was still alive, but she didn't come.

The remains of that spangled era straggled in: Edna Ferber, Deems

Taylor, M. Lincoln Schuster, Margaret Case Harriman (daughter of Frank Case), Rube Goldberg, Ogden Nash, John O'Hara, John Farrar, Lester Markel of the *Times*, Dan Golenpaul. Eulogizers were John Kieran, Marc Connelly, and Rabbi Abraham Burnstein, secretary of the Jewish Academy of Arts and Sciences and chaplain of the Jewish Theatrical Guild, himself an early contributor to the Tower.

Connelly described Frank's high standards and lack of pretensions. "He looked on the world with a lover's fears and a kindly doctor's concern for its health. He hated hateful things." He called Frank "a sternly disciplined craftsman" and claimed that "some of the loveliest of contemporary poetry owes its beauty to Frank's own writing." He said that Frank had stimulated "more young writers in the Twenties and Thirties than any other person," and sat down.

After the rabbi had finished his prayer, everybody remained standing with bowed heads, hushed; then relief came with the organ music and they began talking again, pulling on coats and moving toward the exits. Some came forward to speak to Esther and the family, but most left quickly. Within twenty minutes the place was empty. Frank's body was sent to the Ferncliff crematorium.

Six months after his death, the Players threw a Pipe Night for him, in memoriam. Connelly was Pipemaster. Many old friends came, and it was a warm, gay evening, full of stories about the good old days, about Frank, and about them. After the roast beef and ice cream, Deems Taylor stood to lead the singing. They sang "For He's a Jolly Good Fellow" and "Hail, Hail, the Gang's All Here," "A Bicycle Built for Two," "Break the News to Mother," "After the Ball," "Oh, You Beautiful Doll," "The Band Played On," "Let the Rest of the World Go By," and "My Mother Was a Lady," which goes, "My mother was a lady, like yours you will allow, and you may have a sister, who needs protection now. I've come to this great city to find my brother dear, and you wouldn't dare insult me, Sir, if Jack were only here."

Mimeographed copies of the lyrics were provided, since nobody remembered the words. Had Frank been there, he would have known them all.

APPENDIX A

Books by Franklin Pierce Adams

Answer This One. Questions for Everybody. Compiled by F.P.A. and Harry Hansen. New York: E. J. Clode, Inc., 1927.

The Book of Diversion. Compiled by F.P.A., Deems Taylor, Jack Bechdolt, Aided and Abetted by Helen Rowland and Mabel Claire. New York: Greenberg, Inc., 1925.

The Week-end Companion. Compiled by F.P.A., Deems Taylor, Helen Rowland and Perceval Wilde. Cleveland, Ohio and New York: The World Publishing Co., 1941.

By and Large. Garden City, New York: Doubleday, Page and Company, 1914.

Christopher Columbus and Other Patriotic Verses. New York: The Viking Press, 1931.

Column Book by F.P.A. Garden City, New York: Doubleday, Doran and Company, 1928.

The Conning Tower Book. Being a Selection of the Best Verses Published in The Conning Tower. New York: Macy-Masius, 1926.

In Cupid's Court. Evanston, Illinois: W. S. Lord, 1902.

The Diary of Our Own Samuel Pepys. New York: Simon and Schuster, 1935.

F.P.A. Book of Quotations. New York: Funk and Wagnalls, 1952.

Half a Loaf. Garden City, New York: Doubleday, Page and Company, 1927.

Innocent Merriment. New York and London: Whittlesey House, McGraw-Hill Book Company, 1942.

In Other Words. Garden City, New York: Doubleday, Page and Company, 1912.

The Melancholy Lute. New York: The Viking Press, 1936.

Nods and Becks. New York and London: Whittlesey House, McGraw-Hill Book Company, 1944.

Overset. Garden City, New York: Doubleday, Page and Company, 1922.

The Second Conning Tower Book. New York: Macy-Masius, 1927.

Something Else Again. Garden City, New York: Doubleday, Page and Company, 1920.

So Much Velvet. Garden City, New York: Doubleday, Page and Company, 1924.

So There! Garden City, New York: Doubleday, Page and Company, 1923.

Toboganning on Parnassus. Garden City, New York: Doubleday, Page and Company, 1911.

Weights and Measures. Garden City, New York: Doubleday, Page and Company, 1922.

APPENDIX B

Forewords and Introductions
by Franklin Pierce Adams

F.P.A., JOHN ANDERSON AND OTHERS. *Percy Hammond, a Symposium in Tribute*. Garden City, New York: Doubleday, Doran and Company, 1936.

CONGREVE, WILLIAM. *Love for Love*. Produced by the Players, Directed by Robert Edmund Jones, Introduction by F.P.A. New York: Charles Scribner's Sons, 1940.

DEWEY, BERENICE. *Poems*. Foreword by F.P.A. New York: The Galleon Press, 1933.

DUNNE, FINLEY PETER. Edited by Elmer Ellis. Foreword by F.P.A. *Mr. Dooley at His Best*. Hamden, Connecticut: Archon Books, 1969 (1949).

HILL, WILLIAM ELY. Pictures by Hill, Text by F.P.A. *Among Us Mortals*. Boston and New York: Houghton Mifflin Company, 1917.

NEWSPAPER GUILD OF NEW YORK, *Heywood Broun as He Seemed to Us*. New York: Random House, 1940.

BIBLIOGRAPHY

ADAMS, FRANKLIN, P. *The Conning Tower Book*. New York: Macy-Masius, 1926.

ADAMS, FRANKLIN P. *The Diary of Our Own Samuel Pepys*. 2 vols. New York: Simon and Schuster, Inc., 1935.

ADAMS, FRANKLIN P., et al. *Percy Hammond, A Symposium in Tribute*. Garden City: Doubleday, Doran & Company, Inc., 1936.

ADAMS, SAMUEL HOPKINS. *A. Woollcott, His Life and His World*. New York: Reynal & Hitchcock, 1945.

ADAMS, SAMUEL HOPKINS. *Who and What: A Book of Clues for the Clever*. New York: Boni and Liveright, 1927.

ADE, GEORGE. *The America of George Ade, 1866–1944*. Edited with an Introduction by Jean Shepherd. New York: G. B. Putnam, 1960.

ADLER, POLLY. *A House Is Not a Home*. New York: Rhinehart and Company, 1953.

ALLSWANG, JOHN M. *A House for All Peoples—Ethnic Politics in Chicago, 1890–1936*. Lexington: The University Press of Kentucky, 1971.

ALVAREZ, A. *The Biggest Game in Town*. Boston: Houghton Mifflin Company, 1983.

AMORY, CLEVELAND and BRADLEE, FREDERIC, eds. *Vanity Fair: A Cavalcade of the 1920s and 1930s*. New York: The Viking Press, 1960.

ANDREWS, CLARENCE A. *Chicago in Story—a Literary History*. Iowa City: Midwest Heritage Publishing Co., 1982.

ANOBILE, RICHARD and MARX, GROUCHO. *The Marx Brothers Scrapbook*. New York: Darien House, 1973.

ATKINSON, BROOKS. *Broadway*. New York: Macmillan, 1970.

BAKER, CARLOS, CURTI, MERLE and THORP, WILLARD, eds. *American Issues*. New York: J. P. Lippencott Co., 1960.

BENCHLEY, NATHANIEL. *Robert Benchley*. New York: The McGraw-Hill Book Co., 1955.

BENCHLEY, ROBERT. *The Benchley Roundup*. The favorite selections from Robert Benchley's humorous writings chosen by his son Nathaniel Benchley. Drawings by Gluyas Williams. New York: A Delta Book Published by Dell Publishing Co., Inc., 1954.

BERNSTEIN, BURTON. *Thurber. A Biography*. New York: Dodd, Mead & Company, 1975.

BLAIR, WALTER and HILL, HAMLIN. *America's Humor. From Poor Richard to Doonesbury.* New York: Oxford University Press, 1978.

BLAKEY, GEORGE T. *Historians on the Homefront, American Propagandists for the Great War.* Lexington: The University Press of Kentucky, 1970.

BRENNER, RICA. *Twelve American Poets Before 1900.* New York: Harcourt Brace and Co., 1933.

BROUN, HEYWOOD HALE. *Who's Little Boy Are You? A Memoir of the Broun Family.* New York: St. Martin's/Marek, 1983.

BROWN, JOHN MASON. *The Worlds of Robert E. Sherwood.* New York: Harper & Row, 1965.

BRUCCOLI, MATTHEW J., ed. *The Selected Letters of John O'Hara.* New York: Random House, 1978.

CHAMBERLIN, EVERETT and COLBERT, ELIAS. *Chicago and the Great Conflagration.* New York: The Viking Press, 1871.

CHURCHILL, ALLEN. *The Great White Way.* New York: E. P. Dutton and Co., 1962.

COBB, IRVIN S. *Exit Laughing, an Autobiography.* New York: The Bobbs-Merrill Co., 1941.

CONNELLY, MARC. *Voices Offstage. A Book of Memoirs.* New York: Holt, Rinehart and Winston, 1968.

CONROW, ROBERT. *Field Days.* New York: Charles Scribners' Sons, 1974.

COURTENAY, MARGUERITE. *Laurette. The Intimate Biography of Laurette Taylor.* New York: Rinehart & Co., 1955.

COWLEY, MALCOLM. *—And I Worked at the Writer's Trade. Chapters of Literary History, 1918–1978.* New York: Penguin Books, 1979.

CROMIE, ROBERT. *The Great Chicago Fire.* New York: The McGraw-Hill Book Co., 1958.

DASH, JOAN. *A Life of One's Own.* New York: Harper & Row, 1973.

DAVENPORT, MARCIA. *Too Strong for Fantasy.* New York: Charles Scribner's Sons, 1967.

DEDMON, EMMETT. *Fabulous Chicago.* New York: Random House, 1953.

DENNIS, CHARLES HENRY. *Eugene Field's Creative Years.* Garden City: Doubleday, Page and Co., 1924.

DOS PASSOS, JOHN. *USA.* Boston: Houghton Mifflin Co., 1960.

DREW, JOHN. *My Years on the Stage.* New York: E. P. Dutton & Co., 1922.

DRIESER, THEODORE. *American Diaries. 1902–1926.* Thomas P. Riggio, Ed. James L. W. West III, Textual Editor; Neda M. Westlake, Gen. Ed. Philadelphia: University of Pennsylvania Press, 1983.

DRIESER, THEODORE. Introduction to *The Songs of Paul Dresser*, by Paul Dresser. New York: Boni and Liveright, 1927.

DREISER, THEODORE. *A Book About Myself.* New York: Boni and Liveright, 1922.

DREISER, THEODORE. *An Amateur Laborer.* Edited, with an Introduction, by Richard W. Dowell; James L. W. West III and Neda M. Westlake, Eds. Philadelphia: University of Pennsylvania Press, 1983.

DREISER, THEODORE. *The Color of a Great City*. New York: Boni and Liveright, 1923.

DUNNE, FINLEY PETER. *Mr. Dooley in the Hearts of His Countrymen*. New York: Greenwood Press, 1969.

DUNNE, FINLEY PETER. *Mr. Dooley on Ivrything and Ivrybody*. New York: Dover Publications, Inc., 1963.

DUNNING, JOHN. *Tune in Yesterday. The Ultimate Encyclopedia of Oldtime Radio*. Englewood Cliffs, New Jersey: Prentice-Hall, 1976.

ECKLEY, GRACE. *Finley Peter Dunne*. Boston: Twayne Publishers of G. K. Hall and Co., 1981.

EDMISTON, SUSAN and CIRINO, LINDA D. *Literary New York. A History and Guide*. Boston: Houghton Mifflin Company, 1976.

EDSON, C. L. *The Gentle Art of Columning, a Treatise on Comic Journalism*. New York: Brentano's, 1920.

ELLEDGE, SCOTT. *E. B. White. A Biography*. New York: W. W. Norton & Company, 1984.

ELLIS, ELMER. *Mr. Dooley's America—A Life of Finley Peter Dunne*. New York: Alfred A. Knopf, 1941.

ERNST, MORRIS. *The Best Is Yet . . .* New York and London: Harper & Brothers, 1945.

ERNST, MORRIS. *So Far So Good*. New York and London: Harper & Brothers, 1948.

FANNING, CHARLES. *Finley Peter Dunne and Mr. Dooley, The Chicago Years*. Lexington: The University Press of Kentucky, 1978.

FARR, FINIS. *Chicago, A Personal History of America's Most American City*. New Rochelle, New York: Arlington House, 1973.

FEDERAL WRITERS' PROJECT. *New York Panorama. A Companion to the WPA Guide to New York City*. New York: Random House, 1938; Reprint ed. New York: Pantheon Books with a new Introduction by Alfred Kazin, 1984.

FERBER, EDNA. *A Peculiar Treasure*. New York: Doubleday, Doran & Co., Inc., 1939.

FIELD, EUGENE. *The Complete Tribune Primer*. Chicago: The Mutual Book Co., 1901.

FIELD, EUGENE. *Culture's Garland*. Boston: Tincknor and Co., 1887.

FIELD, EUGENE. *The Tribune Primer*. With original illustrations by John C. Frohn. Boston: H. A. Dickerman & Son, 1900.

FIELD, EUGENE. *The Writings in Prose and Verse*. Boston: Tincknor and Co., 1896.

FISCHLER, STAN. *Uptown, Downtown. A Trip Through Time on New York's Subways*. New York: Hawthorne Books, Inc., 1976.

FITZGERALD, F. SCOTT. *This Side of Paradise*. New York: Charles Scribner's Sons, 1920. (Copyright renewed.)

FORD, COREY. *The Time of Laughter*. Foreword by Frank Sullivan. Boston: Little Brown & Co., 1967.

GAINES, JAMES R. *Wit's End. Days and Nights of the Algonquin Round Table*. New York: Harcourt Brace Jovanovich, 1977.

GELB, BARBARA and ARTHUR. *O'Neill*. Introduction by Brooks Atkinson. New York: A Delta Book published by Dell Publishing Co., Inc., 1962.

GILBERT, DOUGLAS. *American Vaudeville*. New York: Dover Publications, 1940.

GILBERT, DOUGLAS. *Lost Chords*. Garden City: Doubleday, Doran and Co., Inc., 1942.

GILBERT, JULIE GOLDSMITH. *Ferber*. Garden City: Doubleday and Co., Inc., 1978.

GILL, BRENDAN. *Here at The New Yorker*. New York: Berkeley Medallion Books in arrangement with Random House, Inc., 1975.

GOLENPAUL, DAN, ed. *Information, Please*. New York: Simon and Schuster, 1939.

GOLENPAUL, DAN, ed. *Information, Please!* Introductions by Franklin P. Adams, John Kieran and Christopher Morley. New York: Random House, 1941.

GORDON, RUTH. *Myself Among Others*. New York: Atheneum, 1971.

GORDON, RUTH. *My Side. The Autobiography of Ruth Gordon*. New York: Harper & Row, 1976.

GRANT, JANE. *Ross, The New Yorker and Me*. Introduction by Janet Flanner. New York: Reynal and Company in association with William Morrow & Company, Inc., 1968.

GREEN, STANLEY. *Ring Bells! Sing Songs! Broadway Musicals of the 1930s*. Introduction by Brooks Atkinson. New Rochelle: Arlington House, 1971.

GREEN, STANLEY. *The World of Musical Comedy*. Foreword by Deems Taylor. New York: A. S. Barnes & Co., 1960.

HALPER, ALBERT, ed. *This Is Chicago: An Anthology*. New York: Henry Holt and Co., 1952.

HAMMOND, PERCY. *But—Is It Art?* Garden City: Doubleday Page & Co., 1927.

HARMON, WILLIAM, ed. *American Light Verse*. New York: The Oxford University Press, 1979.

HART, MOSS. *Act One. An Autobiography*. New York: Random House, 1959.

HAYES, DORSHA B. *Chicago, Crossroads of American Enterprise*. New York: Julian Messner, 1944.

HAYES, HELEN, with LEWIS FUNKE. *A Gift of Joy*. New York: A Fawcett Crest Book reprinted by arrangement with M. Evans and Company, Inc., 1965.

HECHT, BEN. *A Child of the Century*. New York: Simon and Schuster, 1954.

HELLMAN, LILLIAN. *An Unfinished Woman. A Memoir*. A Bantam Book published by arrangement with Little, Brown & Company, 1970.

O. HENRY. *The Complete Works of O. Henry*. With a Foreword by Harry Hansen. Garden City: Doubleday & Company, Inc., 1953.

HOBSON, ARCHIE, ed. *Remembering America. A Sampler of the WPA American Guide Series*. Introductions by Bill Stott. New York: Columbia University Press, 1985.

JORDAN, ELIZABETH. *Three Rousing Cheers*. New York: D. Appleton, Century Co., Inc., 1938.

ISMAN, FELIX. *Weber and Fields*. New York: Boni & Liveright, 1924.

KAHN, E. J., JR. *The World of Swope. A Biography of Herbert Bayard Swope*. New York: Simon and Schuster, 1965.

KAHN, ROGER. *The Boys of Summer*. New York: Harper & Row, 1971.

KAZIN, ALFRED. *An American Procession*. New York: Alfred A. Knopf, 1984.

KAZIN, ALFRED. *On Native Grounds*. 40th Anniversary Edition. New York: Harcourt Brace Jovanovich, 1982.

KEATS, JOHN. *You Might as Well Live. The Life and Times of Dorothy Parker*. New York: Simon and Schuster, 1970.

KIERAN, JOHN. *Not Under Oath*. Cambridge: The Riverside Press of The Houghton Mifflin Co., 1964.

King's Handbook of New York City, 1893. Boston: Moses King, 1893. Reissued New York: B. B.om, Inc., 1972.

KLEIN, JOE. *Woody Guthrie. A. Life*. New York: Alfred A. Knopf, 1980.

KNIGHT, GRANT C. *The Critical Period in American Literature*. Chapel Hill: The University of North Carolina Press, 1951.

LARDNER, RING. *The Best Short Stories of Ring Lardner*. New York: Charles Scribner's Sons, 1957.

LARDNER, RING. *Some Champions*. Edited by Matthew J. Bruccoli & Richard Layman with a Forward by Ring Lardner, Jr. New York: Charles Scribner's Sons, 1976.

LARDNER, RING, JR. *The Lardners. My Family Remembered*. New York: Harper & Row, 1976.

LAUFE, ABE. *Broadway's Greatest Musicals*. New York: Funk & Wagnalls, 1973.

LEAB, DANIEL J. *A Union of Individuals. The Formation of the American Newspaper Guild*. New York: The Columbia University Press, 1970.

LEVANT, OSCAR. *A Smattering of Ignorance*. Garden City: Doubleday, Doran and Co., Inc., 1940.

LEVANT, OSCAR. *The Unimportance of Being Oscar*. New York: G. B. Putnam, 1968.

LEVIN, MARTIN, ed. *Hollywood and the Great Fan Magazines*. New York: Arbor House, 1970.

LEVY, NEWMAN. *My Double Life*. Garden City: Doubleday & Co., 1958.

LEWIS, JOHN L., et al. *Heywood Broun as He Seemed To Us*. Published for the Newspaper Guild of New York by Random House, 1940.

LONGSTREET, STEPHEN. *Win or Lose: A Social History of Gambling in America*. New York: The Bobbs-Merrill Company, Inc., 1977.

MacSHANE, FRANK. *The Life of John O'Hara*. New York: E. P. Dutton, 1980.

MANGIONE, JERRE. *The Dream and the Deal*. Boston: Little, Brown and Company, 1972.

MAYER, HAROLD M. and WADE, RICHARD C. *Chicago: Growth of a Metropolis*. Chicago: The University of Chicago Press, 1969.

MCELVAINE, ROBERT S. *The Great Depression*. New York: Times Books, 1984.

MCGINLEY, PHYLLIS. *A Pocketfull of Wry*. New York: Duell, Sloan and Pearce, 1940.

MENCKEN, H. L. *A Choice of Days*. New York: Vintage Books, a Division of Random House, 1980.

MENCKEN, H. L. *The American Language*. The Fourth Edition and the Two Supplements, abridged, with annotations and new material by Raven I. McDavid, Jr., with the assistance of David W. Maurer. New York: Alfred A. Knopf, 1977.

MENCKEN, H. L. *The Vintage Mencken*. Gathered by Alistair Cooke. New York: Vintage Books, a Division of Random House, 1955.

MERYMAN, RICHARD. *Mank. The Wit, World and Life of Herman Mankiewicz*. New York: William Morrow and Company, Inc., 1978.

MILLAY, EDNA ST. VINCENT. *Collected Poems*. Edited by Norma Millay. New York: Harper & Row, 1956.

MOTT, FRANK LUTHER. *American Journalism, a History of Newspapers in the U.S.* New York: The Macmillan Co., 1962.

NELSON, RANDY F. *The Almanac of American Letters*. Los Altos, California: William Kaufmann, Inc., 1981.

The New Yorker Scrapbook. Copyright, 1926, 1927, 1928, 1929, 1930, 1931 by F-R Publishing Corporation (*The New Yorker*). Garden City: Doubleday, Doran and Co., 1931.

O'CONNOR, RICHARD. *Heywood Broun, A Biography*. New York: G. P. Putnam's Sons, 1975.

O'CONNOR, RICHARD. *O. Henry. The Legendary Life of William S. Porter*. Garden City: Doubleday & Company, Inc., 1970.

OLMSTED, CHARLOTTE. *Heads I Win, Tails You Lose*. New York: The Macmillan Company, 1962.

OLSON, STANLEY. *Elinor Wylie, A Life Apart*. New York: The Dial Press, 1979.

OPPENHEIMER, GEORGE. *The Passionate Playgoer, A Personal Scrapbook*. New York: The Viking Press, 1958.

PARKER, DOROTHY. *The Portable Dorothy Parker*. Revised and Enlarged Edition with an Introduction by Brendan Gill. First published in the United States by The Viking Press in 1944. Revised and expanded edition published 1973, published in Penguin Books 1982.

PERELMAN, S. J. *The Most of S. J. Perelman*. With a Foreword by Dorothy Parker and a new Afterword by Philip Hamburger. New York: A Fireside Book published by Simon and Schuster, 1957.

PERRETT, GEOFFREY. *America in the Twenties: A History*. New York: Simon and Schuster, 1982.

PETERSON, THEODORE. *Magazines in the 20th Century*. Urbana: The University of Illinois Press, 1956.

ROOT, GEORGE F. *The Story of a Musical Life*. New York: DeCapo Press Reprint Edition, 1970.

ROSMOND, BABETTE. *Robert Benchley, His Life and Good Times*. Garden City: Doubleday and Co., 1970.

SANDERS, MARION K. *Dorothy Thompson: A Legend in Her Time*. Boston: Houghton Mifflin, 1973.

SCHAAF, BARBARA C. *Mr. Dooley's Chicago*. Garden City: Anchor Press of Doubleday, 1977.

SHEAFFER, LOUIS. *O'Neill. Son and Playwright*. Boston: Little, Brown and Company, 1968.

SHEEAN, VINCENT. *Dorothy & Red*. Cambridge: The Riverside Press, 1863.

SILVER, NATHAN. *Lost New York*. New York: Schocken Books, 1971.

SIMPSON, COLIN. *The Lusitania*. Boston: Little, Brown and Company, 1972.

SMITH, PAGE. *A People's History*. Vol. 7: *A People's History of the Progressive Era and World War I*. New York: The McGraw-Hill Book Co., 1985.

SMITH, PAGE. *A People's History*. Vol. 6: *A People's History of the Reconstruction Era*. New York: The McGraw-Hill Book Co., 1984.

STEEL, RONALD. *Walter Lippmann and the American Century*. New York: Vintage Books, a Division of Random House, 1981.

STONE, MELVILLE E. *Fifty Years a Journalist*. Garden City: Doubleday, Page and Company, 1921.

SULLIVAN, FRANK. *Through the Looking Glass*. Edited by George Oppenheimer. Garden City: Doubleday and Co., Inc., 1970.

SULLIVAN, MARK. *Our Times, 1900–1925*. New York: Charles Scribner's Sons, 1927.

SWADOS, HARVEY, ed. *The American Writer and the Great Depression*. Indianapolis and New York: The American Heritage Series of the Bobbs-Merrill Company, Inc., 1966.

TEICHMANN, HOWARD. *George S. Kaufman, an Intimate Portrait*. New York: Atheneum, 1972.

TEICHMANN, HOWARD. *Smart Aleck. The Wit, World and Life of Alexander Woollcott*. New York: William Morrow and Company, Inc., 1976.

THORP, WILLIAM. *American Writing in the Twentieth Century*. Cambridge: Harvard University Press, 1960.

THURBER, HELEN and WEEKS, EDWARD, eds. *Selected Letters of James Thurber*. Boston: Little, Brown and Co., 1980.

THURBER, JAMES. *Alarms & Diversions*. New York: Harper & Row, 1957.

THURBER, JAMES and WHITE, E.B. *Is Sex Necessary? Or, Why You Feel The Way You Do*. With an Introduction by E. B. White. New York: Harper & Row; 1929, 1950. Reprinted by Harper Colophon Books, 1978.

THURBER, JAMES. *Fables for Our Times and Famous Poems Illustrated*. New York: Harper & Row, 1939; first reprint edition published 1983.

THURBER, JAMES. *The Thurber Carnival*. New York: Harper & Row, 1945.

THURBER, JAMES. *The Years With Ross*. New York: Little, Brown and Company in association with The Atlantic Monthly Press, 1959.

TURNBULL, ANDREW, ed. *The Letters of F. Scott Fitzgerald*. New York: Charles Scribner's Sons, 1963.

UNTERMEYER, LOUIS. *From Another World*. New York: Harcourt Brace and Co., 1939.

The Editors of *Variety*. *The Variety Radio Directory, '39 and '40*. New York: Variety, Inc., 1940.

WHITE, E. B. *Essays of E. B. White*. New York: Harper & Row, 1977.

WHITE, E. B. *Letters of E. B. White*. Collected and Edited by Dorothy Lobrano Guth. New York: Harper Colophon Books, 1976.

WHITE, E. B. *Poems & Sketches of E. B. White*. New York: Harper Colophon Books, 1983.

WILLIAMS, WYETH. *Passed By the Censor*. New York: E. P. Dutton, 1916.

WILSON, EDMUND. *Letters on Literature and Politics, 1912–1972*. Selected and Edited by Elena Wilson, Introduction by Daniel Aaron, Foreword by Leon Edel. New York: Farrar, Straus and Giroux, 1977.

WILSON, EDMUND. *The Thirties*. Edited with an Introduction by Leon Edel. New York: A Washington Square Press Publication of Pocket Books, a Simon & Schuster division of Gulf & Western Corp., 1980.

WILSON, EDMUND. *The Twenties*. Edited with an Introduction by Leon Edel. New York: Farrar, Straus and Giroux, 1975.

WINTERICH, JOHN T. *Squads Write!* New York and London: Harper & Brothers, 1931.

WOOLLCOTT, ALEXANDER. *Enchanted Aisles*. New York: G. P. Putnam's Sons, The Knickerbocker Press, 1924.

WOOLLCOTT, ALEXANDER. *The Command Is Forward. Tales of the A.E.F. Battlefields as They Appeared in The Stars and Stripes*. New York: The Century Co., 1919.

YARDLEY, JONATHAN. *Ring. A Biography of Ring Lardner*. New York: Random House, 1977.

ZIFF, LARZER. *The American 1890s, The Life and Times of a Lost Generation*. New York: The Viking Press, 1966.

INDEX